The
CROSSROADS
of CONFLICT

Books by Kenneth Cloke

Mediation: Revenge and the Magic of Forgiveness
Center for Dispute Resolution, Santa Monica, California, 1996

Mediating Dangerously: The Frontiers of Conflict Resolution
Jossey Bass / Wiley Publishers Inc., 2001

Books by Kenneth Cloke and Joan Goldsmith

Thank God It's Monday: 14 Values We Need to Humanize the Way We Work
Irwin / McGraw Hill, 1997

Resolving Conflicts at Work: A Complete Guide for Everyone on the Job
Jossey Bass / Wiley Publishers Inc., 2000

Resolving Personal and Organizational Conflicts:
Stories of Transformation and Forgiveness
Jossey Bass / Wiley Publishers Inc., 2000

The End of Management and the Rise of Organizational Democracy
Jossey Bass / Wiley Publishers Inc., 2002

The Art of Waking People Up: Cultivating Awareness and Authenticity at Work
Jossey Bass / Wiley Publishers Inc., 2003

Resolving Conflicts at Work: Eight Strategies for Everyone on the Job
(Second Edition) Jossey Bass / Wiley Publishers Inc., 2005

The
of CROSSROADS
CONFLICT

A Journey into the Heart of Dispute Resolution

By Kenneth Cloke

JANIS

PUBLICATIONS

THE CROSSROADS OF CONFLICT:
A Journey into the Heart of Dispute Resolution

Kenneth Cloke

Library and Archives Canada Cataloguing in Publication

Cloke, Ken, 1941-
The Crossroads of Conflict: A Journey into the Heart of Dispute
Includes bibliographical references.
ISBN 0-9734396-9-6
1. Conflict management. I. Title.
HM1126.C556 2006   303.6'9'
C2006-901842-1

Editor: Danielle LeClair Rakoz
Book design: CleanPix Corp.
Printing: Marquis Book Printing Ltd.

Publisher:
Published by Janis Publications Inc.
www.janispublications.com

JANIS
PUBLICATIONS

Printed in Canada

TABLE OF CONTENTS

When we look into our own hearts and begin
to discover what is confused and what is brilliant,
what is bitter and what is sweet,
it isn't just ourselves that we're discovering.
We're discovering the universe.
–Pema Chödrön

INTRODUCTION

The Crossroads of Conflict

"Take one step away from yourself—and behold!—the path!"
–Abu Said

Every conflict we experience, no matter how trivial, points us toward a crossroads in our lives. One path leads us into anger, fear, confrontation, and bitterness and draws us into quarrels over the past. This path reveals a deep level of caring about outcomes, yet it also encourages adversarial relationships, sterile communications, contemptuous ideas, negative emotions, and unpleasant physical sensations, blinding us and dissipating our energy and spirit. This is the path of impasse, aggression, and antagonism.

A second path leads us into empathy, acceptance, honesty, and mutual respect and draws us into negotiations over the future. This path reveals a deep level of caring about people, and encourages supportive relationships, improved communications, creative ideas, positive emotions, and pleasant physical sensations, making us more conscious and releasing our energy and spirit from destructive conflicts. This is the path of resolution, collaboration, and mutual problem solving.

In addition to these is a third path branching off from the second and largely hidden from view. This path leads us into increased awareness, compassion, integrity, and heartfelt communications and draws us into awareness of the present. It integrates the honesty and caring about outcomes encountered on the first path with the empathy and caring about people encountered on the second. It encourages openhearted relationships, deep learning, intimate communications, profound ideas, poignant emotions, and physical renewal. It wakes us up, makes us more mindful of ourselves and others, and nurtures our energy and spirit. This is the path of transformation and transcendence, of wisdom, spirit, and heart.

In this way, every conflict leads us to two different crossroads. In the beginning, we face a choice between fighting and problem solving. Later, we face a subtler, more arduous and far-reaching choice between merely settling our conflicts and seeking to learn from them, correcting our behaviors, and moving toward forgiveness and reconciliation.

Initially, conflicts entrap us, tempting us along the first path with rewards that cater to our short-term self-interests with personal advantages, fantasies of victory, righteous anger, vengeful pleasures, and the malignant, self-aggrandizing energy of hatred. Yet by accepting these rewards we place our lives on hold, stoke our anger, and magnify our fear of defeat, shame, and loss of self. At the same time, we gratify our opponents and solidify the very thing we resist or object to, creating knots, insensitivities, and places of blindness inside us. These not only make our pains and sacrifices meaningless, they discourage us from following the more difficult, yet ultimately more rewarding path of negotiation, dialogue, and resolution, and the still more difficult and rewarding path of the heart, leading to transformation and transcendence.

Why do so many of us prefer the first path? Partly because we allow our capacity for respectful communication, open heartedness, and integrity to become *conditional* and dependent on the reciprocal actions of others. Partly because we reserve the full exercise of our empathy and honesty for pleasant experiences and supportive relationships. Partly because we are encouraged by media and culture to accept adversarial approaches to conflict that are physically injurious, intellectually one-sided, emotionally unbalanced, spiritually self-defeating, and socially divisive. Partly because others reward us for adversarial behaviors with attention, sympathy, special privileges, a strong sense of identity, distractions from self-hatred, excuses for failure, and reasons for preserving relationships that might otherwise fall apart.

More deeply, no one gets into conflicts over issues that don't matter to them, even if they seem trivial to others. Every conflict therefore involves an element of caring—perhaps concerning content, process, relationship, or how we are being perceived or treated. Mediators and conflict resolution professionals have largely ignored this element of caring, failing to explore its nature and how it might be possible to turn distorted, negative communications into connections that are direct, positive, and heartfelt.

Adversarial approaches to conflict stress our bodies, close our minds, and magnify our negative emotions. They weaken our spirits, silence our hearts, and undermine our capacity for honest, empathetic communications and intimacy in relationships. They confuse us with false options and dead-end approaches. Worse, they divide us—not only from each other, but from internal parts of ourselves. They cause us to lose perspective and reject whatever our opponents propose. In response, we act defensively, grow intransigent, and ignore or deny whatever *we* contributed to making the conflict worse. As a result, adversarial conflicts weaken our will, make us unhappy, and cause us to learn little or nothing—other than how right we were.

By following the first path we discover that the advantages it promises are ultimately false, cloying, superficial, and dissatisfying. By resisting its pull and discovering its hidden dynamics, we reveal the presence of the second path, consisting of constructive engagement with our opponents and a mutual search for resolution. This path allows us to transform conflicts from adversarial contests in which everyone loses into dialogues and collaborative negotiations in which everyone can win or at least bear their defeats equally.

By following the second path we discover the third path and recognize that our true opponent and adversary in every conflict is always ourselves, and that the real purpose of conflict is, has always been, and can only be to reveal what stands in the way of our learning and growth, our development of character, and our capacity for empathy and honesty, integrity and intimacy, caring and compassion.

In the process, we realize that the very conflicts that get us stuck in pointless, seemingly superficial, adversarial battles are the source of outcomes so weighty and profound, so poignant and beautiful that they are impossible to describe in words, yet nearly everyone has experienced them. We are able to discover, in the thick of discord, how to free ourselves from its all-consuming grip, and how to gain insight into what got us stuck. This insight enables us to transform the ways we interact with our opponents by experiencing criticisms and complaints as suggestions for improvement, allowing us to evolve to higher levels of conflict and resolution.

How to Locate the Third Path

Every conflict presents countless opportunities, both to mediators and parties in conflict, to improve their dispute resolution skills, along with their capacity for wisdom, open heartedness, clarity, balance, and inner peace under trying adversarial conditions. Every conflict therefore leads simultaneously to impasse, to resolution, and to learning, growth, and transcendence. It is this third, subtle, concealed, and profoundly difficult path that is the principal subject of this book.

How, you may ask, in the paroxysm of conflict, can you find your way to these second and third paths? The answer is to

- move skillfully and steadily into the *heart* of conflict and do battle first and foremost with your desire to travel the seemingly easier, more seductive path of demonization, victimization, powerlessness, and self-righteousness;

- resist the temptation to compromise or simply settle disputes, or even resolve the underlying issues that gave rise to them;

- be so deeply committed to yourself and your opponent that you are willing to initiate open, honest, vulnerable conversations and work *through* your conflict, rather than around it;

- consider your opponent not as an enemy combatant, but as a teacher, partner, citizen, and collaborator;

- refuse to accept what is inauthentic or heartless, either in your opponent or in yourself; and

- move heroically into the heart of your conflict, where resolution, transformation, and transcendence suddenly, inexplicably, exquisitely unfold.

Transformation and transcendence are therefore present as *possibilities* at every moment, in every conflict. To locate these possibilities, we need to assume that even the most senseless conflicts have the power to significantly alter and improve our lives and, at the simplest level, they do.

As mediators we can help people turn even trivial conflicts into exercises that improve their skills; for example, by

- asking people to pay careful attention to what is done, said, and felt in conflict;

- pointing them toward the origin of the conflict inside them and their opponents;

- encouraging them to listen with open hearts and minds;

- inviting them to jointly search for solutions that satisfy everyone's underlying interests;

- strengthening their personal and social capacity for empathy, honesty, and integrity;

- making it possible for each person to forgive themselves and others without condoning the harm they or their opponents have caused;

- enabling them to repair and redesign the dysfunctional systems that chronically generated the conflict; and

- assisting others in avoiding similar disputes in the future.

Thus, even minor, insignificant conflicts can be transformed into exercises that improve everyone's skills in listening, collaborative negotiations, and creative problem solving. Each one can deepen our capacity for integrity, patience, compassion, and forgiveness, and increase our ability to learn from our conflicts and transform them into sources of wisdom, insight, and personal and social improvement.

In short, every conflict offers each of its participants an opportunity to overcome what Sigmund Freud called "the narcissism of minor differences" and become better, more balanced, collaborative human beings.

For mediators, a detailed practical and theoretical exploration of how people learn to transform and transcend their conflicts leads to increased effectiveness, even in conflicts that are stuck in impasse or likely to result only in settlement and enduring bitterness. Yet while impasse and settlement can easily be externalized and described objectively, transformation and transcendence are subjective experiences that require us, as mediators, to become fully present and self-aware in order to explore and dismantle our own inherited and instinctual conflict responses. Journeying into the heart of conflict asks us not simply to become better mediators, but better human beings.

For this reason, at its deeper levels, conflict resolution is naturally and automatically a path of character and integrity, of heart and spirit, that begins here and now inside each of us. In the end, of course, there are no paths. The way forward begins wherever you are, and opens whenever you are ready to open your eyes, drop your judgments and expectations, and act authentically.

More fundamentally, we need to learn how to resolve our differences if we hope to ever end the use of warfare and environmental degradation, or assuage national, religious, and cultural hatreds. This requires us not only to focus our resources on learning and teaching the demanding arts and sciences of dispute resolution, but to recognize that we can only succeed in eliminating war and hatred in others by discovering how to eliminate them in ourselves.

Why This Book?

After more than twenty-five years mediating a broad range of disputes, I routinely experience conflicts not merely as physical, emotional, and intellectual, but as profoundly spiritual, heartfelt encounters, both with others and with myself. In thousands of disputes involving vastly different people and issues, transformation and transcendence have transpired so often as to demand a coherent practical and theoretical explanation. While I understand that it may not be possible to fully achieve this goal, each tiny step I take may encourage others to go further, and by clearing one small space in front of me, I can take the next small step into darkness and start exploring again.

My object in writing this book is therefore to gather the strands of my diverse experiences over the last several decades, explore the deeper and subtler aspects of conflict resolution, analyze their practical and theoretical interconnections, synthesize and unify them into a coherent whole, and consider their implications for the future. It is not my intention to *end* disagreements between conflict resolution practitioners, but to offer a way of experiencing, explaining, and understanding them.

I have been guided throughout by a conviction that the whole of conflict resolution is considerably greater than the sum of its parts, and that we have been describing the same essential truths from multiple, equally valid, angles. In the process, we have created a distorted impression that one is somehow better than the others. Yet art and science are both sources of wisdom, and we seem to have missed the forest for the single tree we have become most accustomed to seeing.

My objectives are to reveal the hidden sources of unity in theory and practice, link the different styles and approaches to mediation, and show how techniques associated with heart and spirit flow organically from an understanding of the field as a whole. I use art and science as metaphors and analogies to elucidate the subtle connections between human conflicts and those that occur in nature. I articulate a way of linking the orders of resolution with the principal elements, stages, steps, and phases of conflict as parts of a single, unified practical and theoretical whole.

This task is inherently so audacious that I have sought to perform it with genuine humility, as a work in progress that will require ongoing contributions from a range of diverse perspectives and approaches as it is elaborated, tested, contradicted, and refined. Mistakes and misstatements are inevitable in a project of this nature. The important thing is to begin, so that our future as a profession can proceed from a common understanding of the extraordinary richness of what connects our work and a profound commitment to the human and social values that inspire our field.

How the Book is Organized

I have organized the book in four sections, each of which integrates theoretical principles with practical techniques and applications. The first section explores the hidden elements, components, and ingredients of conflict, their evolution, the varieties of conflict resolution experience, and the practical techniques that characterize and distinguish each of the principal approaches to the subject.

In the second section, I consider a number of discrete, yet largely unexamined aspects of mediation practice in which it can be clearly seen how deeper and more profound resolution practices might be developed concretely. I examine the relationship between ego and I, techniques for transforming conflict stories, and ways of designing rituals to assist in reaching release, completion, closure, and disappearance of conflict.

In the third section, I explore heartfelt and spiritual aspects of conflict and consider the subtle, dangerous, and difficult methods involved in transformation and transcendence. I offer a secular, non-religious definition of spirit and show how to use mindfulness and heart as practical sources of effective, replicable, effective technique.

In the fourth section, I describe the characteristics needed to create a unified theory and the science of conflict as it appears in nature. I present a summary diagramming the theory and linking the elements, steps, techniques, and orders of resolution from previous chapters into a single description. Finally, I propose a vision for the future of mediation and articulate what I see as its shared values.

Each chapter in the first three sections is followed by a case study of a mediation I conducted, sometimes with a co-mediator, in order to illustrate some of the ideas in the preceding chapter and reveal how transformation and transcendence actually occur in real mediations. These case studies are not meant as directives or models to be followed blindly, but as self-reflective practice, revealing what I did in response to particular conflicts in order to stimulate theoretical investigation using real-life, nearly verbatim, yet disguised illustrations. I have included efforts that were unsuccessful, or only marginally successful, along with extraordinary transformations in order to encourage dialogue over the practice of mediation and a search for more skillful approaches.

Finally, this book is dedicated to Joan, whose consistent love, honesty, criticism, support, collaboration, and courageous heart have made it far, far better than it otherwise could have been. Also to Orrin, whose future is very much on my mind. My thanks go to those whose critiques have given it greater focus and precision, to those with whom I have been in conflict over the course of my life, and to those it has been my pleasure to assist in conflict resolution, from whom everything in this book was learned, as often by failure as by success.

Kenneth Cloke
Center for Dispute Resolution
Santa Monica, California

SECTION I:
THE HIDDEN NATURE OF CONFLICT AND RESOLUTION

Ring the bells that still can ring
Forget your perfect offering
There is a crack in everything
That's how the light gets in.
–Leonard Cohen

Chapter 1 Why We Get Stuck in Conflict

Sweet are the uses of adversity,
Which, like the toad, ugly and venomous,
Wears yet a precious jewel in his head.
–William Shakespeare

S weet, indeed, are the uses of adversity, yet this sweetness is often concealed in the ugly, venomous, toad-like aspects of conflict. The precious jewels our conflicts contain are the deeper truths they are capable of revealing to us—the true meaning and significance of the issues that
are in dispute; our character and potential; the hidden rationality, emotions,
and interests of our opponents; and the paradoxical nature of conflict in
general.

What prevents us from recognizing these deeper truths and learning from
our conflicts? What drives us along ugly, venomous, toad-like paths of
aggression and self-destruction, rather than those of dialogue and collaboration? What keeps us locked in impasse? And how can a deeper understanding of the sources of our conflicts help us find these precious jewels
and put them to better use?

The Pervasiveness of Conflict

We all grow up in families, live in neighborhoods, attend schools, work in
organizations, and participate in intimate relationships in which we experience conflict. By the time we become adults, most of us have spent thousands of hours in conflict. Yet few of us, in our families, neighborhoods,
schools, organizations, or intimate relationships receive comprehensive
practical instruction in how to prevent, manage, or resolve conflict. So let us
acknowledge two truths: first, that conflict is endemic and an essential part
of everyone's life experience; and second, that we have not been adequately trained in how to handle it.

As a consequence, nearly everyone behaves badly when they are in conflict, mimicking patterns they learned in their families of origin, and reverting to "fight or flight" default settings located in the amygdala—what is sometimes called the reptile brain—which stimulates automatic reflexes in response to perceived hostility. It is not the activation of these reflexes alone that makes conflict so difficult to handle, but the lack of awareness that they have been triggered and the consequent inability to pursue more constructive, creative, and evolved alternatives.

People in conflict seem unaware that by pursuing alternative approaches and disarming the reptile brain's default responses they can

- dramatically improve their relationships, self-confidence, and skills;

- increase their energy and effectiveness;

- transform arguments into useful conversations;

- liberate themselves from the constraint of unresolved conflict;

- discover more effective alternatives; and

- learn to transcend the conditions that gave rise to their opposition.

In any conflict, we may experience anger, fear, pain, jealousy, guilt, grief, or shame, sometimes simultaneously. We may also experience love, courage, empathy, compassion, joy, forgiveness, or self-esteem, equally simultaneously. This duality and the apparent paradox of concurrently experiencing creative and destructive emotions and, with them, humility and arrogance, divinity and stupidity, comedy and tragedy allows us to recognize that every conflict we experience both keeps us stuck and invites us to become better human beings by learning how to replace destructive with constructive responses. All of these contradictory tendencies exist inside us as unformed, disjointed forces that, given the right catalyst, can keep us imprisoned or set us free.

How people experience their conflicts depends less on the issues at stake than on the awareness, attitude, intention, and self-concept of each person in approaching them. These factors profoundly influence the way people think and feel about the issues, their opponents, themselves, and conflicts in general. Yet these are not fixed, permanent, or in-born features that, once formed, cannot be altered. On the contrary, it is possible to significantly alter people's awareness, attitudes, intentions, and self-concepts by

- changing the *way* they listen to their opponents,

- asking questions that probe beneath the surface of their assumptions,

- drawing them into creative collaborations,

- focusing their attention on the future rather than the past, and

- encouraging them to speak unspeakable, heartfelt, deeply guarded truths—not only to us, their mediators, but more importantly to each other.

Consequently, conflict is both a creative and a destructive force. While this fact is widely recognized, what is not adequately understood is that every conflict is also an opportunity for each of us, mediator and participant alike, to learn and practice more advanced and creative skills, develop higher levels of congruence and integrity, and lead more satisfying lives. To do so, we need to recognize why we become stuck in conflict in the first place, and what can be done to become unstuck.

Ten Reasons Why We Get Stuck in Conflict

There are undoubtedly hundreds if not thousands of reasons we become stuck in impasse and unable to end our conflicts. Here are my top ten, to which you can add your own.

1. *Conflict defines us and gives our lives meaning.* Having an enemy is a quick, easy source of identity, because we *are* whatever they are *not*. By defining our opponents as evil, we implicitly define ourselves as good. Our opponents' apparently demonic behaviors allow us to appear—if not angelic by comparison—at least poor, innocent victims who are entitled to sympathy and support. Yet identifying ourselves

as victims leaves us feeling powerless to resolve our disputes and encourages us to spiral downward into an abyss of fear, pain, anger, and self-righteousness from which it becomes more and more difficult to escape. It makes our opponents seem worse and ourselves better than we actually are. It causes us to lose perspective, resist learning, and hold onto unrealistic expectations.

2. *Conflict gives us energy*, even if it is only the energy of anger, fear, jealousy, guilt, shame, and grief. We can become addicted to the adrenaline rush, the flash point intensity, and the *intimacy* of combat. Yet this energy is ultimately debilitating, providing a quick stimulus that dies just as quickly, in place of the healthier, longer-lasting energy that emanates from compassion, collaboration, and honest, empathetic communication. The negative energy in conflict can keep us stuck and deepen our suffering, causing us to pay a steep physical, intellectual, emotional, and spiritual price in deteriorated health, peace of mind, anxiety, and unhappiness.

3. *Conflict ennobles our misery* and makes it appear that we are suffering for a worthwhile cause. Without conflict, we may feel we suffered in vain and be forced to critique our choices and regret the wasted lives we've led. Yet the effort to assign higher meaning to our suffering encourages us to justify its continuation or to deceive ourselves into thinking our own abusive behaviors serve some higher purpose. It causes us to get angry at people who suggest alternatives and encourages us to hold onto our suffering, rather than learn from it, let it go, and move on to more collaborative, less hostile relationships.

4. *Conflict safeguards our personal space* and encourages others to recognize our needs and respect our privacy. For many of us, conflict seems the only way of effectively declaring our rights, securing the respect of others, restoring our inner balance, and protecting ourselves from boundary violations. Yet conflict also creates false boundaries, keeps out those we want to let in and lets in those we don't, substitutes declarations of rights for satisfaction of interests, secures respect based on fear rather than personal regard, and creates justifications for counterattack and continued abuse. It erects walls that separate and isolate us from each other and prevent us from collaboratively negotiating the use of common space, being authentic, or finding out who we, or they, actually are.

5. *Conflict creates intimacy*, even if it is only the transient, *negative* intimacy of fear, rage, attachment, and loss. Every two-year-old instinctively knows that it is better to be noticed for doing something wrong than not to be noticed at all. Yet negative intimacy is ultimately unsatisfactory because it prevents us from finding positive intimacy in its stead. Many relationships are sustained by invalidating, insulting, conflict-laden communications that simultaneously bring us together and keep us apart, frustrate our efforts to get closer and undermine the lasting intimacy we really want based on positive regard, mutual affection, trust, and shared vulnerability.

6. *Conflict camouflages our weaknesses* and diverts attention from sensitive subjects we would rather avoid discussing. It is a smokescreen, a way of passing the buck, blaming others, and distracting attention from our mistakes. Yet doing so cheats us of opportunities to learn from our mistakes, makes us defensive, diminishes our integrity, and reduces our capacity for authentic, responsible relationships. It impedes our willingness to address real issues, and diverts our awareness from sensitive subjects, falsely magnifying their importance and effect.

7. *Conflict powerfully communicates what we honestly feel,* allowing us to vent and assuage our pain by unloading our emotions onto others. While venting allows us to reduce our own emotional suffering, it increases stress and emotional suffering in others and fails to communicate our respect or regard for them. Venting encourages us to not take responsibility for our choices or address what got us upset in the first place. Venting communicates disrespect, encourages defensiveness and counterattack, escalates underlying conflicts, and does not accurately express who we are capable of being when we are with someone who is genuinely listening and caring.

8. *Conflict gets results.* It forces others to heed us, especially faceless bureaucrats, clerks, and service representatives, who only seem to respond to our requests or do what we want when we yell at them. But yelling turns *us* into angry, insensitive, aggravated people and adds unnecessary stress to the lives of frequently unhappy, alienated, powerless, poorly paid employees who are compelled to pointlessly accept our wrath. It turns us into bullies, and gets us less in the long run than we could get by politely requesting their assistance and eliciting their

desire to be helpful. It discourages us from being genuine and open and produces outcomes that undermine what we really want.

9. *Conflict makes us feel righteous* by encouraging us to believe we are opposing evil behaviors and rewarding those that are good. Our opponents' pernicious actions justify us in giving them what they "rightly deserve." Yet righteousness is easily transformed into self-righteousness, and good and evil are far more complex, subtle, and nuanced than we are prepared to admit. Engaging in conflict reduces our capacity for empathy and compassion. It makes us haughty, judgmental, superior, and less able to be humble, accepting, and egalitarian in our relationships. And, it allows us to cross the line from punishing evil to committing it ourselves.

10. *Conflict prompts change,* which feels better than impasse and stagnation. Many changes only take place as a result of conflict—not because it is actually necessary to achieve a given result, but because people's fear and resistance make it so. Yet conflict also prompts resistance to change, which can be more successfully overcome through inclusion, collaborative dialogue, and interest-based negotiations. Adversarial conflict stimulates a backlash dedicated to minimizing whatever gains it may achieve and polarizing those who might otherwise become its supporters. Worse, as a means, it undermines the ends to which it is ostensibly dedicated. While the deepest and most consequential changes actually *require* conflict, understanding this requirement allows us to design strategies for transforming destructive criticisms into constructive suggestions for improvement and increasing our skills and effectiveness as change agents.

There are many excellent reasons for engaging in adversarial conflict, but there are even better reasons for resolving it and collaborating with our opponents in informal problem solving, unrestricted dialogue, and interest-based negotiations. While adversarial conflicts can produce beneficial outcomes, they can also result in alienation, defensiveness, counterattack, and resistance. Worse, they can create a quality of energy and attitude that gives an appearance of strength while actually sapping it. This weakness makes it more difficult to solve common problems, engage each other constructively, and learn what our conflicts are trying to teach us.

There is really only one great constructive use of adversity: to open our eyes and ears, minds and hearts, and force us to pay attention to what is happening within, around, and between us. Our conflicts are our teachers and liberators because they invite us to wake up and become aware of what we have not yet learned how to handle skillfully. They expose our internal myths, assumptions, antagonisms, misunderstandings, emotional triggers, false expectations, and hidden weaknesses. They direct our attention to wounds that desperately need to heal and problems we urgently need to solve. As Carl Jung presciently wrote, "Everything that irritates us about others can lead us to an understanding of ourselves."

Conflict is therefore simply the sound made by the cracks in a system, regardless of whether the system is personal, relational, familial, organizational, social, economic, or political. Alternatively, it is a warning light pointing at something in our character, relationship, or environment that is not working, either for ourselves or for others. It can be an opportunity for rethinking and innovation, or the birth pang of a new way of being or behaving that is waiting to be born. Equally, it can be a reminder of our interdependence, of the skills we still need to improve, of what is most important in life, of what we need to do or let go of in order to escape its orbit and evolve to higher levels of conflict and resolution.

The principal difficulty with conflict is that we allow *it* to define *us*, usually in the wrong way—for ourselves and against others—rather than for ourselves and with others against our common problems. It deprives us of deep, profound, heartfelt relationships that can only develop through dialogue, problem solving, and collaborative negotiation, and traps us in ancient, profitless, destructive stories that do not allow us to resolve, transform, or transcend what got us into conflict in the first place.

The Components of Conflict

To understand in detail how and why people get stuck in conflict, it is useful to identify the individual components, elements, and ingredients that are required to create a conflict. In my view, for any simple disagreement to turn into a conflict, the first three of the following six components are essential, while the final three help cement it in place and make it intractable.

1. Initially, there have to be two or more people, or two or more opposing parts of the same person, in order to establish a polarity or opposition. We have all heard the admonition "It takes two to tango." We forget that this implies the presence of a corollary: it takes *one* to stop the tango, and that one can be anybody. One person is not enough to create a conflict. Trying to do so is like trying to produce the sound of clapping with one hand. This suggests that we can end our conflicts at any time simply by changing the music or adopting a different dance step, and that introspection, strategic withdrawal, unilateral concession, and forgiveness might be useful techniques in resolving them.

2. Logically, since it is possible for two or more people to interact without creating a conflict, another element is required. A second component is the presence of some difference, disagreement, or dispute regarding an issue over which it is possible to take opposing sides, such as content, process, relationship, or outcome. Yet every opposite is connected along a *line of polarity* just as up and down are connected along a line of height. This suggests that several techniques might be useful in resolving conflict. For example

    -   dialogue over issues,

    -   collaborative negotiation of differences,

    -   small agreements over ground rules and similar details,

    -   brainstorming,

    -   caucusing, and

    -   creative problem solving.

3. Since it is possible for two or more people to disagree and still not have a conflict, something additional is required. A third component is the presence of negative emotions, such as anger, fear, jealousy, shame, guilt, or grief. These emotions fix the conflict, giving it shape, energy, and consistency. Yet emotional intelligence can be both encouraged and developed. People can learn to listen actively, responsively, and empathetically to their opponents expressing negative emotions and

not get upset. This implies that several techniques might be useful in resolving conflict. For example

- recognizing and taking responsibility for emotions,

- listening empathetically,

- venting,

- acknowledging,

- internalizing, and

- translating emotions into practical suggestions.

While negative behaviors are not an essential component of conflict, they are derivative of the first three and represent the acting out of negative emotions and instinctual responses to perceived hostility. Yet negative behaviors can be minimized using several techniques. For example

- mutually agreeing not to engage in them in the future,

- speaking calmly and respectfully and asking open-ended questions,

- calling attention to these behaviors when they occur,

- communicating what it felt like to experience them,

- acknowledging and satisfying the underlying feelings that triggered them,

- clarifying their negative impact, and

- identifying rewards or penalties that might discourage both sides from using them again.

4. The fourth component in conflict is less tangible and consequently more difficult to define. It is the presence of

- an antagonistic spirit, intention, or energy;

- an intolerant or unforgiving goal or aim;

- a weakened or embittered life force, soul, or chi; or

- an attachment to being in conflict that seeks impasse or makes it difficult to discover and discuss what lies beneath the surface.

No matter how skillfully a mediator may dismantle the first three components, failing to address the fourth allows the conflict to continue, since it serves a hidden internal purpose or responds to a larger problem that may have little to do with the people or issues in dispute. Yet in describing their conflict, people provide clues and opportunities for identifying, clarifying, resolving, and transforming these hostile energies and intentions. This suggests that several techniques might be useful in resolving conflicts. For example

- developing a capacity for honesty and empathy,

- introspection,

- centering,

- monitoring intentions,

- listening closely to conflict stories,

- surrendering false expectations,

- releasing and letting go of conflict,

- forgiving one's opponents and one's self, and

- and helping people move on with their lives.

5. The fifth component is similarly difficult to define. It is the presence within the parties of a heart or attitude that is closed, hostile, self-centered, or withholding toward their opponent, themselves, or the

conflict. This attitude is often a result of accumulated pain or repeated trauma, leading people to shut their hearts in order to protect them from further damage. Yet conflict resolution provides multiple opportunities for authentic, heart-to-heart communications, even between people who dislike or distrust each other, suggesting that several techniques might be useful in resolving conflict. For example

- encouraging intimate, empathetic, honest dialogue;

- asking questions that open people's hearts;

- inviting them to engage in poignant, profound, heart-to-heart communications;

- collaborating;

- learning from conflict; and

- reaching reconciliation.

6. A sixth, rarely identified component consists of the presence of an adversarial, bureaucratic, or highly competitive system, context, culture, or environment—be it psychological, relational, familial, organizational, social, economic, or political. Systems manifest their dysfunctions through chronic conflicts that may appear purely personal, yet emanate from systemic sources. These conflicts grow deeper and more profound as a system loses its ability to adapt to changing environments. Systemic disputes may emerge in families, for example, as a result of false expectations, distorted roles, or overlapping responsibilities. In organizations they may emerge as a result of unclear vision or goals, inept leadership, or hierarchical, bureaucratic, autocratic managerial practices; in societies they may emerge as a result of persistent inequalities or unjust treatment. This suggests that identifying and reforming dysfunctional systems, contexts, and environments, including their structures, processes, relationships, and cultures, might be useful techniques in resolving conflict.

The following table summarizes and describes these components, the likely results of each, what is needed, wanted, or missing to move toward resolution, and some possible strategies for intervention in mediation.

Table 1. Components of Conflict

Indispensable Component	Likely Results of Component	What is Needed, Wanted, or Missing	Possible Strategies for Intervention
1. Two or more people (or internal parts of the same person)	Diverse interests, isolation, distrust, competitive relationships	Communication, openness, positive intent, common goals	Ground rules, listening, story telling, empathy, common interests
2. Disagreement over content, process, relationship, or outcomes	Unresolved issues, differences over facts, competing issues, personal solutions common interests	Engagement, logical analysis, neutral identification and discussion of dialogue	Brainstorming, collaborative negotiation, creative problem solving
3. Negative emotion; e.g., anger, fear, jealousy, shame, guilt, or grief	Unexpressed or hostile emotions, incomplete or inadequate compassion and letting go	Emotional closure, introspection, venting, empathy, acknowledgment, self-esteem, rituals, completion	Venting, acknowledgement, caucusing, emotional processing, rituals of closure
4. Antagonistic spirit, intention, or energy; intolerant or unforgiving aim, attachment, embittered life force, soul, or chi	Chronic conflict, illness, injury, blindness to self and others, confusion, spiritual imbalance, feeling stuck, incessant suffering	Forgiveness, mindfulness, insight, expanded awareness, authenticity, acceptance, release, apology, tolerance, willingness to let go	Honesty, empathy, introspection, centering, meditation, rituals, shift from negative to positive energy
5. Closed-hearted hostile, self-centered, or withholding outlook	Dysfunctional relationships, depression, self-centeredness, broken heart	Reconciliation, compassion, positive attitude, heart-to-heart dialogue	Openhearted attitude, communication, confession, learning, acceptance of self and other
6. Adversarial, bureaucratic, or highly competitive system, context, culture, or environment	Inimical social conditions and/or structure or system; e.g., inequity, hierarchical, bureaucratic, and autocratic relations	Systemic change, collaborative relationship, cultural sensitivity, increased equity, equality, and democracy	Transform system, alter or adapt to environment, balance power, build participation, consensus, and ownership

After differentiating and analyzing these components, it is important to recognize that conflict is essentially holistic and cannot be subdivided without rendering it, at a deep level, incomprehensible. While every distinction we invent or discover is a potential key permitting us to unlock impasse at its source, it also allows us to move a little closer to understanding and unlocking the whole.

As these elements swirl and co-mingle in the chaos of conflict, they appear inseparable, and it becomes difficult to recognize what needs to be done to reach resolution. Every conflict thus creates a kind of blindness or confusion regarding the unique, distinct elements that lead to it. This blindness extends to people's impressions of their opponents, and to the root causes of their disagreements, the engrained patterns of their emotions, the attitudes underlying their adversarial behaviors, the deeper spiritual and heartfelt meaning of their conflicts, and the systemic sources of their hostility. Separating these elements and addressing each separately can release people from impasse and lead them to discover the reasons they became stuck—sometimes piecemeal, and sometimes suddenly, in a single stroke.

In truth, there are hundreds of ways of defining and analyzing the components of conflict. Each fresh component or insight can lead directly to some new technique and improved understanding of conflict in general. Ultimately, each component draws the parties' attention back to what *they* did or did not do that made the conflict worse and discourages them from blaming their opponents for what they have not overcome within themselves.

The Circle of Conflict

Another way of describing conflict is to see it as a relationship between polar opposites, a dialectical interplay between countervailing values and principles, a field of forces united in opposition, a dance of antithetical, inimical, refractory possibilities. Because of this contradictory character, conflict can also be defined simply as a state of being stuck or at impasse, as a kind of dysfunctional equilibrium, counterbalance, or stasis in which two equal and opposite forces are drawn into apparently endless rotation around a common hidden center.

What keeps people stuck, going round and round the same issues with no apparent escape? How do they become unstuck and transcend these opposing forces? What releases them from the unfriendly embrace of their conflicts? What triggers resolution, forgiveness, and reconciliation? While an opposition of forces can result in chaos or stalemate, it can also result in a fresh realization, synthesis, and collaboration that transforms and transcends the limits of static order and chaotic opposition.

If we analogize conflict at impasse to circles or ellipses with a double center, we can see that, like planetary orbits, conflicts consist of two equal and opposite forces: a centripetal force that unites and draws them together and a centrifugal one that separates and drives them apart, as illustrated in the following diagram.

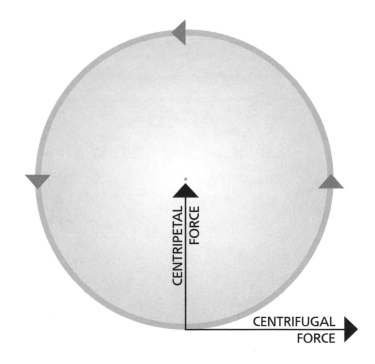

Once we recognize that conflict is a combination of centripetal and centrifugal forces, we can reason logically that it should be possible to end a conflict not merely centrifugally by walking away and leaving it intact, but centripetally by moving toward its hidden center and seeking out its heart, hub, or nucleus rather than trying to avoid, escape, or run away from it. As people advance toward this secret source, they release the energy that fuels and keeps them in orbit, revealing the internal features and holistic character of their dispute.

By thinking of conflict as a circle, ellipse, or three-dimensional sphere, we can understand that the further we go in one direction, after a certain point we begin moving in the opposite direction. And while circles and spheres can be said to possess poles and equators, these are imaginary constructs that can be drawn anywhere. If we combine the circularity of conflict and the repetitiveness of people's arguments with the polarity and one-sidedness of their attitudes and behaviors, we transform circles and ellipses into dynamic geometric patterns that expose the polarized, contradictory, yin/yang nature of conflict arguments, as in the following diagram.

When people experience their conflict as a precise balance between inter-connected, antagonistic positions, as revealed in this diagram, they realize that within it are unified polarized forces similar to the positive and negative poles in an electromagnetic field. In spite of the energy of their opposition, their conflict *connects* them, uniting them along a line of polarity, just as up and down are united along a line of height, hot and cold along a line of temperature, and conflicting parties along a line of caring about the same issues. This line of polarity is also a line of relational energy, intimacy, transformational potential, latent synergy, and transcendence, as will be explored in later chapters.

From Circles to Spirals

Most conflicts are filled with a cacophony and noisome chaos that confuses people about their real meaning. Yet at their center, as in the eye of a hurricane, there is silence and peace, which poet Rainer Maria Rilke described beautifully as "the noise at the entryway to the voiceless silence of a true conflict." When we pay attention to this voiceless silence in conflict—to what people really mean—everything they do or say can lead to the center of their dispute. The parties can locate this center, as with all circles, not by moving outward against their opponents, but by moving inward toward the core of the conflict within themselves.

Whatever we as mediators approach correctly—with the right attitude and intention—leads to its center, or rather from our center it becomes possible to touch the parties' centers, while from our periphery we can touch only their periphery. When we speak and listen empathetically, we automatically encourage empathy in others. When we connect in our hearts with others, we recognize the illusion of our separateness and the reality of our interdependence. We can then see that the invisible lines that divide and polarize us point *directly* at what we most need to learn and overcome.

After analogizing conflicts to circles, we can imagine their transformation into spirals, which can only be done by upsetting their equilibrium and the balance of opposing forces that have kept them in orbit. If every conflict consists of a centripetal force pointing outward toward one's opponent and an equal and opposite centrifugal force pointing inward toward one's self, the outward force represents the desire to avoid, retreat, or find release from the orbit of impasse. The inward force represents the desire to advance closer to understanding what is holding the conflict in seemingly endless rotation, drawing it toward a hidden gravitational center. Transforming circles into spirals means helping people learn what got them stuck, changing directions, improving their skills, and overcoming the equilibrium of forces that are reinforcing the conflict, allowing it to spiral into a more evolved orbit.

Mediation can help people escape circular orbits of impasse by using the polarized energy of their caring to catapult them into higher levels of awareness and understanding. This means exploiting the *centrifugal* force of repulsion to create an energy of disengagement, distance, balance, and equanimity that allows them to break the equilibrium of the status quo. It then means using the *centripetal* force of unity and attraction to create an energy of engagement, empathy, commitment, and caring that allows opponents to discover the hidden core of their conflict. Together, these opposing energies permit people to synthesize the catalytic energy of their opposition, escape the gravitational orbit of their conflicts, and discover what lies hidden at their center.

Surrounding this tension between struggle and accommodation, engagement and renunciation, repulsion and attraction is a field in which these forces can be creatively combined and resolved, and where a third mediating force can blend, transform, and integrate them, encouraging them to spiral into a new orbit connected at their heart or center. This third force, perceptively described by William Ury in *The Third Way*, can be found in the Gandhian integration of non-violence and resistance; the intensity of honest, open dialogue; and the combination of head and heart that, in many Asian and indigenous cultures, is called "thinking with the heart."

The Mathematics of Conflict

The metaphor of circles and ellipses offers an additional insight. Part of the mathematical description of every circle is the number *pi*, an infinitely indeterminate quantity that gives every circle an unending character. So too, every conflict contains something infinite and unending in its logic, revealing a kind of symmetry that can be broken in two fundamental ways: by separating and denying its unity, or by uniting and affirming its wholeness.

When people go round and round the same arguments, it is because there is something fundamental, durable, and infinite at the center of the circle of their conflict waiting to be recognized and addressed. At the same time, there exists a resistance to getting there that keeps them in orbit around it. The longer they remain on the periphery, the more boring, idiotic, and pointless their conflicts seem. The closer people get to what lies at the center of their conflict, the more exhilarating, profound, and rewarding the conflicts become.

Extending this mathematical analogy, it is possible to identify an infinite number of points on a line of any length, each marking a discrete location. Yet not all of these points can be precisely ascertained. Some can only be represented by transcendental numbers, themselves infinite in length. To correctly identify even one such number would require an infinite amount of information, which is beyond the capacity of the most powerful computer imaginable. Thus, at a certain point, precision becomes impossible, and with it, predictability and one-to-one causality. In a similar way, conflicts defy precise definition, upset prediction and causality, resist division, and seem infinite in their depth.

For example, if we ask how far apart people are when they are in conflict we can derive three correct answers.

1. They are an *infinite* distance apart because they are unable to communicate and believe the issues dividing them cannot be resolved.

2. They are *no* distance apart because they are inseparable and intimately connected along the line of polarity created by their disagreement, implying a unity of opposition.

3. They are precisely *one step* apart because either of them can reach out to the other at any time and eliminate their separation.

If we think of the elements of conflict as sources of distance between infinitely divided yet intimately connected people, similar to the points on a line, it is possible to find, as Zeno's ancient parables describe, that if one tries to cross a room by covering half the distance, then half again, repeating half steps, one will never reach the other side. In conflict, this means that an infinite number of reasons can be found for never reaching resolution. Yet each element of conflict can be flipped or transformed from a source of repulsion and opposition to a source of attraction and unity. In this way, two or more can create synergy, disagreements can result in better ideas, negative emotions, attitudes, and intentions can turn into positive ones, and dysfunctional systems can trigger desperately needed changes.

How We Respond to Conflict

Everyone responds to conflict in their own unique ways, which can be charted not only mathematically, but geometrically, through forms and Cartesian diagrams that reveal how seemingly irrational conflict responses can be understood as reflecting underlying symmetries when mapped onto a two-dimensional space.

The two fundamental tensions that characterize most conflict behaviors consist generally of a concern for people and a concern for results. These can be seen to culminate in a variety of different conflict behaviors, as revealed in the chart on the next page, similar to a complex number plane. I have designed the chart based on a simpler version that is concentrated exclusively on the upper right-hand corner, originally created by Thomas and Kilman.

Diagramming conflict responses in this way allows us to clarify what we know intuitively: that people indirectly and unconsciously communicate the kind of relationship they would like to have with their opponents and the results they would like to achieve by the way they behave when they are in conflict.

More importantly, this chart allows us to understand that whenever people accommodate, they automatically communicate that they are more concerned about people than about results, just as they communicate the opposite when they act cruelly or aggressively. We can then appreciate that if we want them to act collaboratively, we can do so by encouraging them to recognize the importance of relationships as well as results.

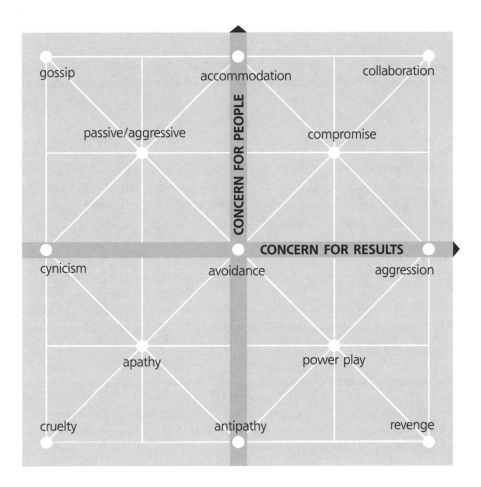

Clearly, none of the responses diagrammed is wrong in principle. Each is simply a choice about how to respond to a given conflict, and there will be times when each may prove necessary, useful, or effective. Conflict choices are fluid and susceptible to change based on how people feel at the time— not only about their conflict, but about themselves, their opponents, and the issues.

Nonetheless, it is clear that only collaboration, among all these options, is able to maximize a concern for people together with a concern for results. To illustrate how understanding these deeper patterns can trigger resolution, forgiveness, and reconciliation, consider the following case study.

Blinded by Conflict—A Case Study

Sara had been blind from birth. She had also been a victim of childhood sexual abuse, and while she had gone on to become a champion downhill skier, karate expert, and horseback rider, she had not been successful in establishing a satisfying sexual relationship.

She met Bill in 1978. They did not marry or live together, but dated for about six months. She said she had not wanted a sexual relationship with him. Nonetheless, according to Sara, Bill had raped her and she had become pregnant. Bill denied doing so, but did not provide an alternate version of their sexual encounter.

Sara said nothing to Bill about the pregnancy and had the baby, Scott, alone. While undergoing counseling regarding the aftereffects of her rape, Sara decided, when Scott was two years old, to confront Bill with his child. At first Bill denied paternity, though his son looked a lot like him. He asked Sara how she knew Scott was his. It took him a while to accept that Scott was his son, and he had many misgivings about Sara not telling him.

He began to see Scott for a couple of hours on Saturdays, then steadily increased the time they spent together. He began to pay child support and agreed in mediation that the amount he was paying was not sufficient. Sara felt she had supported Bill's relationship with Scott and acknowledged in mediation that he had "stuck in there."

Two years previously, at a workshop for single parents and their children attended by Sara, Scott drew a picture revealing sexual content and suggesting possible sexual molestation. An allegation of possible sexual abuse was filed against Sara's mother, who had been Scott's primary caretaker, which both sides felt was unfounded. Scott was taken from his home and from his father and mother and eventually sent to Sara's sisters, who refused to allow Bill to even see him.

Sara and her mother hired an attorney, and while Bill felt he had been supportive of them, he discovered in court that his paternity was not established and he was not recognized as Scott's father. All the latent hostility Sara and Bill felt toward one another came out in court and the child abuse case turned into a bitter custody battle. Bill hired an attorney and was finally able to secure a joint custody order with visitation every other week.

Scott began spending one week with his mother and the next with his father. Sara began a relationship with another man, Ted. They discussed marriage, but Sara had been troubled throughout the relationship, and in the course of several years together they had not had sex with one another.

In August, Sara and Ted decided to move to a small town about four hours from Los Angeles where she and Bill had lived and worked, and where Scott, now age 7 1/2, had gone to school. She gave brief notice to Bill of her decision to move, and none to the court. Bill applied for and received a temporary restraining order preventing her from removing Scott from Los Angeles and applied for sole custody, alleging that Sara was in violation of the court's prior order regarding joint custody and visitation.

Sara appeared in court to oppose the order and lost. School was due to start in one week, both sides were at complete loggerheads, and a trial was set for October, long after school began. They had each spent tens of thousands of dollars on legal fees and were no closer to a solution. In desperation, Sara's attorney recommended mediation.

At first, Bill was reluctant to come to mediation and refused to pay for it. Sara said she was unable to pay. In order to get them started, I agreed to begin the mediation, and indicated that if they felt I had not been helpful at the end of two hours they would not be required to pay. I have done this on several occasions when a couple's conflicts prevent them from agreeing on who will pay for the mediation and I have always been paid at the end of the session.

I asked Sara to start because she seemed the most agitated and untrusting, but she deferred to Bill. But as Bill spoke, she continually interrupted him. Bill threatened to leave if she continued, which created a difficulty because she was unable, due to her blindness, to take handwritten notes for later reference.

I shifted back to Sara, but she was less informative alone than in response to Bill's narrative. I asked her how she felt about the one-week-on, one-week-off schedule, and she said it was not working for her, or, she thought, for Scott, because the transitions were difficult. She expressed concern over changes in Scott's behavior after he returned from Bill's, where there were constant videos and nonstop talk about ninjas, He-Man, Superman, and other escapes into fantasy. She felt these activities were excessive and interfered with Scott's emotional development.

I asked her what she wanted. She said she wanted Scott to be with her for nine months during the school year and was willing to give up all holidays and vacations to support Bill's relationship with him. She said she wanted them to be close and did not want to interfere with their relationship. I asked her to speak directly to Bill and tell him what she wanted and why. She turned to him and repeated what she had said to me, but more directly, emotionally, and in a heartfelt way.

I then asked Bill to tell Sara directly what he wanted and how he felt about what she had said. He said he loved his son and wanted to see him all the time, but recognized that Scott needed his mother and was willing to do whatever was necessary to help him. He felt Sara should have given him more notice and consulted with him rather than just announcing her move. He told Sara he still loved her, but recognized that they were unable to get along. For example, Bill regularly invited Sara to talk, but she always hung up the phone or walked out on him. He agreed that the every-other-week schedule was not perfect. He had moved a few months earlier to an apartment only a block from Sara's so that Scott could walk between their houses. He appreciated Sara's acknowledgment of his relationship with Scott and felt that joint custody was a compromise he had agreed to because it would help Scott.

I thanked them for the honesty of their statements and their willingness to acknowledge their son's need to spend as much time with each of them as possible. I pointed out that they had a much harder time reaching agreement when they discussed what had occurred in the past than when they focused on their son and his future. I summarized their requests and asked whether they would be willing to agree on a solution that would reflect what was best for their son. They agreed.

They also agreed that many parents lived apart and exchanged children during school holidays; that many psychologists counseled against switching children too frequently, or from school to school; that children generally prefer not to switch schools before graduation; that courts often prefer mothers as the primary custodial parents for younger children and fathers for older children, especially boys; and that as Scott grew older he would probably want to have a direct say in where he would live during the school year.

We discussed a number of possible solutions, and they agreed in general that Scott would need to spend his school year with one parent and holidays with the other. We also discussed travel arrangements, improving their communications, and increasing child support. But, in the end, Sara and Bill still each wanted Scott to live with them during the school year. I asked whether they would consider dividing the elementary school grades into two sets, where Scott would spend the third and fourth grades with one parent the and fifth and sixth with the other.

Bill said he was willing to work things out with Sara and be more generous than he had planned before coming to the mediation. He offered to let Scott live with Sara for two years, then with him for the next two years, and that Scott would spend school holidays and every other weekend during that time with the other non-custodial parent. Sara felt relieved and quickly agreed.

I wrote down their principal points of agreement, which included drop-off times and places, and agreements to be flexible, to make these exchanges a priority, to take Scott's wishes into consideration in selecting his junior high and high schools, to meet again to discuss their communication problems and child support issues, and to return to mediation if there were any future problems.

Bill suggested that they see Scott together after the mediation to tell him together what they had decided. Sara agreed. They agreed to tell Scott that they had resolved their differences and were going to support each other more in the future. They agreed that they would do more things together with Scott and not let their past disagreements get in the way of their future cooperation. They agreed to let bygones be bygones, recognize that they both loved Scott more than anyone, and discuss any issues regarding his future and well being with each other before jumping to conclusions.

I congratulated them on their success in reaching these agreements and on their willingness to compromise and acknowledge each other's love for Scott. I told them how lucky I thought Scott was to have two parents who loved him so much. They both began to cry and talked about how much they loved him and wanted the best for him. I said I hoped they would continue to acknowledge and respect each other and recognize how difficult the past few years had been for both of them. I suggested some ground rules for their future communications and we set another date for mediation. Bill offered to pay for the mediation and, as they left, he reached over and hugged Sara, who hugged him back. They both stood and cried for a while, and left arm in arm.

The mediation succeeded because it encouraged them to recognize that in spite of their opposing differences they had one powerful interest in common: they both loved their son. As a result, they were willing to sacrifice their anger at each other for his welfare and commit to finding an imperfect solution outside the legal system and making it work. This result was encouraged by their experience with the costs, delays, uncertainties, and emotional damage they had suffered in the courts.

The mediation allowed them to express their emotions and anger at each other, yet recognize that their anger would not help them make decisions regarding their son. At various points, I made them aware of specific communication problems by asking them to focus on the future rather than the past. I stopped their circular arguments periodically with process interventions, pointed out specific communication problems as they occurred, and occasionally said, "Let's take a look at what just happened in your conversation with each other," in an effort to increase their awareness of *how* they were communicating. I worked with them to create a common agenda, refocused their attention on problems rather than each other, and provided them with information regarding criteria other parents had used to solve similar problems.

The mediation did not become sidetracked in endless, collateral arguments over whether Bill had actually raped Sara years earlier, whether their son had been molested, etc., since none of these issues, in their minds or mine, ought to have determined where Scott would go to school. Sara's blindness was acknowledged and addressed openly, but not allowed to dominate or distort their negotiations.

In closure, I encouraged them to acknowledge their mutual love for their son and suggested that they might actually become friends over time. While the session began with acrimony and accusation, it ended with both of them speaking from their hearts to each other. They started to reach forgiveness and reconciliation the moment they agreed to tell their son together what they had decided and try to minimize his feeling that one of them had been treated unfairly or had greater power than the other. In this way, they took a small, significant, collaborative step toward joint parenting, transcended the issues and conditions that had led them into litigation, and learned the power of collaboratively negotiating their interests and communicating from their hearts.

In short, they were able to transform their conflict and successfully create a collaborative parenting relationship in place of the competitive one that had developed over time—not just as an idea, but as a real experience. They were able to break through their animosity and reestablish a more integrated family system, even at a distance. Finally, they were able to speak honestly to each other, deepen their relationship, and transcend the centripetal orbit of their earlier relationship.

In a follow-up mediation I conducted several months later, Bill and Sara both reported that their agreements had held up and their communications had never been better. Scott was doing well, the transitions had become less difficult, and their new relationship had reduced his level of anxiety, hostility, and acting out. They both felt they were starting to become friends again.

Chapter 2 The Evolution of Conflict and Resolution

Give me a fruitful error any time,
full of seeds, bursting with its own corrections.
You can keep your sterile truth for yourself.
–Vilfredo Pareto

Without conflict, quite simply, there would be no learning, growth, or change. This is not merely because learning, growth, and change require a release from obsolete circumstances, but because every human being, relationship, organization, and system stabilizes itself by means of integration and order, yet is only able to evolve to higher levels of functioning by means of disintegration and disorder, expressed primarily through conflict.

The more desperately a given change is required, the greater the risk that it will threaten the balance of power within a system, making both its continued existence and precise resolution uncertain. This uncertainty can provoke fears that change will become chaotic or necessitate higher levels of skill than may currently be available to successfully resolve the underlying problem, thereby promoting increased resistance, defensiveness, and calculated impasse.

Thus, breakdowns inevitably precede breakthroughs, and chronic conflict is the first sign that fundamental shifts are taking place within a person, relationship, organization, or system. Breakdowns result from an accumulation of chronic conflict due to anomalies, dysfunctions, and difficulties that have not and cannot be completely resolved or transcended within the confines of an existing system. Yet, for this very reason, they are also potential sources of innovative ideas, fresh perspectives, creative thinking, inventive solutions, and higher levels of order.

Chronic conflict is therefore not only a sign that a person, relationship, organization, or system is breaking down, but an indication that its problems can and increasingly *must* be resolved in order for it to evolve. When our conflicts are easily resolvable, we experience only isolated, episodic, situational disagreements. Chronic conflicts occur only when we can no longer function optimally under given conditions and require release from whatever is preventing us from evolving.

The Evolutionary Dance of Conflict and Resolution

Conflict and resolution are thus a dance, inextricably linked in their logic, essence, and evolutionary rhythms. Together, they suggest a punctuated equilibrium model of development, as described by the late evolutionary biologist Stephen Jay Gould, in which periods of equilibrium are interrupted by intervals of rapid transformation.

Chronic conflicts represent the emergence—within a person, relationship, organization, or system—of an environmentally induced need to change that cannot be addressed without evolving to a higher level of order. These conflicts are distinguishable primarily by their

- repetition,

- low orders of resolution,

- incongruity between high level of emotion and apparent triviality of the issues over which people are fighting,

- being commonly mistaken for miscommunications or personality clashes,

- tolerance of disrespectful and adversarial behaviors,

- seeming irrationality,

- accidental misunderstandings,

- idiosyncratic circumstances, and

- underlying similarities.

In truth, an organism and its environment are one. If any person, organization, or system wishes to improve, change, or evolve, in response to either internal needs or environmental demands, it is first necessary to actively seek out the internal and external obstacles that block advancement, as well as the processes, methods, and techniques by which those obstacles can be identified, analyzed, and overcome. This means asking questions that reveal the internal and external sources of conflicts and what can be done to prevent, resolve, transform, and transcend them.

Evolution can occur not only in the content or substance of conflicts (*what* people fight about), but also in their contour or form (*how* they fight about them), and in their context or meaning (*why* they fight about them). Resolution, therefore, means working through the content, or underlying reasons for conflict, and abandoning the old ways of thinking and behaving that led to them. Transformation means altering the contour, form, or shape of the conflict, both within the parties and in their relationships, communications, and perceptions of the issues over which they are fighting. Transcendence means moving beyond form and content to change the context, system, environment, and meaning of the conflict. This implies that the parties have learned how to evolve, outgrow, or rise above what was keeping them stuck, and are now ready to handle a higher level of conflict and order of resolution.

Lower level conflicts require only lower order resolution techniques, which do not encourage higher order results to emerge. Higher order resolution outcomes require more advanced techniques to elicit or bring them forth, and can only be used successfully by transcending or working through lower level conflicts and lower order resolution outcomes. It is therefore highly unusual for people to reach forgiveness by using techniques designed to stop them from fighting, such as caucusing, or to achieve reconciliation by using settlement techniques, such as identifying criteria.

The depth and quality of questions the mediator is able to ask and the parties are able to entertain will largely determine the depth and quality of the answers that are likely to emerge and the level of conflict and order of resolution that are possible for them to achieve. The subtlety and skill of the mediator can have a powerful influence on what the parties are able to learn from their conflict. The greater our willingness as mediators to learn from conflicts, especially our own, the more effortlessly we will be able to assist others in moving from impasse to resolution, transformation, transcendence, and prevention, allowing them to evolve to higher levels of conflict and orders of resolution.

For these reasons, conflict can have no existence apart from resolution, any more than sound can exist without silence, light without darkness, or good without evil. Together, they create a complementarity, which physicist Neils Bohr defined as "a great truth ... whose opposite is also a great truth." The consequence of this recognition is not merely that a deeper understanding of conflict may lead us to deeper resolutions, but that more skillful and creative approaches to resolution can allow us to experience higher levels of *conflict*, and as a result, increase our capacity for learning, growth, and evolution.

Ten Philosophical Propositions on Conflict Resolution

To understand the evolution of conflict and resolution at a deeper level, it is useful to consider a set of fundamental propositions regarding the human reality and context in which they occur. The following ten philosophical propositions regarding conflict resolution help explain its constantly changing, highly intuitive, deeply subtle, transitory character and ability to regularly result in resolution, transformation, and transcendence.

1. *No two human beings are the same.* Everyone is different, and while we share certain characteristics, at a given level of nuance or subtlety, nothing that happens between two people is more than grossly predictable. Therefore, no conflict resolution technique, however evolved or skillfully executed, will succeed with everyone.

2. *No single human being is the same from one moment to the next.* Not only is it impossible to step into the same river twice because it is continuously flowing, *we* are continuously flowing and different from one moment to the next. Therefore, no matter how stuck we are, we can become unstuck at any moment.

3. *The interactions and relationships between human beings are complex, multidetermined, subtle, and unpredictable*, if only because they involve two or more different, constantly changing individuals. Therefore, while it makes sense to plan and strategize how we are going to resolve conflicts, it also makes sense to improvise and refuse to allow rigid plans or strategies to stand in our way.

4. *Conflicts are even more complex, multidetermined, subtle, and unpredictable.* Many conflicts involve intense emotions, negative behaviors, miscommunications, contrasting cultural norms, jumbled intentions, false expectations, inconsistent attitudes, and dysfunctional systems, any one of which can increase the level of chaos and complexity. Therefore, linear, scientific, logically rigorous approaches to resolution need to be combined with holistic, artistic, creative ones.

5. *Most conflicts take place beneath the surface, well below the superficial topics over which people are fighting, and often hidden from their conscious awareness.* What lies beneath the surface in many conflicts are emotions, interests, longings, memories, self-images, secret desires, the history and trajectory of people's relationships, the systems in which they are operating, where, how, and why they got stuck, and the *meaning* of their conflict to each of them. Therefore, every conflict leads toward the center, not only of the issues in dispute, but also the minds, emotions, and hearts of those who are stuck.

6. *Chronic conflicts are systemic, and all systems, be they personal, familial, relational, organizational, social, economic, or political, defend themselves against change, even when it is essential for their survival.* Thus, the greater the need for change and the deeper the potential transformation, the greater the resistance, the more intense the conflict, and the more difficult it becomes to even imagine resolving or letting it go.

7. *Every conflict is holographic and systemic, so that each part contains and recapitulates the whole.* Therefore, every issue in conflict, no matter how trifling or insignificant, is capable of invisibly altering the whole by transforming any of its parts, allowing even minor interventions to trigger major resolutions.

8. *Every conflict reveals an internal crossroads, with each path branching and leading off in radically different directions.* As outlined in the introduction, every conflict contains at least three paths: one moving backward toward impasse, enmity, and adversarial relationships; one moving forward toward resolution, respect, and collaborative relationships; and one moving deeper into the heart of the conflict toward evolution and learning, transformation and transcendence. Therefore, every conflict allows people to choose how they will define their attitudes toward past, future, and present.

9. *Every conflict offers opportunities to evolve to higher levels of skill and awareness in how people respond to their opponents and problems.* Therefore, every conflict is a rich source of learning, improvement, and wisdom, both for people and for systems. More importantly, every conflict subtly and implicitly points attention toward these sources.

10. *At the center or heart of every conflict lies a pathway to resolution, forgiveness, and reconciliation.* Therefore, conflicts have the capacity to ensnare and entrap or liberate and transform people, along with their ideas, feelings, intentions, attitudes, relationships, and the systems that created or fueled them. By opening our minds, emotions, and hearts in conflict, we *automatically* initiate an evolution to higher orders of conflict and resolution.

Several practical conclusions flow from these propositions. First, it is clear that each person's attitude, intention, intuition, self-awareness, environment, and capacity for empathetic and honest communication will significantly impact that person's experience of conflict and capacity for resolution. Second, because each person is different, each conflict is different, and both are different from moment to moment, no one can conceivably know objectively or in advance how to resolve a given conflict, as anything that is chaotic or rapidly changing cannot be successfully predicted or managed. Third, for this reason, it is impossible to instruct anyone in detail on the best way to resolve a particular conflict, other than to develop their skills, increase their self-confidence, and develop a broad range of techniques that may or may not succeed depending on unpredictable conditions. Fourth, to resolve the underlying reasons for a dispute, learn, or evolve, it is necessary to probe beneath the superficial issues people are arguing about and bring the *meaning* of their conflict into conscious awareness. Then they may be able to increase their empathy, engage in dialogue, resolve issues collaboratively, and negotiate interest-based solutions, which can lead to a profound understanding of the systemic sources of their conflict and ways of working collaboratively to change them.

Finally, evolving to higher levels of conflict and orders of resolution eventually requires everyone to learn to navigate, not just the physical and intellectual, but also the emotional, spiritual, heart-based, and systemic components of their conflicts. The ability to do so can significantly alter the dance of conflict, the durability of impasse, the depth of resolution, the decision to collaborate in finding constructive alternatives, and the capacity to evolve to higher levels of conflict and resolution.

The Orders of Resolution

Multiple outcomes other than impasse are possible in any conflict, yet each order of resolution allows people to respond skillfully to successively higher levels of conflict. In my experience, there are six fundamental orders of resolution.

1. We can stop the fighting and de-escalate the confrontation. This is useful and important, and most mediators understand the basic skills and techniques needed to be successful, such as separating people, speaking to them calmly, and listening empathetically to their stories.

2. We can settle the issues over which people disagree and end their dispute. This requires them to discuss the issues and negotiate a compromise. Most mediators understand the basic techniques needed to be successful, such as setting ground rules, identifying issues, articulating reasons for settlement, caucusing separately with each side, and negotiating compromises.

3. We can resolve the underlying reasons that gave rise to the dispute and will continue to generate new disputes until they are resolved. This transforms the conflict by moving the parties' conversations inward toward their common center and unlocking them. Few mediators have been adequately trained in these techniques, although it is possible to intuit and learn them as we go, albeit at different rates and levels depending on our own issues, characters, and skills.

4. We can forgive our opponents and, finally, ourselves. Forgiveness consists of releasing ourselves from the burden of our own false expectations, or as Annie Dillard wrote, "giving up all hopes of having a better past." Forgiveness is a sweeping transformation of the conflict, and few mediators are skilled in methods of reaching forgiveness, especially when it comes to forgiving ourselves.

5. We can reconcile with our opponents and renew our relationships. In reconciliation, we come full circle and our conflicts disappear. At the highest level of reconciliation, conflicts become powerful sources of learning, fresh synthesis, and higher order relationships. Mediators know least about how to achieve this last order of resolution, as it not only involves completely letting go, but learning, transcending, and evolving.

6. We can design preventative systems, structures, cultures, and environments that make it more difficult for future conflicts to occur, manage them better, and resolve them faster, deeper, and with less effort.

Each of these orders, like the Richter scale for earthquakes, requires exponentially greater skill and sensitivity than the one beneath it, along with greater integrity, commitment, and permission to proceed on the part of everyone involved. Each takes longer to achieve, goes deeper into the heart of the problem, and permits a different set of issues and resolutions to emerge. Each leaves less of the conflict remaining after it is completed.

If we simply stop the fighting but fail to settle the issues, most of the conflict will remain. If we settle the issues but do not resolve the underlying reasons that gave rise to them, a large portion of the conflict will disappear, but anything lying beneath its surface can reappear unexpectedly and trigger future conflicts. If we resolve the underlying reasons for the conflict but do not reach genuine forgiveness, most of the issues will dissipate, but part of our energy and attention will remain trapped by whatever we are unable to forgive. If we reach forgiveness but do not achieve reconciliation, the conflict will nearly vanish, yet some infinitesimal fragments will remain to remind us, sometimes in our sleep, that it is not completely over. Only with full reconciliation can the conflict finally cease to exist and completely vanish. This may seem unimportant compared to active fighting, but when people cannot reach reconciliation, small residues accumulate over time, leading to divorce, loss of employment, depression, stress, illness, chronic anger, and an inability to find release, learn, grow, or evolve. Following reconciliation, the conflict may still reoccur if people do not work preventatively to redesign the system, context, culture, or environment that produced it, encouraged it, and allowed it to thrive.

Consequently, every conflict can be seen as an opportunity to improve the parties' skills and behaviors, acknowledge their opponent's interests, learn from their negative experiences, and evolve to higher levels of conflict, resolution, and insight or wisdom. Each order of resolution can allow them to advance to more complex and nuanced conflicts, practice more subtle resolution techniques, invent more creative outcomes, and develop higher levels of skill, understanding, and relationship. For example, by shifting the style of communication from debate to dialogue, people can improve their communication, replace competition with collaboration, redefine the meaning of their conflict, and reveal solutions they could not have imagined beforehand.

The Dimensions of Resolution

Another way of understanding the evolution of conflict and orders of resolution is to visualize them using a mathematical metaphor. In mathematics, a physical dimension is a measure of the number of quantities required to define an object's location in space or, more interestingly, it is a degree of freedom, measured by the number of directions or ways an object can move. It is possible to shift from lower dimensions to higher ones by dragging the lower dimension 90 degrees in a new direction. Thus, a plane dragged 90 degrees in a new direction turns into a cube. Each new dimension can be described as a transformation, which in conflict resolution can be understood as shifting the parties' conversations 90 degrees in a new direction.

For example, if we are operating in zero dimensions, represented by a point, no information is required to define where an object is located, and there is no freedom of movement. This is analogous to impasse in conflict resolution, where either or both parties are stuck or unwilling to change, and no solutions or movements are seen as possible.

One dimension, which is created by dragging a point 90 degrees in a new direction to form a line, allows us to create a single degree of freedom. This is analogous in conflict resolution to stopping the fighting or de-escalating the confrontation, which can be achieved simply by separating the parties and asking them singly to identify what they want, or by imposing a solution on them, which requires only a single piece of information to define a solution space.

A second degree of freedom is created by dragging a line 90 degrees in a new direction, producing a plane that possesses both length and breadth. In conflict resolution, this can be analogized to settling the dispute, which can be achieved by both parties identifying their positions, or what they want, and negotiating a result. Every outcome in a two-dimensional space represents a compromise, as it consists of some combination of two parameters on a positional plane, with vertical and horizontal axes or vectors representing the limits or boundaries of what each person wants.

A third degree of freedom can be symbolized by a cube, which possesses depth in addition to length and breadth. Depth can be analogized to resolving the underlying emotional issues in a dispute or negotiating a result based on interests. These allow the parties to move beyond adversarial or positional bargaining and solutions based on compromise to emotionally satisfying, interest-based solutions that allow the parties to move beyond compromise to identify creative solutions that could not have been imagined in two dimensions.

We can also imagine a fourth physical dimension, represented by a hypercube created by dragging a cube 90 degrees in a nearly unimaginable new direction. In conflict resolution, this can be analogized to forgiveness. This fourth dimension is more difficult to define, but represents the spirit, intention, energy, life force, attachment, or chi of people in conflict, as described in Chapter 1. Adding a fourth dimension allows forgiveness to be explained in ways that would appear magical to anyone operating in only three dimensions, just as three-dimensional solutions would appear magical to anyone who is unable to perceive depth.

Similar, yet even more difficult to visualize, is a fifth dimension represented by a geometrical figure that cannot be drawn adequately on a two-dimensional page, but can be analogized to reconciliation, based on an attitude that is now heartfelt, positive, open, and compassionate. Including attitude as a dimension allows intangible elements such as heart-to-heart communications and expressions of apology and compassion to trigger transcendence.

We can also imagine a sixth dimension that represents the *space* within which all these dimensions become manifest and constantly change, along with the systems, contexts, cultures, and environments in which they occur. This dimension expresses the holographic nature of space, or what physicist

David Bohm calls the enfolded element that contains a hidden implicate order. Without this dimension, we might forget that there must be a field, stage, structure, or backdrop on and against which each of the lower dimensions is revealed.

When we consider any dimension—for example, a single dimension consisting of a line—we need to ask: a line in or on what? Each of the first five dimensions describes a direction in space, which represents the background or context in which conflict occurs. Without identifying a sixth dimension, these implicate elements might pass unnoticed and unexamined.

Finally, we can imagine a seventh dimension representing the unidirectional flow or *arrow* of time. This dimension expresses the natural impermanence of even the most hardened conflicts, the ability of people to become stuck in the past, and the enduring possibility of change, resolution, transformation, and transcendence—not only in the conflict, but in the system, context, culture, and environment within or against which it occurs, all of which are themselves constantly changing. For practical purposes, following Einstein, we are able to combine the sixth and seventh dimensions in a single entity representing the field of space-time.

The first four of these dimensions are illustrated on the following page. The fifth and sixth are left to your imagination, while the seventh can be thought of as any movement, evolution, or transformation in the first six. While additional dimensions are possible, perhaps even an infinite number as in higher mathematics, they are unnecessary to this analysis of conflict.

Dimensions of Conflict Resolution

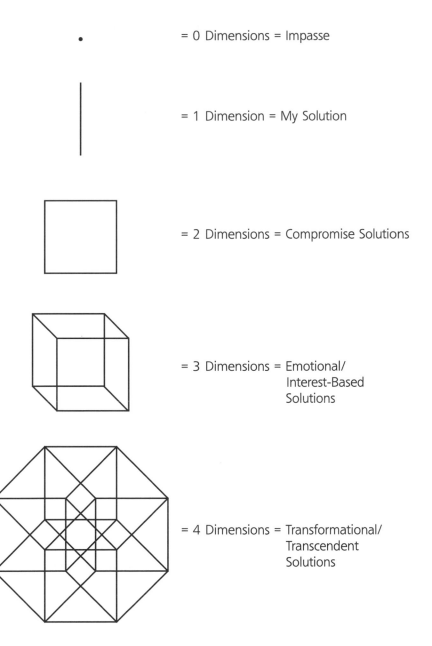

= 0 Dimensions = Impasse

= 1 Dimension = My Solution

= 2 Dimensions = Compromise Solutions

= 3 Dimensions = Emotional/
Interest-Based
Solutions

= 4 Dimensions = Transformational/
Transcendent
Solutions

Using dimensionality as a metaphor, we can recognize that every new approach to conflict confers an expanded degree of freedom, potentially resulting in a higher order of resolution. This suggests a rational explanation for the role played by intention, attitude, spirit, and heart in dispute resolution. It also helps explain the magic that so often happens in mediation that allows people to resolve, transform, and transcend their conflicts in ways that seem to defy rational explanation. Finally, it suggests that for conflict to disappear completely there must be transformation and transcendence not only in personal attitudes and intentions, but in *conflict space*, which includes the systems, contexts, cultures, and environments in which it occurs.

The Dimensions of Communication and Organizations

We can now easily extend this dimensional analogy to include forms of communication and varieties of organizational structure. Thus, zero dimensions can be analogized to coercive silence in communication and dictatorship or slavery in organizational structures.

One dimension can be analogized to monologue in communication and hierarchical, bureaucratic, and autocratic forms of organization in which power is arranged vertically, from the top down.

Two dimensions can be analogized to debate in communication and cross-functional teams that are able to work horizontally across otherwise hierarchical organizational structures.

Three dimensions can be analogized to dialogue in communication and organizational depth created through collaboration, leadership, vision, and shared values in matrixed organizations, where there is both hierarchical reporting to a boss and horizontal reporting to a team.

Four dimensions can be analogized in communication to understanding another person's meaning without words, and integrating strategically across organizational boundaries.

Five dimensions can be analogized to poignant, profound, heartfelt communications, and the experience of organizational synergy.

Six dimensions can be analogized to recognizing the impact of systems, context, culture, and environment on communications, and designing organizational structures and systems to prevent conflicts and minimize dysfunctional interactions.

Seven dimensions can be analogized to timing in communications and organizational change.

Combining these dimensional analogies allows us to draw a connection between conflicts, communications, and organizational architectures; to strategically identify ways of releasing individuals, relationships, and the systems in which they interact simultaneously from lower-dimensional conflicts, miscommunications, and constricted organizational structures; and to design strategically integrated, evolutionary approaches to all three. I believe the combination of these dimensional elements and their application to personal, organizational, social, and political conflicts constitutes the future of conflict resolution.

Example: A Multidimensional Approach to Organizational Disputes

Countless organizational disputes arise between managers who adopt hierarchical, bureaucratic, and autocratic methods of communication and employees who respond in defensive, adversarial, or resistant ways. These behaviors produce cycles of miscommunication, petty power struggles, and chronic conflicts. Both sides' communications invite negative responses, which justify, reinforce, and perpetuate the very communications they oppose, provoking negative attitudes, behaviors, and work styles in response.

In many cases, upper management decides to impose a one-dimensional solution by hierarchically transferring the employee or commanding obedience to management orders, or micromanaging and second-guessing the manager's decisions. This may sometimes stop the fighting, but more commonly results in driving the conflict underground and preventing its full resolution.

A human resource manager may decide instead to impose a one-dimensional solution by directing the parties to stop fighting and avoid talking to each other or may try to broker a two-dimensional settlement based on a compromise that allows each side to save face through limited, temporary concessions limited to communications and short-term results, leaving the original conflict in place and setting the stage for future disputes.

In contrast, a three-dimensional approach would allow a mediator, ombudsman, or human resources manager to acknowledge each side's pent-up emotions, identify their underlying interests, and negotiate consensus-based solutions that encourage them to coordinate their efforts, communicate more respectfully, and work together to achieve agreed-upon results. This may allow the parties to resolve the underlying reasons for their dispute and continue working together after it is over.

While more difficult to achieve, a four-dimensional outcome would consist of transforming the manager and employee into partners or team members who collaborate to achieve common goals. By clarifying intentions, vision, and values, agreeing on goals and responsibilities, developing leadership capabilities, and strategically integrating work across organizational lines, it is possible to transform the conflict and formulate innovative solutions.

A five-dimensional solution would mean seeking to alter the parties' attitudes toward each other and inviting them to communicate openly, honestly, and compassionately from their hearts about who they are and what they really want. As a result, they may learn to act synergistically create a better relationship and transcend the attitudes and conditions that led to their conflict in the first place. On these rare, magical occasions, they may happily surrender their failed strategies, agree on solutions they could not have imagined, and evolve to higher levels of interaction and relationship.

Finally, on a sixth (and seventh) dimensional level, a conflict resolution systems designer might work with both sides and the organization as a whole to preventatively redesign their communications and relationships, along with the systems, structures, processes, and cultures that fueled the conflict. Instead of acting in isolation, they reengineer the entire communication system and initiate an organization-wide dialogue and change process that focuses on how they can learn to be more effective in preventing and resolving future conflicts and achieving their common goals.

Example: A Multidimensional Approach to Teenager-Parent Conflicts

To make this multidimensional metaphor more concrete, consider a different example, such as a typical parent/adolescent dispute over curfew. In zero dimensions, both sides remain at impasse and simply exchange insults or accusations that lead nowhere. A single dimension might be represented by the parent "laying down the law," and insisting on 10 p.m. as the hour to return home, leaving the teenager with three options: blind obedience, passive-aggressive behavior, or open rebellion and consequent punishment.

Two dimensions require two inputs, suggesting that both sides get to advance their own unique positions. This can be represented by the parent continuing to uphold 10 p.m. and the teenager arguing for 2 a.m. as the proper time to return home. The natural outcome is likely to be a compromise ranging from 10 p.m. to 2 a.m., based on their relative power. In many families, the ability of teenagers to state their position and have it heard suggests a significant transformation in the parent-child relationship.

Three dimensions introduces the idea of depth, represented by each side clarifying the interests that underlie their positions. This might consist of a parent articulating the need for safety (while minimizing or denying the importance of independence), and a teenager battling for independence (while minimizing or denying the need for safety). Yet which of these values can be disregarded or defeated without jeopardizing the other? Who should win or lose this conflict?

The only sensible solution is for both sides and their respective interests to win. It is not safety *versus* independence, but safety *plus* independence that yields the highest outcomes in the end. The best solutions will be those that recognize the intrinsic unity that underlies these seemingly opposite interests. Doing so requires the parent, first and foremost, to affirm and support the teenager's desire for independence, and the teenager to affirm and support the parent's desire for safety.

More profoundly, they may decide to speak openly to each other about their emotions and tell each other stories about the experiences that produced them. The parents may be motivated to insist on 10 p.m. by feelings of fear and underlying love for the teenager, perhaps because of some incident that occurred when they were teenagers. The teenager may be motivated by feelings of shame before schoolmates and peers as a result of derogatory comments that were made because the teenager was required to leave before everyone else did.

A fourth dimension can be triggered by both sides recognizing that the family as they have known it is about to die, since the teenager is getting ready to leave home forever. Both sides may be feeling grief, joy, fear, and excitement in anticipation of their impending separation, yet the chances are quite good that neither has spoken openly to the other about the life-altering changes that are covertly influencing their negotiations.

In a fifth dimension, they may sidestep their conflict over curfew to discuss sensitive, heartfelt questions, such as: Who will they be without each other? What will happen to their love for each other? How will they be able to function? How can they learn to accept and trust each other? What can each of them do now to improve their relationship and keep the family together? These unspoken, heartfelt questions surreptitiously yet profoundly affect their conflict over curfew and will allow them to evolve not only to higher levels of communication, relationship, and decision making, but to higher levels of conflict and resolution as well.

In a sixth and seventh dimension, they may discover ways of improving their family's conflict culture and redesigning now-outmoded family systems and environments to accommodate their future transition from childhood to adult relationships or to allow for different outcomes at different agreed-upon stages.

Their dimensions of communication and conflict resolution, beginning with impasse, can be diagrammed as follows:

	Focus	Parent	Teenager
0.	Insults and Accusations	"Irresponsible"	"Bossy"
1.	Parent's Position	10 p.m.	Obedience or Punishment
2.	Both Positions	10 p.m.	2 a.m.
3.	Interests and Emotions	Safety (Fear)	Freedom (Shame)
4.	Spiritual Reality	Death of the Family	Loss of Security/Support
5.	Heartfelt Desire	Love and Acceptance	Love and Trust
6.	Family System	Prevention, Redesign	Supportive Relationship

Ultimately, we can see that there are only two goals or purposes for any conflict over curfew: to transfer responsibility for safety from the parent to the teenager consistent with freedom, and to transition from a family system based on parental control to one based on voluntary, consensual, adult relationships grounded in familial love. These only begin to become possible at Level 3, yet many families never get beyond Level 2. Nonetheless, we can see in retrospect that this was precisely what the conflict taught them by occurring.

We can also see that each transition to a higher dimension can be triggered by a few relatively simple questions. For example, starting at one dimension, a mediator might ask the parties

- what they want,

- why they want it,

- what they are feeling,

- what deeper realities they are about to face,

- what kind of relationship they really want with each other in their hearts, and

- what they think they might do to make their family system and conflict styles more effective in the future.

Underlying much of the resistance to adopting higher dimensional approaches and evolving as a family is the reality that doing so requires them to surrender their denial about the loss of their old relationship, genuinely transfer power from the parent to the teenager, and transform the way conflicts are resolved in ways that reflect a wide-ranging evolutionary shift from power and rights to interests.

Power, Rights, and Interests

Over thousands of years, we have resolved disputes using three fundamental methods. First and foremost, we have resolved them based on power. Power is the most ancient, instinctual, and efficient method, at least in the short term, though the means by which power has been exercised have evolved considerably over the centuries with advances in technology. As Sigmund Freud wrote to Albert Einstein, analyzing the causes of war:

> To begin with, in a small human horde, it was superior muscular strength that decided who owned things or whose will would prevail. Muscular strength was soon supplemented and replaced by the use of tools: the winner was the one who had the better weapons or who used them more skillfully...but the final purpose of the fight remained the same...

Power-based conflict resolution techniques, including war, violence, and coercion, generate a great deal of collateral damage because they create winners and losers, destroy important relationships, and draw future disputes in their wake. As Lord Acton famously wrote, "All power corrupts and absolute power corrupts absolutely." Thus, when one group regularly wins power contests, those who lose are repeatedly stereotyped and prejudged. This, however, encourages them to surrender, resist, or revolt and escalate the conflict until their needs are met. Under these conditions, it is nearly impossible for individuals, families, organizations, or nations to evolve without experiencing harmful, cataclysmic conflicts.

For these reasons, rights-based methods such as legislation, litigation, adversarial negotiations, and written policies and procedures were instituted to place limits on the exercise of power, allow disputes to be finally resolved, salvage important relationships, and encourage individuals, systems, and nations to stabilize and interact more peacefully. Freud located the origin of rights in the organized power of community, defining rights as "the might of a community," in opposition to those who are in power. Thus, legal rights are simply a subtle, collective form of violence.

> The only real difference lies in the fact that what prevails is no longer the violence of an individual but that of a community. But in order that the transition from violence to this new right or justice may be effected, one psychological condition must be fulfilled. The union of

the majority must be a stable and lasting one...The community must... draw up regulations to anticipate the risk of rebellion and must institute authorities to see that those regulations—the laws—are respected and to superintend the execution of legal acts of violence.

Rights are limitations on the exercise of power, yet they are also based on power and correctly perceived by those in power as curtailing their authority. Rights are therefore fragile and contingent on the continuing willingness of those in power to acknowledge and authorize their existence. Rights-based processes similarly generate collateral damage, winners and losers, corruption, and lesser, muted versions of all of the problems created by power. Moreover, as Freud recognized, rights-based processes uniquely generate bureaucracy, which diminishes the ability of people and systems to reach higher orders of resolution and evolve.

While power-based processes focus on preserving hierarchy and obedience, rights-based processes focus on enforcing contractual language and technical compliance. Interest-based processes such as mediation and collaborative negotiation, on the other hand, focus on commonality, identifying the reasons people seek power or rights, and revealing and resolving the underlying reasons that generated the conflict.

Interests therefore reflect not merely *what* people want, but *why* they want it, and as a result, encourage them to communicate at a deeper level, learn from each other, work more collaboratively, and redesign and transcend the antiquated, dysfunctional power- and rights-based systems and structures that caused, aggravated, or sustained their dispute.

Freud believed that power leads ultimately to the development of rights, and that rights inevitably lead to increased "emotional ties between the members of a united group of people—feelings of unity that are the true source of its strength." The development of community-based emotional ties permits a far broader expansion of interest-based methods and institutions by encouraging evolution from hierarchical power and individualistic rights to community responsibility for resolving conflicts based on egalitarian satisfaction of interests.

Interests are unique and diverse, yet also potentially compatible and synergistic. When parents argue with teenagers over curfew, power-based solutions are likely to result in perfunctory obedience, passive-aggressive behaviors, or open rebellion. Rights-based solutions are likely to result in solutions the teenager skirts, discovers loopholes in, or responds to as though they were power-based solutions. Interest-based solutions, on the other hand, are likely to result in open, egalitarian dialogue over why safety and independence are important, and a joint search for solutions that satisfy both sets of concerns.

Because interest-based processes require consensus, they are less likely to result in unacceptable collateral damage, win/lose outcomes, entrenched positions, bureaucracy, abuse of power, corruption, and resistance to implementation. For this reason, on a societal level, interest-based approaches invite deeper levels of community, encourage conflict to emerge, permit more advanced resolution outcomes to be imagined, and allow people and systems to evolve to more complex, collaborative, mutually satisfying interactions and relationships.

If we view conflict as a source of opposition and resolution as a source of unity, interest-based processes allow these forces to intersect, creating a living, evolving, spiraling, double-helixed relationship in which separation and combination, expansion and contraction, dissension and harmony commingle in a self-organized, iterative process. This new relationship produces combinations that could not have been imagined at lower dimensions and that strengthen adaptation, evolution, learning, collaboration, and change.

This does not make progress or evolution inevitable, but suggests that power- and rights-based processes naturally resist higher-level evolutionary outcomes because they are focused on suppressing or settling conflicts rather than on resolving, transforming, transcending, and preventing them. In these ways, interest-based processes increase everyone's ability to evolve and learn from conflict.

While there are times when resolution is more important than conflict, there are also times when conflict is more important than resolution, primarily because people, relationships, and systems continue to evolve and grow. For this reason, it may initially be useful for parents and teenagers or divorcing couples to argue, as one way—albeit costly—of ending their denial and freeing them from relationships they no longer want, need, or are afraid to end. But those who would have resolution without conflict, or conflict without resolution, miss the evolutionary opportunity to reach higher levels of each, and the beauty of the dance that brings both into existence.

The Evolution of Interest-Based Processes

Over the last several decades, we have developed a multiplicity of interest-based methods for achieving resolution that can be distinguished based on a variety of factors, including the number of people involved in the resolution process. There are, for example

- single-party processes such as reflection, observation, meditation, and introspection in which individuals search alone for insight into their role in conflict, its meaning for them, and what they are going to do about it;

- two-party processes such as coaching, mentoring, informal conversation, negotiation, and private dialogue in which two people discuss what is not working in their relationship and agree on possible solutions;

- three-party processes such as mediation, facilitated negotiation, and advisory arbitration in which third parties assist people at impasse to reach consensus on solutions, clarify their issues, or agree on how they are going to disagree; and

- multi-party processes such as facilitated meetings and organizational retreats, collaborative public policy negotiations, environmental mediations, and public dialogues in which external mediators, facilitators, and negotiators assist groups or communities in discussing their problems, agreeing on solutions, and improving their relationships.

It is also possible to distinguish conflict resolution approaches based on whether they are assisted or unassisted, binding or non-binding, costly or cheap, or based on power, rights, or interests. Many conflicts are resolved through pleasant social interactions, informal problem solving, brainstorming sessions, team building, agreement on shared values, visions for the future, an experience of collaboration, or a charismatic leader who unites people around common goals. Conflicts can also be resolved through organizing, lobbying, elections, direct action, non-violent resistance, lawsuits, delegation, and deferral to hierarchical decision making.

Why Mediation Works

Among these methods, mediation is perhaps the most advanced and satisfying. In its simplest form, mediation is merely a facilitated conversation designed to solve a problem. It does so, at a simple level, by making the conversation voluntary, private, confidential, collaborative, and informal, and led by someone who is outside the problem, yet experienced in the issues. The mediator commonly succeeds by

- encouraging active, empathetic, and responsive listening;

- allowing private conversations to take place in caucus;

- facilitating collaborative forms of bargaining;

- directing conversations toward interests and the deeper reasons for the dispute;

- balancing power and treating everyone as equals; and

- ensuring that decisions are made by consensus or unanimity.

In short, mediation creates a positive context within which negative emotions, substantive disagreements, and personal differences can be surfaced and discussed without destroying the core of what people have in common.

Mediated conversations reinforce respectful behaviors and support openness, honesty, authenticity, and integrity. They invite people to participate in meaningful dialogue over issues that matter to them, reduce blaming and faultfinding, encourage emotional and diverse forms of intelligence, and support creativity and informal problem solving. At a subtler level, mediation achieves these results by:

- moving from angry interactions over boundary violations and fear of differences to respect for boundaries and dialogue over differences;

- converting communications from sullen silences or acrimonious complaining to candid, acknowledging conversations and collaborative negotiations;

- shifting processes from exclusion and competition based on positions to inclusion and collaboration based on interests;

- discovering the real reasons why people are stuck, freeing them from those reasons, and helping them forgive and let go;

- opening closed minds and hearts by inviting people to listen and be honest, vulnerable, and receptive;

- changing people's actual experiences of each other from hostile, mistrusting, and aggressive to friendly, cooperative, and respectful; and

- helping people resolve, transform, and transcend conflict, improve communications and relationships, and correct the systems that created or nourished the conflict.

In order to do so, mediators must occupy a space that is not merely between the parties, but above, below, before, behind, and around them. At a still deeper level, every conflict generates opposition between self and other, subject and object, actor and acted upon. By locating the lines that separate these opposites within ourselves and uniting them, we can improve our ability to cross the boundaries that define the context, space, or field in which conflicts occur and achieve higher orders of resolution.

For this reason, the most critical and subtle element in interest-based conflict resolution methods does not concern what we *do* as mediators, but who we *are* and are capable of becoming in the presence of conflict. We become mediative when, in the midst of conflict, we are able to

- show up and be present;

- listen empathetically for what lies hidden beneath words;

- tell the truth without blaming or judgment;

- be open-minded, openhearted, and unattached to outcomes;

- act collaboratively in relationships;

- display unconditional integrity and respect;

- consistently act in accordance with our core values and principles;

- draw on our deepest intuition;

- be on both parties' sides at the same time;

- encourage open, authentic, heartfelt communications;

- be ready for anything at every moment;

- seek completion and closure; and

- let go, yet abandon no one.

The highest goal in conflict resolution is not simply to increase our own skills and those of the parties in resolving disputes, but to assist everyone to evolve personally and socially by becoming more meditative as human beings—both in our conversations and relationships with conflicted parties, and in the very core of our being. To do so, we are ultimately required to surrender our power to compel, coerce, or manipulate results, and our right to insist that others obey our rules and follow uniform procedures.

Yet through these surrenders, we evolve and gain access to far greater powers and rights. These flow from powerlessness and the equal right of everyone to satisfy their interests; act with integrity; participate in community and collaborative relationships; and resolve, transform, and transcend their conflicts. To illustrate how personal evolution and transcendence are linked, consider the following case study.

Weeding Out Conflict—A Case Study

Ramon came to California from Mexico and spent twenty years doing odd jobs as a gardener to feed his family. Finally, he received the offer of a lifetime: a full-time gardening position on the estate of a wealthy retired businessman named Sam. Ramon worked for Sam for several years and received frequent accolades for his devotion and responsibility. Sam hired a manager, Luis, to oversee Ramon and other employees. On one occasion, Luis told Ramon to clear away some wood and take it to the dump. Ramon asked if he could use the wood since it was of very high quality but not useful on the estate and Luis told him he could.

Ramon and Luis got along fine until Luis decided to bring in a subcontractor to trim some ailing trees. Ramon did not like the way the subcontractors attacked the trees and noticed that the truck they were using did not have a license plate. He checked and found out they did not have a license to trim trees and reported this information to Luis. Luis became furious and told Ramon to mind his own business. After that, their relationship deteriorated.

One day when Luis was on vacation, Ramon decided to take three pieces of wood that had been thrown away and could not be used on the estate to repair his house. When Luis returned he complained to Sam, who called Ramon into the office and summarily fired him. Ramon was shocked and tried to explain, but Sam would hear none of it. Ramon returned the three pieces of wood, but felt so humiliated by the experience that he decided to sue for wrongful termination.

At the mediation, both attorneys began by indicating that neither they nor their clients would make any opening statements, but wanted to move directly into separate rooms to conduct settlement negotiations. I met with each side privately and recommended against this process. Based on my observation of the discomfort their clients were experiencing and my intuitive sense of what lay beneath the surface of their dispute, I asked if there were things the clients wanted to say to each other that had not yet been said. Both said there were, and the attorneys agreed to allow Sam and Ramon to speak directly to each other.

Sam asked to go first, and told Ramon how disappointed he was in him. He said he liked Ramon and felt his gardening work was excellent, but his trust had been shattered and he could no longer keep him on the estate. Ramon asked Sam why he had not allowed him to explain what happened at the time he was terminated, and Sam said he had asked if he had taken the wood, heard that he had, and that was all he needed to know.

Ramon told him the circumstances that had led him to take the wood and said he had never stolen anything in his life. He agreed that he ought to have waited for Luis to return from vacation to ask permission as he had done in the past, but that he knew the wood was being thrown out and Luis had given him permission in similar situations before.

Sam thought the unresolved conflict between Ramon and Luis made the whole situation impossible and felt he had to accept what Luis had told him. I asked whether either side would like to bring Luis into the mediation to tell his story, but both sides felt there would be no point since Ramon had found a new position and did not want to return to working at the estate.

Based on an empathetic sense that had I been in their shoes I would have wanted to say more, I asked them if there was anything either of them wanted to apologize for. After a moment of silence, Ramon apologized to Sam for having not checked with him before taking the wood and not being able to resolve his conflict with Luis. Sam then apologized to Ramon for jumping to conclusions and said he now understood that Ramon had not stolen the wood. He said he felt sorry that he had not listened to Ramon when he tried to explain what happened and asked if there was anything he could do to make up for it. Ramon told Sam he had found another job, but wanted to be paid for the six months he had been out of work and receive a positive letter of recommendation in case his present job did not work out. Sam immediately agreed.

To give them an opportunity to reach completion, I said this was probably the last time they would see each other and was there was anything else either of them wanted to say in parting. Ramon said he had really appreciated working on the estate, that it had helped him provide security for his family and purchase a home of his own. He said he wished Sam well. Sam thanked Ramon for all the work he had done to make the estate a beautiful place to live. He said he had no problem writing a very positive letter of recommendation because Ramon had really been a wonderful employee. He wished him well and said he would miss him.

To move the conversation further in the direction of learning, I asked them each to identify one thing they would do differently as a result of this experience. Sam said he would communicate better and not avoid difficult conversations that could require him to change his mind. Ramon said he would not ever take anything that belonged to anyone again because it wasn't worth it. He said he would not let future conflicts with coworkers go unresolved, but would work hard to prevent bad feelings from building up.

I asked them if they now felt the conflict between them was really over and whether they would be willing to shake hands as a way of symbolizing that it was finished and wish each other well in the future. They shook hands, then hugged each other with great emotion, cried, and spoke privately and intimately for several minutes while their attorneys sat wondering what happened.

Had the mediation been conducted as the attorneys had originally wished, along the lines of power or rights, none of this could have happened. No amount of simply shuttling between the parties would have conveyed the open, honest, heartfelt spirit they brought to their communications, which could only have taken place between them. While the litigation might still have settled, the underlying reasons for the dispute would have gone unresolved and the parties would not have reach forgiveness or negotiated an agreement that was very different from what each side initially demanded. Only their direct communication, heart-to-heart engagement, willingness to apologize for what they had done, and genuine appreciation for each other as human beings allowed them to walk away feeling good about themselves and each other and reach genuine closure in their conflict.

By speaking honestly and empathetically to each other they were able to transform their intentions and attitudes toward each other, and their conflict became a direct, open, honest, empathetic conversation, a vehicle of learning and increased awareness, a way of evolving in their understanding and approach to conflict and resolution, and a means of transformation and transcendence.

Chapter 3 The Varieties of Resolution Experience

The greatest discovery of my generation
is that human beings can alter their lives
by altering their attitudes of mind.
–William James

Nowhere is it more apparent that attitudes can alter our lives than in conflict. The attitudes people form toward their opponents, themselves, and the meaning of their conflicts and the attitudes mediators form toward the parties and their behaviors, toward their role in resolving conflicts, and toward the many varieties, orders, and approaches to resolution significantly alter the course of a conflict and result in vastly different outcomes. Ultimately, as psychiatrist Victor Frankl recognized based on his concentration camp experience, "Everything can be taken from a man but...the last of human freedoms – to choose one's attitude in any given set of circumstances, to choose one's own way."

Regarding attitudes, we can distinguish two broad classes of mediators: those who view conflict as destructive, seek to control it, distance themselves from the parties through professionalism and neutrality, and encourage settlement through caucusing and compromise; and those who view conflict as constructive, seek to learn from it, empathize with both parties, and encourage resolution, forgiveness, and reconciliation through interest-based dialogue and risky emotional communications.

These radically divergent attitudes and approaches to conflict resolution serve as self-fulfilling prophecies, resulting in outcomes that reinforce the attitudes that create them. Similarly, we can distinguish attitudes and approaches to conflict resolution based on the locations of conflict and the styles of mediation and variety of resolution techniques that flow from each location.

Where Conflicts are Located

When asked where their conflicts are located, most people initially point to their heads, or to various parts of their bodies where they feel stress, or toward their opponents. Closer observation reveals that conflicts manifest themselves in six distinct yet indivisible locations.

- In our physical bodies, where stress is internalized and translated into chemicals that prepare us for aggression or defense.

- In our minds, where distinctions and judgments are formed that bolster our positions and justify aggressive or defensive reactions.

- In our emotions, where anger, fear, jealousy, guilt, shame, and grief emanate and strive for release.

- In our spirits, where intentions, energy, life force, or chi become attached, intolerant, or unforgiving.

- In our hearts, where attitudes become closed or open, withholding or forthcoming, self-centered or compassionate, revengeful or forgiving.

- And in our systems, where cultures, contexts, conditions, and environments become adversarial or egalitarian, competitive or collaborative, autocratic or democratic.

If we concede that conflicts arise in these six locations, is it not apparent that our efforts to resolve them will be not be complete and precise until we develop skills and methodologies that allow us to reach deeply into each of these areas to prevent, stop, settle, resolve, transform, and transcend them at their source? And is it not equally apparent that, of all of these locations, we know least about how to work skillfully with the last three?

In the absence of a synchronous set of techniques and traditions for responding to *all* of the sources and locations of conflict, we have developed resolution models and practical techniques eclectically, working from the periphery rather than from the center, using mainly our heads rather than our hearts and heads. We accept without question the biases of our culture, and we learn accidentally rather than systemically. As a result, we have largely failed to recognize that indigenous cultures have done the opposite, and have a great deal to teach us regarding the deeper holistic aspects of conflict resolution.

Conflict Resolution in Indigenous Cultures

In Native American, First Nation, aboriginal, and indigenous cultures, it is widely recognized that these six primary locations of conflict correspond to six fundamental attitudes and six compass directions, including one that points inward toward the heart and one that points outward toward the environment. These are reflected in the following generalized diagram of a Native American Medicine or Spirit Wheel.

Native American Medicine or Spirit Wheel.

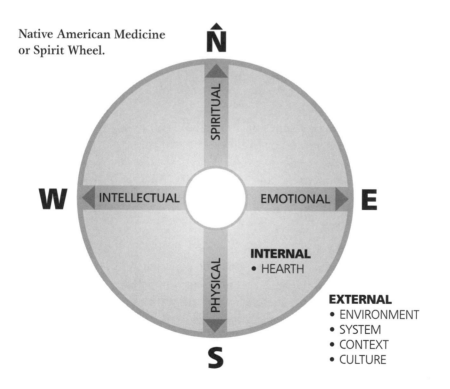

This depiction of the locations of conflict suggests the possibility of developing a diverse yet holistic set of approaches to the resolution process that allows each location to be accessed and resolved in its own way while recognizing the possibility of resolving all of them at a single stroke through heartfelt or systemic intervention.

For this reason, indigenous cultures commonly open mediations with a spiritual invocation, a deep collective silence, the passing of a peace pipe, or a comparable ritual through which those who are gathered manifest their conciliatory, collaborative, heart-based intentions at the northern end and center of the diagram, only later moving into the intellectual, emotional, and physical locations. Many US and European mediators, on the other hand, regard spiritual and heart processes as pointless, diversionary, or touchy-feely. They open instead with intellectually based introductions and agreements on ground rules at the far western end of the diagram, sometimes working with emotions or the body, but rarely engaging the conflict in its spiritual, heart, or environmental locations.

Unfortunately, US and European mediators have been handicapped in learning these spiritual methods by a long history of dismissal, dismemberment, degradation, and destruction of indigenous cultures around the globe. This history has caused and continues to cause enormous damage to these cultures, has resulted in a disparagement of techniques for influencing spirit, heart, and environment, and has led to an incalculable loss of subtle knowledge, ancient wisdom, and spiritual techniques that might have been preserved, translated, and adapted through collaborative interaction and mutual respect across cultural lines.

This history, which includes enslavement, imperial conquest, patriarchal domination, environmental exploitation, and genocidal attacks on Native cultures, encouraged US and European authorities to suppress empathy and honesty, resist collaboration, refuse to engage in joint problem solving, and deny spiritual kinship with those they sought to suppress. This was achieved partly through xenophobic ideologies that provoked fears of racial difference, condemned physicality (especially in its sensual and sexual forms), repressed honest dialogue, discounted emotionality, demolished non-Christian spiritual traditions, and viewed the environment as something to conquer.

These acts strengthened adversarial conflict cultures by championing the superiority of physical power, intellectual achievement, technology, and material wealth over sensual pleasure, emotionality, intellectual integrity, social affinity, spirituality, and ecology. The more emotionally and spiritually oriented cultures of indigenous populations were seen as soft, heretical, feminine, and sinful by those who championed intellect, aggression, patriarchy, and wealth, and conflict resolution as a whole passed out of favor.

For these reasons, we lack deep appreciation today of how to even talk about, appreciate, or understand the spiritual and heart locations of conflict, or recognize how intimately they are connected to all the others. We have lost the ability to recognize how they subtly influence and are influenced by the environment, culture, system, and context of conflict, and how essential they are to learning, improvement, and evolution.

To regain this understanding, reclaim our larger humanity, and fashion a unified theory and practice of mediation, we need to develop a set of advanced, nonreligious, culturally generic, inclusive, nonjudgmental, spiritual, heart, and systemic techniques for working with people in conflict at levels deep enough to skillfully and repeatedly nurture settlement, resolution, transformation, transcendence, and prevention.

This should not mean mindlessly copying indigenous cultural traditions, but learning from the spiritual practices of ancient cultures and merging these lessons with an understanding of the subtle, complex nature of conflict. We can distill, meld, and adapt each culture's best practices, and design innovative, integrated, cross-cultural, spiritual, heart-based, and systemic interventions that take us deeper and farther in resolving conflict than we ever could using physical, intellectual, and emotional techniques alone.

To do so, we need to form a better understanding of what spirit, heart, and systems are, how they fit into the whole of conflict resolution, and how they work—not as religion, mystique, new age jargon, abstract theory, or wishful thinking—but as practical, ubiquitous, replicable methods that are available to everyone and susceptible to both scientific analysis and artistic intuition.

Maps of Experience

In an effort to show how spirit connects to the material world, psychologist Carl Jung formulated the idea of synchronicity, indicating the presence of hidden connections between events and feelings based on meaning rather than conventional ideas of causality. Jung's ideas are summarized in the following diagram showing the subjective, internal universe. Jung's therapy patient, Nobel Prize winning physicist Wolfgang Pauli, tried to make Jung's ideas consistent with quantum physics by constructing his own diagram to explain the objective physical universe that follows it.

Maps of Experience

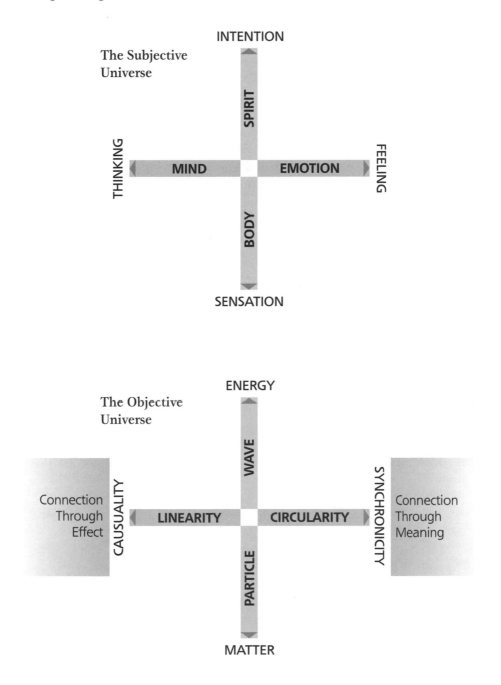

It is easy to see a connection between these charts and the Medicine or Spirit Wheel and to imagine these three maps overlapping to create a three-dimensional intersection between objective and subjective universes. While not accepting these diagrams as scientific fact, we can appreciate them as metaphor and allow them to lead us to a deeper understanding of conflict resolution that might explain its seemingly magical qualities.

The most important element in these diagrams, for our purposes, is the implied opposition and connection, on the one hand, between *intention* moving through spirit and energy as waves versus sensation moving through body and matter as particles, and on the other hand, between *thinking* moving through mind and connection as causality versus feeling moving through emotion and connection based on meaning. Thus, spirit, intention, energy and waves all emanate from the same location, as do physical sensation, body, matter, and particles; thinking, mind, causality, and linearity; and feelings, emotions, and connection through meaning and circularity.

By placing these maps on top of one another, we can see that each set of locations contributes to our understanding of the complexity of conflict, suggests very different mediation styles, and allows us to deduce useful techniques for resolution that are unique to each location and style.

Seven Styles of Mediation

We can use this metaphor to visualize the six locations of conflict as corresponding to six principal styles, models, and approaches to conflict resolution. We can then identify a primary location for each intervention and a methodology appropriate to each site, along with a seventh location that draws from each and floats between them.

1. A conciliative style aimed chiefly at reducing the fighting and primarily uses physical calming and spatial tools such as separation, reassurance, sympathetic tone of voice, and caucusing.

2. An evaluative or directive style aimed mainly at settlement and primarily uses mental calming and logical tools such as analysis, distinction, debate, instruction, compromise, and reductionism.

3. A facilitative style aimed chiefly at resolution and primarily uses emotional calming and affective tools such as listening, empathy, acknowledgement, summarization, reframing, and dialogue.

4. A transformative style aimed principally at the value of personal transformation and primarily uses relational calming and meaning-altering tools such as recognition and empowerment, along with participation, responsibility, and relationship building.

5. A spiritual, heart-based, or transcendent style aimed mostly at personal letting go, forgiveness, and reconciliation and primarily uses attitude calming and heart-based tools such as centering, mindfulness, direct heart-to-heart communication, compassionate inquiry, wisdom, and insight.

6. A systems design style aimed at preventing systemic dysfunctions and primarily uses systems thinking and design principles to alter the context, culture, and environment in which conflicts occur.

7. An eclectic style that uses all of these approaches more or less simultaneously, responding to each moment, person, and conflict differently and moving between them as opportunities for resolution present themselves.

Each of these styles or models of mediation has been successful in resolving disputes, partly because each employs a distinctive set of techniques to unlock conflict in ways that are uniquely appropriate to each location or incorporate techniques that have proven successful in other locations.

Mediation Techniques by Location

Over the last few decades, the principal techniques for resolving conflicts in their physical, mental, and emotional locations have largely been identified and developed, though not completely or consistently. However, we have yet to develop highly skillful approaches to spirit, heart, and even systems design. Nonetheless, it is now possible to identify some of the principal resolution techniques that have proven successful in each location.

1. *Physical Techniques*–Paying attention to body language, physical movement, and sensory awareness allows us to speak *directly* to the body and resolve conflicts at their physical source. For example, we can encourage people to stop fighting and de-escalate their conflict by

- moving out from behind our desks into an open circle of chairs;

- modulating our voices;

- arranging our bodies to subtly mirror the parties' postures;

- lowering our height to appear less threatening;

- making eye contact with our non-dominant eye;

- nodding to encourage trust;

- using hand gestures to communicate calm;

- moving closer to communicate sensitive information;

- using body language to counteract aggressive or defensive postures;

- using touch to anchor negative feelings in one physical location and positive feelings in another;

- indirectly embracing the space around the parties with our arms;

- lightly touching someone to soothe their wounded feelings;

- leaning forward to interrupt fruitless exchanges, or backward to open a space for direct communication;

- holding up our hands to stop a combative communication or block an aggressive party from becoming violent;

- closely observing body movements to monitor shifting states of mind, emotion, and attitude; and

- expanding body awareness by asking questions about how someone is physically sensing themselves, others, or the conflict.

2. *Mental Techniques*—We have learned a great deal about how to resolve conflicts mentally, logically, sequentially, and intellectually. For example, we can help conflicted parties move toward settlement by

- clarifying and explaining the parameters of the resolution process;

- establishing clear ground rules;

- listening to facts and explanations;

- identifying the issues requiring settlement;

- setting an agenda listing issues for discussion;

- contracting and agreeing to work toward solutions;

- caucusing to explore hidden agendas;

- brainstorming options;

- clarifying interests;

- accumulating points of consensus;

- using law, research, and expert opinion to resolve differences;

- evaluating arguments and proposed outcomes;

- facilitating negotiations;

- urging settlement for objective and subjective reasons;

- making recommendations and evaluations to promote settlement;

- drafting agreements; and

- reviewing and solidifying commitments.

3. *Emotional Techniques*–Resolving the underlying emotional reasons for conflict requires a subtle, sensitive, facilitative, empathetic approach. For example, we can help moderate negative emotions and resolve the underlying emotional reasons for conflict by

- listening to and naming the emotions that parties express;

- acknowledging and accepting emotional declarations;

- normalizing and validating emotional concerns;

- mirroring emotional affect;

- releasing hidden emotions by asking probing questions;

- reframing to raise or lower emotional intensity;

- searching for emotional triggers;

- connecting emotions to vulnerability and internal issues;

- revealing the benefits gained from intense emotion;

- empowering people to tell others how they feel and set limits;

- eliciting and surfacing repressed emotions;

- reducing emotional resistance and ego defenses;

- redirecting emotion from people to problems;

- separating intentions from effects;

- shifting focus from emotions to behaviors;

- agreeing to change behaviors in the future;

- connecting emotions with underlying interests;

- modeling appropriate emotional responses; and

- acknowledging and apologizing for negative, disrespectful, or counter-productive communications.

4. *Spiritual Techniques*–Spirit may be easier to translate into techniques by substituting the words intention, energy, life force, attachment, or chi. For example, we can assist people in moving beyond resolution to forgiveness and increased mindfulness or awareness by

- centering, relaxing, and balancing internally;

- releasing past recollections, emotions, and judgments;

- releasing future expectations, goals, plans, and desires;

- expanding present awareness;

- clarifying and concentrating energy, spirit, intention, or chi;

- setting the physical stage for intimate conversation;

- opening with an appeal to the parties' highest intentions;

- sitting in silence and slowing the pace of conversation;

- watching the energy flowing within, around, and between the parties;

- using compassion to understand the parties' deepest intentions, motivations, and desires;

- asking questions that clarify people's deepest intentions;

- using silence, pacing, body language, tone of voice, and emotional vulnerability to communicate sincerity and positive intentions;

- asking questions that encourage responsibility for intentions, attitudes, and choices;

- encouraging forgiveness, acceptance, and letting go;

- identifying all the reasons for not forgiving, what is wrong with those reasons, and the price for not forgiving; and

- designing rituals of release, completion, and closure.

5. *Heart Techniques*—The greatest deficit in current models of mediation is our lack of skill in responding to conflict in its heart location, yet we can assist parties in engaging in heartfelt conversations and reaching reconciliation by

- welcoming people with an open heart;

- opening with a question, invocation, or invitation directly to the heart;

- asking people to tell each other why they want to resolve the conflict, or what kind of relationship they would like to have;

- eliciting the heart meaning of conflict stories;

- opening our hearts and using them to search for questions that invite the parties to speak and listen from theirs;

- asking direct, honest questions that encourage integrity and trust;

- being vulnerable and encouraging vulnerability in others;

- honestly communicating our heartfelt insights, preferably in the form of questions;

- encouraging people to ask each other heartfelt questions and answer them openly and honestly;

- focusing attention and awareness on what is taking place at the center, core, or heart of the dispute;

- bringing humor and play into the conversation;

- encouraging participation in activities likely to result in positive, collaborative, openhearted experiences;

- asking each person what they learned for themselves from the conflict;

- identifying what each person is willing to do differently as a result;

- encouraging complete reconciliation;

- jointly designing new consensual relationships; and

- ending with heartfelt acknowledgements and appreciation.

6. *Systems Design Techniques*—Attempting to resolve the systemic, contextual, cultural, and environmental sources of conflict in ways that can prevent future conflicts allows us to work preventatively and systemically in response to chronic sources of conflict, for example, by

- conducting a conflict audit to identify the chronic sources of conflict within an organization or system;

- analyzing and targeting the chronic sources of conflict, including their connection to systems, structures, culture, communications, strategies, change, values, morale, motivation, styles, and staffing;

- viewing conflicts not as isolated events, but as part of a stream of disputes originating in systemic dysfunction;

- identifying the core cultural ideas, traditional approaches, and informal mechanisms already in place for resolving conflict;

- supplementing these with enriched alternatives that emphasize prevention, skill building, and early intervention;

- approaching conflict resolution in multiple, diverse ways that allow many people to work on the conflict from different perspectives with different methodologies;

- emphasizing integrated conflict resolution systems over individual or discrete procedures;

- focusing on interest-based rather than rights- or power-based solutions;

- expanding the number and kind of resolution alternatives available internally and externally;

- arranging these procedures from low to high cost;

- encouraging early informal problem solving;

- including a full range of options from process changes to binding arbitration;

- providing low-cost rights and power backups;

- creating loopbacks to informal problem solving and negotiation;

- encouraging consultation before, feedback and facilitation during, and evaluation afterward;

- using dialogue, coaching, and mentoring to alter entrenched behavior patterns;

- instituting practices that support inclusion, empowerment, equity, dialogue, collaboration, and consensus, and other organizational techniques for reducing conflict;

- developing training programs in conflict resolution and ways of implementing and sustaining preventative systems;

- simplifying policies and procedures and adopting measures to encourage widespread use of resolution procedures;

- increasing motivation, skills, support, and resources to make these interventions work; and

- continually evaluating why these succeed or fail, and improving the design.

The Uses of Location Techniques

Ultimately, all of these locations and techniques are interconnected, yet each is unique in ways that augment our ability to use the others. Increasing our skills in responding to conflicts in their physical location may simultaneously increase our competency in assessing and responding to their intellectual, emotional, spiritual, and heart aspects or locations.

In addition, while physical techniques may be useful in stopping people from fighting, they will be less useful in settling disputes. Similarly, intellectual techniques may be highly effective in settling disputes, but less likely to resolve the underlying emotional issues in the conflict. Emotional techniques may be successful in resolving the underlying issues, but less likely to encourage forgiveness. To reach forgiveness, spiritual techniques are required. To achieve reconciliation, it is necessary for people to open their hearts, explore what triggered the conflict internally within them, reconnect with their opponents, and transcend the reasons that gave rise to their conflict. Yet even reconciliation techniques may not prevent systemic disputes. To act preventatively, systems design techniques are required to discourage and dismantle conflicts at their systemic source.

While many conflicts will never settle or resolve and only a fraction will result in forgiveness, reconciliation, or systemic prevention, the infrequency of these outcomes does not render these deeper locations and levels of skill useless or irrelevant. On the contrary, the ability to work through conflict in all of its stages and locations can only increase our skills and effectiveness in responding to conflict at any level and location.

In my experience, what makes conflict difficult to resolve is its presence in one of these deeper locations, combined with my own lack of understanding, skill, or permission from the parties to reach and unlock it there. Conflicts naturally occur in these deeper locations because they are well camouflaged and contain hidden, metaphorically coded life lessons that the parties have chosen to suppress, yet subconsciously recognize and are quick to recognize once they emerge in awareness, and the defenses and disguises that conceal them are released.

Mediators can improve their understanding and skill by becoming more aware of these deeper locations within themselves and using multiple forms of intelligence to encourage movement beyond resolution to transformation, transcendence, and prevention. Indeed, it is *precisely* in their spiritual, heart-based, and systemic locations that conflicts are transformed from destructive into constructive forces, allowing them to become sources of learning and systemic change.

Setting the Stage for Negotiations—A Case Study

Several years ago I was asked to facilitate a pre-negotiation meeting between the superintendent and negotiating team for a large urban school district, and the president and negotiating team for a frustrated militant teachers' union. The goal of the session was to set the stage for the round of collective bargaining that was about to begin and resolve a number of intense conflicts that had arisen out of years of miscommunication and adversarial relationships that were threatening to create an impasse before negotiations even began.

I opened the process by interviewing the top negotiators for each team to find out what had worked and not worked in their last round of negotiations, and what they thought might improve their communications and behavior in the next round of negotiations. I then brought both teams together in a large meeting room with a huge conference table in the center. As they arrived, each group seated themselves on opposite sides of the table from their adversaries.

After greeting everyone and expressing my hopes for a useful meeting, I went to a flip chart and drew a diagram of the table they were seated at, with X's on one side and O's on the other, as depicted on the following page.

How not to design the table

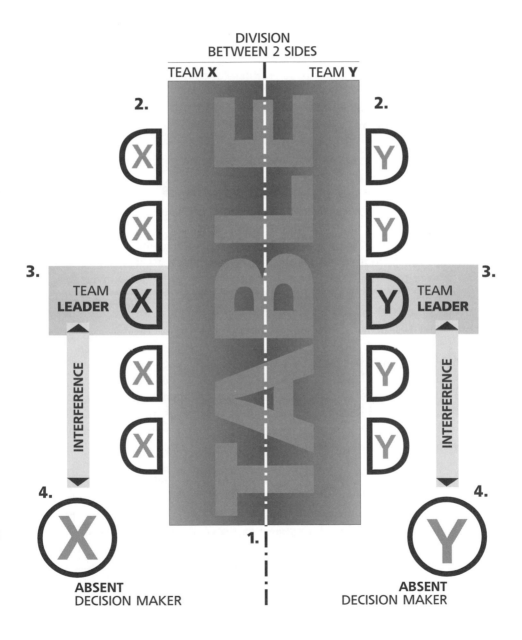

I asked the group, "What kind of conversations are likely to take place at a table arranged like this?" After a moment of poignant silence, they began to answer, and I wrote down their key words, which included "adversarial," "positional," "pointless," "argumentative," "grandstanding," "lack of listening," and "going nowhere fast." I asked them what impact the table might have on their negotiation process, and they identified the following principal results (displayed in the previous diagram).

1. Polarize into adversarial sides regardless of commonalities.

2. Coalesce into loyal teams that require individuals to publicly support their team whether they agree with it or not.

3. Empower team leaders to the detriment of team members.

4. Concentrate authority in absent decision makers who second-guess the team's decisions and accuse them of selling out.

After agreeing that the way they were sitting would likely be counterproductive, I asked them to get up and rearrange their seats in whatever way they wished to increase their chances of having a productive conversation. They switched seats so that union and district representatives sat next to each other, as did people who had similar expertise or were each other's counterparts.

As they moved into new seats, they smiled and exchanged informal personal greetings with each other. Afterward, I asked them how this new arrangement felt compared to the way they had originally been seated. They said it was much easier to talk this way and felt less defensive and positional. They agreed that it would be useful to meet later in smaller teams and have informal conversations away from the formality of the table.

I next asked them to introduce themselves, indicate what role they played, how long they had played it, and identify one thing they felt was at stake in the conversations they were about to have. Their responses to the last question were heartfelt and profound, and included the following answers:

- saving the district and public education from bankruptcy;

- the well being and economy of the city and the region;

- the credibility of the union and the district;

- a future in which kids in outlying areas could continue to be part of the district;

- whether teachers would survive;

- the futures of our children;

- the direction of public education;

- my son and hundreds of thousands of kids and their families;

- public trust and the credibility of our system;

- public confidence that these two organizations can get something done;

- the lives of all children in urban schools who are looking to us for direction;

- putting the agenda for kids ahead of the agenda for adults;

- hope, because everyone in the state is watching what we do here; and

- so the district can do for all children what it did for my family that allowed me to succeed.

I asked them to imagine that all the children in their schools and families and all the stakeholders and people they had mentioned were present in the room watching what we were about to do today. I asked them if they would be willing to consider these high stakes in evaluating any proposal presented for negotiation and to measure every proposal made by either side by whether it would enhance student learning. They unanimously agreed.

Because the press was actively interested and watching what was happening in the negotiations, I asked them to agree on a set of ground rules for communications with the outside world during the course of negotiations.

They agreed on the following communications ground rules.

- The two primary leaders for both sides will jointly agree on all communications that will be made to the public.

- All inquiries will be directed by everyone else to these two leaders.

- While both teams are engaged in this process, all reporting to their respective Boards of Directors will be done by those leaders or their designates.

- Communications to these Boards will indicate that the key interests of both parties are being addressed.

- All communications will avoid indicating or characterizing progress or lack of progress until there is a complete agreement or an agreement to proceed otherwise.

I next asked each side to meet separately, select a facilitator and recorder, and identify their goals for their relationship with each other. When they returned, each side presented its goals, and they discovered to their surprise that they were in agreement or accord on every goal. After some group brainstorming and wordsmithing, they rapidly reached consensus on the following goals:

- commitment to student achievement,

- collaboration and partnership based on mutual trust and dignity,

- a professional working relationship based on mutual respect,

- a problem-solving orientation based on equal power sharing and accountability,

- credibility and restoration of public trust,

- recognition of each side's legitimate roles in educating children and representing its constituencies, and

- continued commitment to achieving our common goals.

Because their relationship had been rocky and adversarial for many years, I asked each group to meet separately and identify what their side had done in past negotiations that had jeopardized or undermined the goals they just created for their relationship. After each side presented their behaviors, the other side had an opportunity to add, subtract, or correct the other side's list. The presentations and discussion were funny, risky, and extremely honest. They quickly reached consensus that neither group would engage in any of the following behaviors, as it would undermine their ability to build a more trusting relationship:

• lie, mislead, withhold information, or use threats;

• impose changes unilaterally before the conclusion of negotiations;

• engage in regressive bargaining;

• delay the release of information;

• have either of the principal leaders not fully participate;

• not act respectfully or follow the ground rules;

• promise what they can't deliver;

• approach issues with a closed mind; and

• refuse to work together and search for creative solutions.

I asked each participant if they would be willing to personally commit to avoiding these behaviors, and they all agreed to do so. I then asked whether it would be acceptable for other people to remind them of their commitments if they failed, and they agreed that it would, especially if the person was a member of their own team. I asked if they were ready to start acting on their commitments right now, and they said they were.

I then stopped, and asked them to reflect for a brief moment, in silence, on what they had accomplished so far in the meeting, opening a heart space before moving on to the next step in the process. I asked for their responses, and everyone spoke warmly, positively, and supportively of what they had achieved so far. I asked whether what they had done so far felt like collective bargaining and they all agreed that it did not. I said that, regardless of what they thought, they had been negotiating collectively over how they would work together, and could do so successfully even over substantive issues without using adversarial negotiating techniques.

I asked them to meet again in separate teams to prioritize their bargaining issues, explain to the other side why each was a priority for them, and how it might enhance student learning. Again, many priorities were the same, so we combined them and picked the lowest priority items to tackle first. An equal number of volunteers from each side met in teams to discuss each priority thoroughly, brainstorm all the solutions they could imagine, identify all the interests each side had in the issue, and rank each solution based on its ability to enhance student learning and satisfy both sets of interests.

The teams then presented their top solutions to the reassembled group, not as final recommendations, but as prioritized options for consideration, and I began to write down and accumulate points of consensus on each issue. On several issues, the group reached consensus immediately, though it was understood that final approval would be necessary from the school board and union membership.

We then focused on mid-priority issues and achieved similar, though less rapid results. In the end, only the top priority issue of wages remained. At this point it became clear that, in order to succeed, both groups needed to expand the scope of bargaining to include a number of non-mandatory subjects that stemmed from parts of their relationship that were not working, including participation in planning, budgeting, and collaborative decision making.

On the issue of wages, each team was asked to come up with a monetary proposal, then indicate what it would want or need in non-monetary items, without restrictions, in exchange for agreeing to the other side's proposal. The resulting discussion exposed underlying issues in their relationship that had not previously been seen as priorities, and led to a negotiated solution that both sides felt was a win/win solution.

The teams worked together over several sessions to finalize their decisions and fine-tune language, and ultimately succeeded in negotiating a contract that pleased both sides. Their process worked, partly because it opened with relationally oriented, interest-based, personal communications that set the stage for dialogue, clear and open communications, and a more trustful, collaborative, consensus-based relationship. None of these topics were traditional topics for bargaining, yet by touching people's hearts, the parties rebuilt their trust in each other, reduced adversarial behaviors, and nourished consensus.

Consensus, of course, is not the same as unanimity. Consensus requires willingness on the part of both sides to live with the group's decision and to vigorously dissent if they prefer a different alternative. It means everyone affected by a problem should have a voice in its solution and participate in making decisions that affect their lives. If the group makes a wrong decision, it will try to learn from experience and do better next time, but the possibility that a group will decide incorrectly does not justify their exclusion from the responsibility of deciding.

Communication does not always result in consensus. It increases the chances of reaching agreement by encouraging people to act respectfully toward each other, listen as though to a friend rather than an opponent, and ground their communications in what is deeply important to both of them. As Abraham Lincoln advised, "When I'm getting ready to reason with a man, I spend one third of the time thinking about myself—what I'm going to say—and two thirds thinking about him and what he is going to say."

Even in the most adversarial, crisis-ridden labor management negotiations, it is possible for passionately committed advocates to agree to avoid behaviors that undermine their relationship. Doing so encourages them to recognize that they are in the same boat, and it ultimately does not matter whose end of the boat is sinking. By acknowledging and affirming what each side wants, needs, and has in common, they are drawn to think about their opponents' needs, as Lincoln advised, and improve their relationship as well. In doing so, they increase their capacity to emerge victorious without anyone leaving defeated.

SECTION II:
ALTERNATIVE APPROACHES TO PRACTICE

Forget safety.
Live where you fear to live.
Destroy your reputation.
Be notorious.
–Jelaluddin Rumi

Chapter 4 Who, Exactly, is in Conflict?

Let us speak of the I, the true I. At least, let us try. What I call the I is that
animation, that impulse, that allows me to make use of the four elements of
this earth on which I live, also of my intelligence and of my emotions – yes,
even of my dreams. It is, in sum, a force that imbues me with a power afforded
by no other force on earth: the power to live without waiting for life to come to
me. The ego needs things, the greatest possible number of things – be they
money, fame, approbation, power, reward. The I makes no such demands,
When it is present, when it is at work, it sets its own world up against the other
world, the world of things. The I is wealth in the midst of poverty. It is vital
interest when all around are bored. It is hope, when all rational basis for hope
is gone. From out of the I springs man's whole world of invention. And, finally,
it is what we still have left when all else has been taken from us, when nothing
comes to us from outside and yet our forces are sufficient to overcome the void.
–Jacques Lusseyran

Jacques Lusseyran suddenly became blind at the age of eight. He went on
to attend the Sorbonne and become a leader in the French Resistance
during World War II. His blindness increased his sense of hearing, and
he was able to tell by listening to people's voices whether they were sincere or concealing something, and so became a chief recruiter and leader
in the Resistance. Eventually, he was captured by the Nazis and sent to
Buchenwald, yet he somehow managed, under horrific conditions, to survive. In a chapter titled "Poetry in Buchenwald," he wrote of the profound
effect that hearing the following poem by Apollinaire had on his capacity
for survival:

> I know all sorts of people
> Who are not equal to their lives
> Their hearts are poorly smothered fires
> Their hearts
> Open and close like their doors.

Lusseyran suddenly realized that unhappiness is a result of a closed heart, that it is stimulated by ego, and that it happens

> ...because we think ourselves at the center of the world, because we have the miserable conviction that we alone suffer to this point of unbearable intensity. Unhappiness is always to feel oneself imprisoned in one's own skin, in one's own brain. For a few moments there was none of this: the poets, the great poets, spoke the universal... It is in part because of this experience that I will say without ceasing, man is nourished by the invisible...He dies from preferring [the visible].

Poetry provided nourishment even to the brutalized prisoners of Buchenwald because it revealed the invisible, fanned the poorly smothered fires of their hearts, freed them from the prisons of their egos, led them to moments of lightheartedness, and revealed the I that lies at their center. The same nourishment and lightheartedness can be found in the midst of conflict.

Ego and Conflict

The central problem in conflict resolution concerns the relationship between self and other, and therefore also between ego and I. Ego, which is Latin for I, is often defined as the focal point of self-awareness, or the ability to create an integrated understanding of the external world that lies outside us and the internal world that lies within. Ego can also mean egotistical or self-centered. In *The Devil's Dictionary*, Ambrose Bierce humorously defined an egotist as "a person of low taste, more interested in himself than in me."

Sigmund Freud defined ego as the part of our personality that maintains contact with the external world through perception; integrates inner and outer worlds; remembers, plans, and evaluates; and responds to external experience, especially the experience of conflict. The ego mediates internal conflicts between the instinctive, impulsive id that relishes and enjoys conflict, and the conscientious, controlling superego that is frightened by it and continually strives for settlement, generally through avoidance, accommodation, and compromise. Ego, then, is the central point from which we perceive, interpret, experience, defend against, and settle conflicts.

Psychologist William James disagreed with Freud about the nature of the ego, writing that "passing states of consciousness" create a false sense that the ego runs the mental show, which actually consists of distinct and separate mental processes. Modern neuropsychology similarly points to a conglomerate sense of self that brain injuries are able to fracture and split off from one another.

In Lusseyran's terminology, the ego sees itself as distinct from the external world, which it regards solely in relation to its own internal needs. The I recognizes that it is indistinguishable from the external world and has no needs or attachments. The ego is congealed, discrete, superficial, and either for or against, while the I is flowing, diffuse, profound, and neither for nor against. Integrity, balance, and creativity all spring from what Lusseyran considered "the true I," as opposed to the "false I," which he defined as ego.

Similarly, the Buddhist principle of "no self" asserts that there is no stable, fixed thing, as suggested by the ego, that can be located internally and differentiated from the flow of moment-to-moment experience. Ego, in this sense, is a story we construct about who we are in order to influence others, make sense of conflict, or protect ourselves, as opposed to the I, which is who we are when nobody is looking, and the one the ego is trying to protect. As Shunryu Suzuki writes:

> If you think, 'I breathe,' the 'I' is extra. There is no you to say 'I.' What we call 'I' is just a swinging door which moves when we inhale and when we exhale. It just moves; that is all. When your mind is pure and calm enough to follow this movement, there is nothing: no 'I,' no world, no mind nor body; just a swinging door.

While the ego is closed, narrow, and self-serving, the I is open, broad, and generous, and for this reason, able to engage in authentic, collaborative relationships with others. Ego-oriented relationships regard others merely as extensions or projections of the self, which solidifies the self. I-oriented relationships regard others as different from the self in ways that promote learning, insight, authenticity, and synergistic relationships, which allows the self to grow.

Ego is responsible for organizing a sense of identity, or self, out of multiple, conflicting sources, including genetic determinants, sibling order, gender, sexual orientation, ethnicity, place of work, social class, religion, politics, physical appearance, and a multitude of others elements that are constantly in flux. Ego can therefore be thought of as a conglomerate, a byproduct of internal conflicts between divided or warring parts of ourselves, and external conflicts with parents, siblings and peers. The greater the conflict, the more precarious and defended the ego, whose work it is to harmonize these warring tendencies.

The ego is therefore highly vulnerable to conflicts that could threaten internal balance and stability. As a result, significant conflicts trigger a set of ego defenses that are designed to protect the self, cement its relationship with the external world, and defend a synthesized or mediated sense of identity, even one that is based on an unstable, artificial version of the self. Yet these same ego defenses also block its ability to listen, understand, change, or learn the lessons only conflict can teach it.

Ego defenses play a variety of complex aggressive and defensive roles that help explain why people get into conflict, why they get stuck, and why they resist resolution. Anna Freud helped define the principal ego defense mechanisms, including *repression,* which develops as young children learn that some impulses, if acted upon, can be dangerous, and seeks to suppress conflict by sweeping it under the nearest rug. Some other ego defenses include

- reaction-formation, which conceals repressed hatred in loving, conscious ideas;

- projection of conflicted feelings onto others;

- internalization of angry feelings;

- sublimation of aggressive impulses,

- divorcing ideas from feelings or arguing over issues to protect wounded feelings; and

- identification with the aggressor, in which victims imitate their perpetrators by turning aggressively against others.

Each of these ego defense mechanisms denies, disregards, or devalues the underlying internal reasons for conflict, making deeper orders of resolution more difficult to achieve. Yet for each defense, there are multiple ways of responding to it that diminish its power and encourage listening and learning. In general, ego defenses can be disarmed, for example, by

- telling the truth in an amiable, non-adversarial, acknowledging way;

- using empathy, apology, and acknowledgement to deliver potentially threatening messages;

- asking questions that reveal the internal sources of the conflict; and

- separating the person from the problem and shifting from positions to interests.

The most effective antidote to most ego defenses, however, is the development of a strong, internally balanced, relationally oriented sense of self or I.

Ego, I, and Relationship

Combining the insights of Lusseyran with those of Sigmund and Anna Freud and others, we can describe the self-oriented ego as a superficial, publicly presented, conglomerate way of defending the self against internal and external conflicts. We can describe the I, on the other hand, as relationally oriented and, naturally, at its core, integrated, aware, and beyond self-defense. Those with a relationally oriented I are thus better at listening compassionately, speaking authentically, and resolving conflicts with people who differ from themselves. Ultimately, it is the I that unmasks and releases the ego, and that resolves, forgives, and reconciles conflict.

This distinction is more easily understood by contrasting feelings, qualities, or attributes that appear similar, yet differ significantly based on their orientation to I or ego, relationship or self. For example, love and attachment look quite similar, yet with love there are two participants, self and other, whereas with attachment there is only one, the self-oriented ego. The same can be said of other qualities, a few of which are listed on next page.

Relationally Oriented I	Self-Oriented Ego
Love	Attachment
Compassion	Pity
Curiosity	Prying
Helping	Controlling
Kindness	Weakness
Courage	Recklessness
Honesty	Aggression
Integrity	Self-Righteousness
Passion	Addiction
Acceptance	Indifference
Collaboration	Manipulation
Feedback	Judgment

The gap between these attributes is narrow and the line separating them difficult to define, making it easy to mistake one for the other. Yet we can notice that

- the self-oriented ego gets into more intractable, antagonistic conflicts than the relationally oriented I;

- adversarial conflict behaviors are reinforced more powerfully by ego than by I; and

- it is easy for the ego to become confused and mistake itself for the I.

Relational attributes can be transformed into their ego opposites simply by forgetting about, refusing, or being incapable of understanding others. More importantly for conflict resolution purposes, ego attributes can be transformed into their relational opposites by developing authentic, empathetic, and collaborative relationships with people, ideas, and emotions different from our own. By modeling relationally oriented behaviors, mediators strengthen the I, weaken the ego, and create healthier, stable, integrated, self-confident relationships.

In the short term, creating an authentic, empathetic, relationally oriented I requires significantly more energy and effort than maintaining a fractured, dysfunctional self-oriented ego. Only in the long term does a satisfied, relational I become less costly to maintain than a dissatisfied, isolated ego. Ultimately, ego is a mask or pose that can be set aside once conflict is resolved and fear, anger, shame, guilt, and distrust have dissipated, allowing it to become apparent that the ego has no enduring substance. The ego is counterproductive, and cannot participate in collaborative relationships or communicate who the I really is, which is simply who remains after ego disappears.

Reinforcing the I in Mediation

There are countless ways of shifting from ego-oriented to relationally oriented behaviors, such as

- meeting together and discussing common problems,

- agreeing on ground rules and agenda items,

- brainstorming options,

- listening to stories,

- engaging in dialogue,

- collaboratively negotiating solutions,

- building consensus, and

- jointly implementing agreements.

In these ways, ego involvements are reduced and I-based relationships are strengthened. Even inconsequential collaborative relationships and minor team efforts subtly reinforce the I. A recent study using functional magnetic resonance imaging (fMRI) revealed that even small acts of cooperation and collaboration produce significant electrical responses in the pleasure centers of the brain, resulting in a release of endorphins and increased pleasure. This helps explain why reaching consensus, even on non-content issues such as process, ground rules, and shared values, or agreeing to avoid negative behaviors in the future relaxes people's moods and makes it easier for them to resolve difficult issues afterward.

Every conflict conversation allows us to transform closed, untrusting, inauthentic, ego-oriented debates into open, trusting, authentic, relationally oriented dialogues. For example, here is a conversation I facilitated during a marital mediation in an effort to reduce ego involvement and reinforce the relationally oriented I.

He: "She is always yelling at me for no reason."

Me: "So you really don't understand why she is yelling at you?"

He: "No."

Me: "Would you like to know why she is yelling at you?"

He: "...Yes..."

Me: "Why don't you ask her right now?"

He: [Turning to her with curiosity] "Why are you always yelling at me?"

In this initial intervention, I helped move their conversation from closed, ego-based assumptions to an open, relational inquiry at a relatively low level of connection. Without outside assistance, they would probably have remained stuck because they lacked the skill or were afraid to ask the questions that could produce the answers they most wanted (or did not want) to hear. In my experience, these are always relational and heart-based in nature.

I proceeded to flip their conversation from negative to positive by moving it in an openly relational direction.

She: "I'm not always yelling at you. You're the one who is always criticizing everything I do."

Me: [Transforming her accusation into a request] "Instead of criticizing you, is there anything you would like him to *thank* you, or acknowledge you for?"

She: [Still fuming] "Yes. He could thank me once in a while for X."

Me: [Shifting to the relational I] "Why don't you turn to him right now and tell him *directly* what you would most like him to thank you for?"

She: [To him, somewhat calmer and more positively] "I would like you to thank me for X."

Me: [Legitimizing and reinforcing the positive in her request] "Would you be willing to thank her for X?"

He: "Yes, but she never..."

Me: [Interrupting ego defense and reorienting to relationship] "Without saying 'yes, but,' could you just thank her for X, and we will come back to the 'but' later? [He does so.]

Me: [Afterward, to him] "Great. Now, can you tell her one thing you would most like her to thank or acknowledge you for?" [He does so.]

Me: [Later, to both] "How did it feel just now to acknowledge and be acknowledged by each other?"

[Perhaps followed by] "Why was that so difficult for you to do at the beginning?"

"What do you think would happen to your relationship if you could do that all the time?"

"Is that what you want?"

"Can you tell each other right now why you want that?"

"Can you both agree to do more of that in the future?"

"How and when will you do that?"

"What got your acknowledgement off track or made it less generous?"

"Is there any way you might sabotage your efforts?"

"What do you need to do to make sure this really happens?" And so on.

"Now let's return to the 'buts' and see if we can reach agreement on what each of you can do to make your relationship more satisfying."

In a different example involving a workplace mediation, a female employee said, regarding her manager, "He thinks I'm a terrible employee." The obvious exaggeration in her statement clearly indicated that she did not really intend this as an ego-oriented declaration of fact, but as a relationally oriented request for contradiction, reassurance, and relationship, as when one says, "You don't love me," hoping the answer will be a denial and an affirmation of affection.

I turned immediately to her manager, trusting that I knew how he would respond, and asked, "*Do* you think she is a terrible employee?" He said, "No, I don't, but she doesn't..." Again, I interrupted, suggesting he hold the "but" part of his answer until later and we would come back to it, and said [gesturing in her direction]: "Can you give her an example of something she did well?" He turned to her and gave an example, and she immediately began to melt. I asked him to give her several more, which he offered freely and in detail. Afterward, I asked her how it felt to hear him praise her this way. She said it felt wonderful and that she had no idea he thought anything positive about her. I asked her if she would now be willing to say something positive about him, which she did, after which they easily reached agreement on ways of improving their relationship, and made sure the "yes, buts" got resolved.

In both examples, the level of conflict was reduced by shifting the conversation from grasping, negative, unacknowledging, self-oriented, ego-based statements, accusations, and defenses, to generous, positive, acknowledging, relationally oriented, I-based *inquiries*, recognitions, and acknowledgements. Acknowledgment, recognition, and praise are not the only means of transition from ego to I in conflict. Asking any question that calls for a relational answer, or for vulnerability, compassion, affirmation, authenticity, or honest introspection, including apology, can nudge a conversation from debate toward dialogue, and from ego toward I.

Me, Myself, and I

In practice, it is difficult for anyone in conflict to surrender their ego or create a closer relationship with someone they do not like or trust. Partly this is because the ego performs a useful function in stabilizing a sense of self and protecting people from the consequences of aggression and poor self-esteem. Partly it is because of a confusion concerning the first person pronoun.

For example, if someone says, "I love myself," or "I hate myself," who exactly is this I who is referenced? Who is the one who loves or hates and who is the one who is loved or hated? If someone says, "I am angry at you," is the part that notices they are angry *also* angry? If the answer is no, where did their anger go? Where was it to begin with? How is the I-as-describer different from the I-as-described? What about all the other I's that coexist inside them? Does the anger actually have anything to do with the I? And who is the you they are angry at? Is it *really* you, or some projection or image of you that was created or contorted by their ego, or yours, or both through some kind of silent conspiracy?

There is an important paradox here concerning how we discover who we are. Many of us learn who we are by negation or opposition to others. But we can also discover who we are by affirmation or collaboration with others. Each of these approaches is reflected in an orientation to self and relationship. In Buddhism, the non-self can be revealed through an internal meditative process, sometimes expressed in the following Zen paradox.

1. The way to awareness is to study the self.

2. To study the self is to forget the self.

3. To forget the self is to become the self.

We can think of these statements as describing different manifestations of the self, either as ego or as I. We manifest the I-self by moving beyond the ego self to no self. The I self is located and concentrated through self-reflective awareness practices such as mindfulness meditation, insight, and direct experience, but can also be located in conflict through relational practices such as interest-based negotiation, collaborative problem solving, dialogue, mediation, and consensus decision making. Thus, transformation and transcendence in conflict resolution can be said to consist of conversations and relationships that calm the ego's defenses, revealing linkages between self and other, and inviting the active participation of the I.

Some people find their self by identifying with something larger or more important than themselves, as by feeling passionately about a person, idea, cause, or thing. In their passion, they resonate and become one with the object of their attention, merging with it, forgetting the ego self, and in the process, become the true self or I, and find deeper satisfaction than ego alone could provide. Others locate the self by focusing awareness inward, studying the self, and gaining insight into the false, transitory nature of ego. Both methods moderate ego-based desires, disappointments, and antagonisms, and assuage conflict fears that sap energy and stimulate ego defenses. Both encourage direct, integrated, unmediated, unselfconscious being. Both occur naturally, without intention, artifice, manipulation, or idealization.

Paradoxically, while having a strong sense of self *seems* to require an ego orientation, the opposite is true. In ego-oriented interactions, the self is formed in isolation or opposition to others, rather than in partnership with them, whereas with I-based interactions, a strong sense of individuality leads to higher levels of collaboration than could have been achieved through isolation or opposition. Consequently, the smallest human relational unit is not one, but two, and the highest levels of individuality occur not in isolation, but in collaborative relationship between self-realized individuals. This led South African novelist Nadine Gordimer to write: "The real definition of loneliness is to live without social responsibility."

Equally paradoxically, in order to improve I-based relationships in conflict resolution, mediators sometimes need to increase people's ability to fight in order to strengthen their self-awareness and personal boundaries, without which they may surrender, lose focus, adopt ego-defending behaviors, or negotiate poorly. With a strong sense of self, they can begin to take responsibility for their actions, listen for the deeper meaning of what their opponents are saying, and search collaboratively for solutions that result in mutual gain.

In this sense, self-effacement and self-aggrandizement are equally ego oriented, though in opposite ways. Indeed, one of the principal challenges in life is to discover that all the labels the ego uses for self-protection, self-defense, and self-aggrandizement have nothing whatsoever to do with the deep, authentic I that remains once these labels disappear or shift because of changing circumstances. "Who am I?" is a question we all attempt to answer, without realizing that the answer is already hidden in the question. We are simply, in the language of Zen, "riding an ox in search of an ox," or "putting legs on a snake."

Our purpose as mediators is neither to deny or attack the ego, nor to falsely elevate or inflate it, but to develop a strong sense of self and other that are equally entitled and inextricably interrelated. By strengthening people's awareness of themselves in relation to others, they become more authentic, forget about themselves, feel more relaxed, and are able to participate more intimately and collaboratively in relationships without feeling manipulated or losing their sense of identity.

Manipulation vs. Involvement

It is tempting for people in conflict to try to manipulate others into giving them what they want rather than to involve them in jointly defining problems and collaboratively negotiating solutions that satisfy mutual interests. When people manipulate, their relationships become one-sided and they get drawn into selfish, controlling, insincere, emotionally provocative behaviors that, in calmer moments, they *know* are counterproductive. They denounce their opponent's ego-based actions, blame others for their own ego defenses, and by manipulating others into doing what they want, discourage their opponents from feeling responsible for implementing solutions, thereby reducing the possibility of collaboration, resolution, learning, and transcendence.

We all understand the difference between being manipulated and being involved. Manipulation employs seduction, operates unilaterally, and uses means that ultimately undermine its ends. Involvement employs dialogue, operates collaboratively, and uses means that reinforce its ends. Manipulation encourages autocratic decision making, demands unquestioning loyalty, promotes conformity, and suppresses opposition. Involvement supports democratic decision making, seeks critical feedback, promotes individuation in partnership with others, and invites constructive dissent.

When mediators adopt ego-oriented approaches, they seek to manipulate, coerce, or seduce the parties into settlements they would not otherwise accept. This often occurs when mediators neglect or discount I-oriented approaches that focus on interests, emotions, and relationships. Ego approaches may settle conflicts, but at a lower order of resolution that does not resolve their underlying causes.

I-oriented approaches to conflict resolution require involvement rather than manipulation, which takes more time, but makes higher orders of resolution possible. Involvement means securing permission as we go and allowing each party to decide what they want to communicate and resolve, thereby increasing their ability to act with integrity, maintain positive self-esteem, and participate voluntarily and responsibly in authentic I-based relationships.

While manipulation may give an appearance of integrity and positive self-esteem, these are ultimately defensive and do not truly recognize the legitimacy of interests other than one's own. Involvement, on the other hand, builds integrity and positive self-esteem by encouraging principled, constructive, mutually rewarding interactions with others, even if they are conflicted.

Superficially, all resolution efforts can be considered manipulative because it is impossible to secure permission in advance for conversations whose outcomes could not have been imagined before they occurred. Nonetheless, there is a fundamental difference between what I think of as benign, or I-oriented manipulation, and its malignant, ego-oriented cousin in that the latter helps others get where *the mediator* wants them to go, while the former takes them where *they* want to go. Deep resolutions only transpire when mediators drop their egos, aid everyone in getting where they genuinely want to go, and encourage them to believe they did it themselves.

In the end, involvement means understanding that conflicts do not belong only to one party, but collectively to both, and to the community or environment in which they transpire. It means accepting that few people ultimately want to be manipulated, even into reaching agreements that are to their advantage. For this reason, having a strong sense of I means being able to act democratically, involve others as full partners, and work toward genuine consensus.

Overcoming Overcompensations

One reason people in conflict attempt to manipulate their opponents rather than involve them is that their egos are chronically insecure and tend to excessively build themselves up or tear themselves down. These overcompensations are triggered by a lack of inner conviction, consistency, and balance in maintaining a positive image of themselves, usually originating in their families of origin. As a consequence, their egos oscillate between self-aggrandizement and self-loathing, neither of which promotes learning, collaboration, or change, or directs attention toward what most needs to be resolved, transformed, and transcended.

Many conflicts are triggered by failed efforts to compensate for what people perceive as faults in their character or weaknesses created by experiences in their families of origin that they project onto others. They overcompensate for these weaknesses by developing countervailing strengths, largely in response to what their families did or did not do. They strive to fulfill needs their families failed to satisfy, and resist others they satisfied to excess. As a result, they are easily drawn into conflicts with people who manifest similar or opposite overcompensations.

If, for example, they grew up in families in which there was constant change, they may become frightened of anything new and resist change, or try to control its every minor detail so they don't feel out of control. Perhaps they become addicted to change and enjoy uncertainty and chaos. Either response can provoke conflicts with those who take similar or opposite approaches, as in the following examples.

1. I mediated a dispute with a corporate executive who was stuck in unresolved patterns from her family of origin. She was the older sister of a brother she found threatening because she saw him as brighter and more cared for by her parents. She had four younger men reporting to her out of a staff of eight. While she was in other respects highly respected, her relationships with these men were tense, controlling, belittling, and distant. She was critical of everything they did, distrustful of the quality of their work, and constantly micromanaged them. In a mediation session, a female colleague asked her why she was treating these men like they were her little brothers. She suddenly realized she was overcompensating based on a family pattern, as her

parents had consistently downplayed her contributions while overlooking her brother's shortcomings. Once she had identified the source of her overcompensation, she was able to participate in cross-gender relationships more fully, listen more empathetically, be less judgmental, calibrate her responses, and solicit feedback so she could continue improving.

2. In a large company, a woman was being fired for resisting her boss's advice. In separate caucuses, she said he reminded her of her father who had tried to control her every move, while her boss said she reminded him of his incompetent, alcoholic parents who had been unable to function without his constant intervention. In response, I asked them to tell each other their family histories, and they immediately recognized their underlying patterns. She was overcompensating for feeling controlled by resisting his advice, causing him to overcompensate by offering advice designed to control her, which increased her resistance to being controlled, and so on. To break this cyclical pattern, he agreed to tell her what results he wanted and leave it to her to determine how she would deliver them. She agreed to thank him for his advice and tell him she would be responsible for figuring out how to achieve the results he wanted in her own way. They both agreed to meet once a week to discuss each project, improve their communications, and search for ways of breaking their interlaced overcompensation patterns.

3. In a dramatic example, a supervisor and an employee were constantly in conflict. Before our session, while waiting for a meeting room to be unlocked, I casually asked them to tell me something about their backgrounds. It turned out they *both* came from families with thirteen children! Amazingly, the supervisor was firstborn and highly experienced in bossing others around, while the employee was lastborn and not about to be bossed around by anyone else. Stunned, I asked them: "How did you *find* each other?" They laughed and their conflict disappeared before the mediation even began. Once they realized their contrasting overcompensations were fueling the conflict, it simply evaporated and they were able to improve their relationship. They not only joked about it publicly, but turned it into a source of pride and unity, which totally transformed their relationship.

The principal way most of us learn to overcome overcompensation is through conflict, which exposes the overcompensation, allowing us to reverse it by involving people rather than manipulating them, by participating in open, authentic, intimate I-oriented relationships, and by avoiding the ego traps of self-aggrandizement and self-blame that fuel anger, fear, guilt, and shame.

Interestingly, every escalation of conflict can also be seen as a regression, or reverse maturation, in which the parties move backward into more infantile states in which advanced mental functions such as the I are overwhelmed by primitive emotions and ego defenses. Regression prefers manipulation over involvement and dismisses collaboration, empathy, and altruism as idealistic and inferior in power to contention, hatred, and selfishness.

More deeply, many people subconsciously choose their conflicts, including their opponents and issues, precisely because they contain concealed, critical lessons that can stimulate their growth, learning, and development. They seem to innately know that a resolution of their conflict could help them expand their awareness, overcome overcompensation, develop skills in involvement, and achieve a higher sense of self. In this sense, conflict is merely the disguised ego voice of the I, asking to learn and evolve.

As people in conflict learn to transcend their ego limitations, overcome whatever they experienced in their families of origin, and develop a more authentic, integrated, balanced sense of self, they become free to decide how they will live, relate, and respond to each other without overcompensating. If they do not, they are likely to continue pretending to be people they are not, triggering recurrent conflicts and experiencing poor self-esteem.

Mediating Dysfunctional Family Systems

Our earliest experiences with conflict occur in our families of origin, where we first learn how to react when we make mistakes, or things do not go our way, or other people become angry or upset at what we say or do, or make mistakes. These early family patterns were reinforced by who our parents were, including systemic dysfunctions in their relationships and those of their parents, and by the space and support allowed within the family for alternative responses to conflict. These patterns become engrained after years of rewards and punishments, successes and failures, and, to the degree that they remain unconscious and outside the realm of choice, are brought intact into each new relationship.

Removed from their sources, these patterns generate fresh conflicts whose roots remain hidden. Yet behaviors that appear irrational may have rational, resolvable causes when traced back to their origins. While mediation is a place where the family origins of conflict might be discussed and learned from, many mediators lack an understanding of why or how to do so. To begin, we need to understand more about the family as a crucible of conflict.

People who grow up in dysfunctional families often feel they have limited options, which is one of the ways their dysfunction expresses itself. The principle choices they recognize are those that, in one way or another, allow the dysfunction to continue. These include

• denying the existence of the dysfunction and sweeping it under the rug;

• adapting, accommodating and becoming dysfunctional oneself;

• becoming apathetic or cynical, going with the flow, and putting a minimum amount of energy and effort into resolving disputes;

• gossiping, complaining, judging, spreading rumors, encouraging others to fight, or becoming professional victims;

• blaming or directing anger at those who are dysfunctional and taking time from creative efforts to engage in equally dysfunctional battles with them; and

• choosing not to surround oneself with dysfunction, and leaving.

None of these responses eliminates the dysfunction. Each traps the person in something equally dysfunctional and cheats them out of learning and growth. Indeed, all dysfunctional systems seek to replicate themselves, based partly on the assumption that only equally dysfunctional responses can justify negative behaviors, overcome guilt and shame, impart a false sense of power, and rationalize the initial dysfunction by making it appear normal.

In contrast to these responses are strategies for escaping and recovering that do not replicate the dysfunction. These responses require courage, support, and determination to implement because they break with the past, prevent the destructive behavior from moving forward, and acknowledge the need for renewal and healing. These include

- choosing, at whatever cost, not to become dysfunctional oneself;

- seeking assistance from experts such as therapists, counselors, facilitators, and mediators in resisting the dysfunction;

- openly discussing the dysfunction and joining with others in a search for the underlying reasons that created it;

- negotiating agreements with those who engage in dysfunctional behaviors to cease or marginalize the dysfunction;

- joining with others to collaboratively eliminate the need to engage in dysfunctional behavior;

- choosing to publicly call attention, limit, or break contact with those who are dysfunctional or toxic and trigger dysfunctional reactions in others; and

- using mediation to better understand, oppose, and transcend dysfunction.

These choices fundamentally boil down to a shorter list: we can either tolerate the dysfunction and adapt our thinking and behavior to it, or we can act to change it by transforming the way we think and behave in its presence. Whichever choice we make will be based partly on what we learned in our families about our ability to overcome dysfunction, and partly on our skills in the deeper levels of conflict resolution. When we learn to oppose dysfunctional behaviors successfully, without replicating them—even in small ways—we feel more powerful in resolving disputes and able to confront the next dysfunctional encounter with greater self-confidence.

Exploring Family Patterns in Mediation

Mediators rarely inquire into the family backgrounds of those with whom they mediate. However, unless we address these early family and peer experiences it will prove difficult for those who sincerely want to change to recognize the source of their difficulties or learn how to unravel and become free of them. By seeking permission to ask questions that direct people to their own inner truths about their experiences, we can help them complete these experiences and move on.

This is dangerous territory. Many mediators feel uncomfortable probing into family histories or believe they lack the skills to do so. Others consider it an intrusion into intimate, non-conflict-related areas. This is especially true for mediators who have not resolved their own family experiences. Yet by failing to examine and discuss these issues, we ignore the most important causal factors in shaping dysfunctional attitudes, habits, and behaviors. Worse, we condemn people to continue blindly following unconscious family patterns.

It is important to step lightly in these conversations. If the inquiry takes place in caucus, privately, empathetically, constructively, and in the context of trusting, ongoing dialogue, it is possible to ask about family issues without sparking embarrassment, defensiveness, or resistance. For example, we can simply request permission to ask questions about family history. If we probe gently, tentatively, and empathetically to assess each parties' level of comfort with this topic or line of inquiry, we can obtain permission to go a little further. We can then ask progressively more probing questions while sensitively monitoring verbal and nonverbal signals, stopping wherever there is resistance, and providing supportive feedback as important stories, insights, and revelations emerge. Here are some initial questions I have found useful.

- Can you each tell me a little something about yourself and your family background?

- Is there anything about [the other person] or issue that reminds you of someone or some problem from your family of origin? If so, who and how?

- How did you respond then? What happened when you did?

- What were some of the unwritten rules and unspoken expectations about conflict that were communicated in your family of origin?

- Do you have any feelings or reactions left over from the past that are similar to those you are feeling now?

- Have you ever found yourself in this position before? When? What did you do? What was the outcome?

- From whom did you first learn how to behave in conflict? What did you learn? Was it successful then? Is it successful now?

- Do you believe your family background has affected the way you are approaching the issues or difficulties you are facing today? How? What messages did your family communicate regarding this issue or problem?

- Do you want to achieve a different result now? Why? Would you be willing to say that to [the other person]?

It may also be useful to assign homework that allows people to probe deeper into their family issues. The mediator may ask each person to talk with parents or siblings and find out their version of what happened. Or, the mediator may ask them to write down all the words that describe their opponent, and afterward write the name of the family member who behaved most similarly, or perhaps to keep a journal or diary and record their insights and thoughts regarding the person or problem and then look back over it for patterns.

It may also be useful to agree on ground rules for future behavior, request support in making needed changes, and invite feedback when old behavioral patterns resurface. The mediator may

- recommend counseling or offer support to keep the person on track and follow through to see whether their responses over agreed-upon issues actually change;

- ask the person to solicit on-the-spot feedback from their opponent, friends, family members, or colleagues;

- ask them to identify the words, signals, or gestures their opponent uses that push their buttons, or might use in the future to avoid doing so;

- set up periodic check-in sessions;

- coach them on how to communicate that dysfunctional behaviors are not acceptable; and

- make the change process more casual and enjoyable by negotiating low-level prizes or rewards and agreeing on penalties for regression.

Dysfunctional family patterns and systems often reveal themselves in small, subtle ways as parties participate in the mediation process, as in the ways they signal that their connection with the family system is undergoing a transformation or phase transition. Here are a few examples.

- *Ways of Entering Mediation*—The complex, even Byzantine negotiations parties engage in to enter mediation may symbolize their role in the relationship and perception of how they are valued by the other person. Frequently, their attitudes toward each other are self-descriptive, revealing wounded self-esteem, frustrated desires, and unrealistic expectations: "She'll never agree to anything I say." "He won't listen." "She's totally irresponsible about money." "If he agrees to pay for the whole thing, I'll come."

- *Cancellations*—As the system begins to unravel, the parties often cancel their appointments, sometimes as a ritual way of rejecting the future and clinging to the past, and sometimes in preparation for moving on to the next phase of the process.

- *Promptness*—A frequent indicator of denial and transformation, or phase transition, is tardiness. Rage is more frequently on time.

- *Blaming*—Often, there is a need to represent the other person as an incarnation of evil. Abandonment and betrayal of trust are often felt to require public humiliation in return for the earlier humiliation. The mediator may empathize, as a friend might, with each party's emotional needs regarding the betrayal without becoming judgmental. A party who needs to blame may have a strong desire for loyalty, perceive neutrality as rejection, and blame the mediator.

- *Procedure*—If one party speaks first the other may have difficulty "listening to all the lies." Confidential caucuses with one may become a focus of suspicion by the other.

- *Language*—There may be increased sensitivity to nuance in the use of language, placing heavy meanings on otherwise neutral terms.

- *Drawing Lines*—Whenever parties put their foot down and say no, they signal the mediator regarding what is really at stake. Some people cannot say no and need to be encouraged to do so; otherwise, they feel taken advantage of later and betrayed by the mediator. This is a kind of victim behavior that hopes to return to the earlier relationship and avoid responsibility for outcomes. Wherever a firm line is drawn, wherever expected behaviors no longer take place, the system breaks and the parties become free to create separate lives.

- *Interruptions*—Linking interruptions to the ideas being expressed can reveal underlying emotional concerns that may have to be surfaced, acknowledged, or resolved before moving on. Asking interrupters to hold their comments can establish a boundary and be gratefully accepted by parties who have difficulty recognizing their own boundaries or those of others. Yet allowing interruptions to occur can reveal underlying power dynamics, efforts to create a smokescreen to hide something important, or dynamics that need to be surfaced or broken.

- *Accusation as Confession*—Parties often accuse each other of what they have done themselves. Mediators can adopt this assumption as a hypothesis and pose questions to discover whether it is true.

When parties allow painful experiences from their families of origin to dominate and preoccupy their interactions in the present, these experiences deplete their energy and subvert their relationships. This continues until they self-critically examine their experiences and release or transcend them. The first act of maturity, and thus of wisdom, freedom, and the I, consists of *becoming aware* of old dysfunctional patterns. The second consists of *transforming* behaviors by choosing to act differently. The third consists of *transcending* dysfunctional patterns by being authentic and inviting others to do the same.

Questions on Self-Esteem

Beneath many conflicts lie issues of poor self-esteem that conflicted parties have internalized or projected onto their opponents. For this reason, it is possible for mediators to resolve conflicts by helping the parties become more introspective, develop self-awareness, and acquire a more positive, relationally oriented, congruent, and collaborative understanding of themselves, their issues, and their opponents.

Ultimately, the reason for transcending family systems is to achieve an integrated sense of self and others. As people do so, they magnify their capacity to achieve the results they want, graduate from their families of origin, and become who they want to be. The primary obstacle to doing so is poor self-esteem, which blocks them even from imagining how their lives might be different. They are afraid to let go of past conflicts because they don't know how to live in the present. They have accepted an image of themselves as inadequate or unlovable, are afraid to let go of their anger because doing so means they will have no one to blame or focus on other than themselves, or are frightened of being alone, unloved, and dying.

The more negatively people feel about themselves, the more unbalanced and polarized they feel internally, the stronger their adversarial and defensive ego responses to perceived insults, and the more hostile their communications are with their perceived opponents. As a result, they become less able to listen empathetically, think creatively, reach consensus, or develop collaborative relationships with those who stimulate or remind them of their negative feelings about themselves. In its extreme form, negative self-esteem turns chronically self-destructive, causing them to find and initiate fights with people who will predictably reinforce their negative self-image.

Self-esteem prompts people to become open or guarded, expansive or fearful, accepting or denying, collaborative or adversarial. Whether the issue is one of spending money, expressing emotions, taking risks, responding to criticism, or working on teams, people with positive self-esteem are more open, uninhibited, and accepting, which allows them to resolve conflicts more quickly and easily. Those with negative self-esteem are more guarded, constrained, and rejecting, causing them to experience longer, deeper, and more entrenched conflicts.

Asking parties about their self-esteem is also risky, and can be considered prying or judgmental. It is therefore both dangerous and helpful to explore self-esteem issues in conflict. Here are a few questions I have found useful in doing so. It is important for us to begin by answering these questions ourselves; build a strong base of empathy; ask them humbly, cautiously, and privately; back off quickly if we encounter resistance; and apologize for our error if anyone takes offence.

- What lessons did you learn about yourself from the conflicts in your family of origin? What impact did these earlier experiences have on your self-esteem? Did they make you stronger? Weaker? How did they contribute to what you experienced in this conflict?

- Have you experienced conflicts like this one before? When? With whom? What does that conflict have in common with this one? Is there anything you are doing that could be causing it to happen again? Is any part of your past still controlling your present?

- What judgments do you have about yourself? How have these judgments influenced your choices? Your conflicts?

- How has your self-esteem affected what has happened in this conflict? How would your perception of this conflict shift if your feelings about yourself were different?

- List some things you *didn't* do in this conflict but think you should have. What kept you from doing them?

- List some things you *did* do but think you should not have. What compelled you to do them?

- Who wrote the script for what you should or should not do? When did they write it? Why? What myths or false assumptions about you shaped it?

- Against what standard are you measuring yourself? Who created it? Why? Who do you know who actually lives up to it? At what cost?

- What are the most important lessons about yourself that you have learned from the conflicts in your life? How could you use these lessons to improve your life?

- What price have you paid for poor self-esteem? How long do you intend to continue paying it?

- What benefits have you gotten from poor self-esteem? Could you receive those benefits any other way?

- Can you imagine letting go of this conflict and releasing it forever? If you did, what kind of person would you become? What would it take for you to do so?

Any of these questions can unlock poor self-esteem at its source. But it is less the questions and answers than the attitude and self-esteem of the mediator, the process of open self-examination, and the receipt of honest, empathetic feedback that are important in building positive self-regard. The right question at the right time can turn a futile, superficial, circular, self-defeating conversation into a transcendent realization that resolves a conflict and ends a cycle of destructive self-esteem.

Karma and the Iron Law of Integrity

The principal reason for addressing issues of ego and I, manipulation and participation, overcompensation, and self-esteem is to recognize that these are filters through which everyone understand their conflicts and shapes them to fit their self-image. For this reason, they are a potent source of self-fulfilling prophecy, *karma*, and what I call "the iron law of integrity." This means that these issues are also ways of recognizing the emptiness of conflict and creating future pathways to increased self-awareness, the I, participation, and enhanced self-esteem.

The Hindu notion of karma reveals a subtle connection between people's attitudes toward themselves, what they have done in the past, and what they expect to occur in their future. At its simplest level, without requiring any belief in reincarnation or past lives, karma merely suggests that there are future consequences to past acts. It is a law of action and reaction, cause and effect, applied to everything we do, feel, say, and think. Tibetan Lama Thubten Yeshe offers a practical definition:

Karma is not something complicated or philosophical. Karma means watching your body, watching your mouth, and watching your mind. Trying to keep these three doors as pure as possible is the practice of karma.

It is not difficult to recognize that when people act unethically, lack integrity, treat people with contempt, or behave cruelly, conflicts are more likely to appear in their wake. What is more difficult to recognize is that ego-oriented behavior, overcompensation, manipulation, dysfunctional family patterns, and negative self-esteem generate a polarized internal field that results in blindness to self and others and attracts conflicts.

Whoever we are and whatever we do, feel, say, and think generates a kind of momentum, a vibration, wave, ripple of energy, or probability field that does not remain in our past, but moves forward into our present and future, influencing and resonating with everything and everyone we encounter. By carefully monitoring what we do, feel, say, and think, especially when we are in conflict, we can all become better at communicating, correcting our mistakes, and resolving our conflicts. This allows us to choose the effects we want to follow us into the future and abandon those we want to leave behind.

In truth, there is no difference between karma and integrity, or between integrity and the I, or between the I and the heart. In essence, they are the same, though they differ in form. As a result, mediators can resolve conflicts simply by

- shifting from ego-oriented to I-oriented interactions,

- rejecting manipulation and encouraging involvement,

- overcoming overcompensation,

- dismantling dysfunctional family patterns,

- promoting positive self-esteem, and

- encouraging people to consistently act with integrity, even over trifles.

Each of these methods alters the parties' attitudes toward themselves and their opponents, thereby creating a momentum or field of possibility leading in the opposite direction toward resolution, forgiveness, and reconciliation.

The quality of our lives depends on our ability to evolve and sustain a clear, coherent, positive sense of ourselves, which depends in turn on our ability to develop a strong sense of ethics, values, and integrity, which, whether we are aware of it or not, profoundly influences our self-image and relationships with others, even when no one is watching. Hungarian novelist Sandor Marai writes:

> One's life, viewed as a whole, is always the answer to the most important questions...Questions such as: Who are you?...What did you actually want?...What could you actually achieve?...At what points were you loyal or disloyal or brave or a coward? And one answers as best one can, honestly or dishonestly; that's not so important. What's important is that finally one answers with one's life.

The Iron Law of Integrity is really quite simple. Whenever we act without integrity, even at a tiny, subtle, subconscious level, we subdivide into separate, dissimilar, opposing parts, somewhat like the cartoon image of a devil over one shoulder and an angel over the other. One part recognizes that what we are doing is wrong, while the other wants to go ahead and do it anyway. One feels like acting with integrity, while the other feels like behaving badly and disregarding the consequences. As a result, we become internally divided.

In a wonderful Native American story, an elder tells a child he has two warring wolves inside him, one filled with hatred, fear, and distrust, and the other filled with love, compassion, and acceptance. The child asks which one will win, and the elder tells him "Whichever one you feed." Every time we insult our opponents, we feed something insulting within ourselves. Every time we hate someone, a wave of hatred gathers and coalesces inside us. When we act without conscience, it is always ourselves we betray. And when we extend love, compassion, or forgiveness, love, compassion, and forgiveness grow within us.

When we behave disrespectfully to others, or act in ways we know are wrong, whether as a result of poor self-esteem or anger or fear, we weaken our integrity, spirit, heart, and sense of self, even if we can rationalize or justify our actions. Sometimes we weaken our integrity in microscopic ways, but these microscopic weaknesses produce macroscopic effects. Ultimately, these microscopic cracks accumulate and reach a point where they create a crisis or crossroads, making possible a return to unity and an end to a divided self.

Acting without integrity is common in conflict, giving rise to subconscious feelings of guilt and shame, along with a fear that they will be found out. As George Sewell wrote, "Fear is the tax that conscience pays to guilt." Even small, nearly unnoticeable feelings of guilt, fear, and shame accumulate in conflict communications, making it difficult to hear what the other person is saying or to see them as they actually are. In this way, their own lack of integrity trips them up and causes them to lose balance.

The word *integrity* has multiple meanings. On the one hand, it means being integral, or whole. On the other, it means having values, behaving ethically, and acting justly and fairly toward others. Integrity is often confused with purity or honesty, and while purity and honesty may contribute to integrity, they are not identical to it. For example, one can have integrity without being honest, as when people lied to the Nazi SS about the location of Jews they were hiding. One can also be honest yet possess little integrity, as when people told the SS the truth about where they were hiding. Integrity requires a clear sense of values and beliefs and a willingness to act on them, even at high personal cost.

Integrity is weakened when people stereotype or demonize their opponents, when they cannot empathize with others or acknowledge their legitimate interests, when they think or feel one thing and say another, when they become defensive and counterattack, and when they behave in ways that contradict their values. On the other hand, integrity is strengthened when people respect their opponents and affirm their humanity, when they empathize and acknowledge their positive characteristics, when they are deeply honest, when they listen and collaborate, and when they act in accordance with their values. When they do these things, even to the detriment of their short-term interests, they become stronger, more balanced, internally integrated, and no one's enemy. Writer Michael Ventura makes an even stronger claim:

> People who assume the burden of their own integrity are free—because integrity is freedom (as Nelson Mandela proved), its force can't be

quelled even when a person of integrity is jailed. The future lives in our individual, often lonely, and certainly unprofitable acts of integrity, or it doesn't live at all.

Building integrity requires conflicting parties to separate their ego from their I, clarify their values and principles, and act according to their own highest standards and beliefs. It requires them to improve their capacity for awareness, acceptance, and see themselves and others without masks or filters. In addition, it requires them to do these things not in isolation, but collaboratively with their opponents.

The negative effects created by a lack of integrity can be cured by offering restitution to those who have been injured, by self-forgiveness, and by repeated acts of integrity and generosity toward others. In the end, integrity simply means wholeness of self, which requires seeing the I beneath the ego, both in themselves and in others. For this reason, as critic Terry Eagleton declared, "Seeing things for what they are is, in the end, possible only for the virtuous." To understand how integrity influences conflict resolution, consider the following case study.

Partnership in Decay—A Case Study

Bob and Fred were dental partners who worked together for many years and said they liked each other, but were mired in conflict. Neither really wanted to dissolve their partnership, and both hoped to avoid litigation if they could. As a result, they agreed to come to mediation.

After welcoming them, introducing the mediation process, and agreeing on a number of ground rules, I asked them where they felt stuck in their relationship. Bob spoke first and said he thought their basic disagreements were over financial inequities, unequal contributions to the partnership, and unequal participation in the profits. He felt the profit participation issues masked a set of philosophical differences that could also be seen in the decisions they had made about marketing and maintaining a high quality of customer service.

Fred said he felt the whole conflict was Bob's problem and was happy with things exactly as they were. He had agreed to mediate because they disagreed about the fairness of their original agreement, which Bob wanted to change. Fred said he felt he was better at management and Bob was better at administration. Both agreed that they would have to separate if they could not resolve their disputes.

In an effort to draw their attention to what was working in their relationship and the positive reasons for their partnership, I asked them why they had decided to practice together in the first place. Fred said he had graduated from dental school in 1980 and set up a practice with a classmate named Tom that was ongoing and highly successful. He made sure I knew Bob had graduated from a less prestigious dental school, needed to take the licensing exam three times before passing, and came to him to propose that he set up a second practice. Fred had been a mentor to Bob in those early years, but that had begun to change as Bob learned, grew, and developed their practice.

Fred continued to maintain two offices, working with Bob in one office and Tom at another location. As Fred was the more experienced of the two, they agreed that Bob would work more hours in their joint office. In arranging their compensation, they had created a distinction between per diem pay, which favored Bob, and profits, which were funneled back into the partnership, but when paid rewarded them equally, regardless of their efforts.

Their per diem rate was $200 a day, which they agreed was average for dental offices, and Fred was willing to see it go up to $300 a day, which he said was the highest amount paid under comparable conditions by dental partnerships in the area. Bob, on the other hand, said he felt compensation should be entirely per diem, with no allocation for profits because he was now doing considerably more work than Fred in making the practice function and grow.

A year ago, Bob went to Fred and asked that their per diem rate be raised. Bob was then working four days a week to Fred's two, but Fred was bringing in twice as much patient work as Bob, so they decided to each take 50% of the profits. Six months later, Bob had again increased his workload, and they went back to a per diem / profit split, but with the per diem set at $250 a day, which was the going rate at the time.

Bob felt Fred had brought his superior dental and management experience to the partnership and should be compensated fairly for risking his money in a new venture. But now that risk was much smaller and Bob was spending a great deal more time than Fred administering the office on a daily basis, handling all the accounts payable and receivable, resolving personnel problems, deciding on bids, and completing other time-consuming work. Fred responded that Bob's idea of office management consisted of paying the bills, and if he wanted to perform that task, that was fine. They each had different styles of management, and Fred said he would be willing to bear part of the burden of compensating someone for time spent on office management, no matter who did it.

Bob objected that Fred did not really understand what was involved in doing the work and didn't seem to appreciate his efforts. We were now nearing the end of our first session, and their exchanges were becoming increasingly heated as they moved closer to the underlying emotional issues in their relationship. In an effort to defuse their negative emotions before leaving, I asked Fred if he would be willing to acknowledge the administrative work Bob had done, and he did so, but without much enthusiasm. I then asked Bob if he would be willing to acknowledge Fred, and he thanked him for starting the practice and being willing to acknowledge his contribution.

I wanted to test their ability to work together on creating a plan for the future, and altering the work systems and environment that were contributing to their conflict, and asked them if they would be willing to complete a homework assignment. I asked them to meet together before our next session, list all the administrative and management tasks that needed to be performed in the office, and try to divide the tasks between them, either 50/50 or 60/40 or any other way they wanted. They agreed.

At the next session, they announced that they had successfully worked out a 50/50 division of administrative responsibilities, with Fred being responsible for promotion and growth, accounts payable, and accounts receivable, and Bob doing the rest, but taking responsibility for managing office personnel, since they both agreed he was good at it. They were quite proud of what they had accomplished, and of the improved quality of their communications.

I complimented them on the success of their negotiations, reinforced their positive attitudes, and asked them what they had done differently. They said they felt encouraged by their open communications at the end of the first mediation session, and as a result, had been able to avoid their past pattern of hostility and hurt feelings during their meeting. This enabled them to successfully divide their office responsibilities. They each said they had not changed their minds, however, about the need to reach a new agreement regarding their compensation plan. I encouraged them to continue meeting together to address office problems, and they agreed at their next meeting to discuss how they could create a more acknowledging office culture.

We began the collaborative problem-solving process regarding compensation by breaking it down into smaller constituent elements and tackling the easiest ones first. They quickly agreed that their basic profit arrangement did not need changing. Their 50/50 division of office responsibilities made a 50/50 split of their profits now seem completely fair. The only remaining issue was how much they should be paid per diem.

In order to shift their attention away from power-based solutions and prevent their positions from hardening, I attempted to elicit their interests by asking them why per diem was important to them. They said they felt per diem was like a wage and should represent compensation for time actually worked. I drew their attention to the future, and asked them what changes in conditions or circumstances ought to translate into changes in per diem. After considerable dialogue and discussion, they agreed on the following criteria that they would use in adjusting their per diem.

- Changes in the cost of living.

- Comparison with other practices.

- In making this comparison, include:
  - partners with similar arrangements,
  - associates on a percentage basis with similar experience, and
  - an additional 10% to 20% for financial participation.

Fred and Bob agreed that these criteria established a fair basis for setting future increases in per diem, and while the mediation could have stopped there, I felt there were still unresolved issues in their relationship that could threaten their partnership in the future. I asked Bob how he felt about these criteria, and he complained that the incentives were still not great. For him to be willing to spend long hours building their practice, he needed to see a larger increase and felt the current per diem schedule still favored Fred. Bob said he felt their present arrangement was unfair because he felt Fred really didn't care as much about their joint practice as he did about his practice with Tom.

Because of this intimation of jealousy on Bob's part and a long history of reluctance to talk openly with each other about emotional issues, I decided to caucus separately with Bob and Fred to explore the deeper emotional issues I suspected were driving their dispute and hoped would allow them to discover why they had become stuck in their positions.

In the caucus, I began by asking Bob how he felt about Fred, and how he thought Fred felt about him. Bob said he felt completely undervalued by Fred. He had worked hard from the beginning of their partnership and never really felt acknowledged by Fred for his efforts. While Fred had certainly started with greater knowledge and experience, they were now professional equals, yet their unequal relationship had never changed.

Bob said he felt that Tom, as Fred's other partner, was like the other woman in a marriage. It felt to him like Fred was having an affair and signaling his lack of commitment to their relationship. There was also a philosophical difference in Bob's eyes, as he wanted to emphasize building a neighborhood practice and providing a high quality of customer service and patient care, while Fred was more interested in marketing, profitability, and high turnover.

I asked Bob if he was certain he wanted to continue the partnership, as these differences in character and philosophy could either be a source of strength or weakness in their practice. Bob said he was clear that he wanted to continue working with Fred if their relationship could "be more fair." After their cordial discussion during the homework assignment and fair division of administrative tasks, he now felt this was possible. I asked Bob if he would be willing to tell Fred directly, when we returned, how he felt about their relationship and what he wanted from him by way of acknowledgment. Bob was shocked at the idea of actually saying this to Fred, but agreed to try.

I next met with Fred, who was direct and to the point. He said he felt Bob wanted to be seen as a nice guy, and was "keeping things close to his chest." I asked him if he knew what Bob was keeping close to his chest, and he said he had no idea. Fred described himself several times as not afraid of being seen as pushy or a hard bargainer. He felt he "put things out there" and took the consequences, whereas Bob just seemed to capitulate. I asked Fred if he would be willing, when we returned, to draw Bob out more, get him to "put things out there," and talk about what he was keeping close to his chest. He said he would.

Fred said he was willing to change the number of days they worked, though he knew that Bob was unwilling to cut back. He said he knew when they started the partnership that Bob would want to work more days that he did, which was why he wrote the contract the way he had. Very simply, he said, Bob "made a bad deal," and as far as he was concerned, Bob was stuck with it. He said he had come to mediation so I would tell Bob that he had to live up to his agreement. When I asked Fred whether he wanted to end the partnership, he said he wanted to continue working with Bob if possible.

I asked Fred if he would be willing to be generous in acknowledging the work Bob had done in expanding and managing their partnership. Fred hesitated, so I asked him if he would agree to tell Bob that there was now a greater equality in their skills and abilities than had been the case when they started. Fred felt that this was accurate, and said he would be happy to say so directly to Bob.

We returned to a joint session and I thanked them for their comments and suggestions. I asked Bob if there was anything he wanted to say to Fred. Bob spoke eloquently about his feeling of being undervalued by Fred, that he now felt he was Fred's equal as a dentist and a partner and no longer wanted to be treated as an inferior. I asked Fred if he would respond directly to Bob. In a genuine and heartfelt way, Fred told Bob he really appreciated all the work he had put into the practice. He agreed that they had begun in a mentor/student relationship, but now were really equals and colleagues. If anything, Fred said he felt Bob was now more skilled than he was in dentistry. Bob was shocked and thrilled to hear him say this, and immediately altered his attitude and demeanor.

Fred said he really wanted to continue the partnership and was willing to make whatever changes Bob needed in order to make it work. He said he would make their practice a priority over his practice with Tom in order to do so. He reiterated that he felt their relationship was really one between equals, though with different strengths, and he was sure they could not have created a successful practice without each other. Bob for the first time opened up completely and said he really appreciated Fred's acknowledgment, support, and superior marketing skills, which meant a lot to him, and said he also wanted to make their partnership a priority. He sincerely thanked Fred for all he had done to help him grow and create a successful practice, and for his generous comments.

I complimented them on their willingness to acknowledge each other and asked how their financial arrangement might be designed to reflect their new, more equitable relationship. They had divided their administrative tasks equally, agreed on a 50/50 division of profits, and set in place a mechanism for adjusting their per diem in the future. The only remaining issue to resolve and complete their partnership was the level of per diem pay.

Fred said that since Bob felt there was little incentive for him to work hard to build the practice, he would agree to allow the per diem to float according to the criteria they had agreed on. He also suggested a new category of incentive pay that would give Bob a bonus for building the practice. They agreed that their average rate of net growth had been about 15% per year. Anything over that rate would be considered a bonus that would be divided between them based on their average per diem.

Bob felt satisfied and pleased with this result, and they both were smiling and said they felt the dispute was now fully resolved. They agreed to return to mediation if their agreement broke down, and I congratulated them again on their ability to work through their disagreements. I recommended that they meet once a week to review how their relationship was working, talk openly about emotional issues as they had done in mediation, and go over any difficulties they might have with how they were working and communicating with each other. As we finished, they got up and hugged each other.

Their conflict moved from settlement to resolution, forgiveness, and reconciliation by shifting their dialogue from an ego orientation at the surface of their dispute to an I or relational orientation at the center of what was not working for both of them. This meant not merely addressing their disagreements, but exploring, expressing, and transforming their stories about each other, disarming their ego defenses, shifting their interactions from manipulation to involvement, altering their self-esteem-based negative behaviors, and changing the systems that were reinforcing their conflict.

The mediation invited them to turn them inward, release themselves from the burden of their past unequal relationship, and acknowledge what they had generously done for each other. It encouraged them to engage in open, heartfelt communications, which transformed their intentions and attitudes toward each other. It leveraged their newfound respect, commitment, equality, and diverse strengths to collaboratively negotiate optimal solutions that satisfied both their interests.

For their partnership to succeed, they had to learn quickly how to overcome ego and poor self-esteem and to ask for what they really wanted. In the course of the mediation, they learned to shift their focus from positions to interests, break issues down into smaller units so they could be solved individually, make their office systems and culture more collaborative and acknowledging, nail down agreements on practical issues involving roles and responsibilities, develop criteria for making economic decisions, focus on the future rather than the past, openly and honestly communicate emotional issues to one another, and collaboratively explore creative solutions. For either of them to have learned even *one* of these skills would have been accomplishment enough, and continued coaching was needed to keep them from slipping back into their old patterns.

After the mediation, I coached them separately and met occasionally with both of them over a period of several months. Bob had to be encouraged not to slip back into his old patterns of deference to Fred, give up his defensiveness, tell Fred what he wanted, be enthusiastic about the partnership, and on some level, take care of Fred as Fred had taken care of him. Fred had to be encouraged to make the partnership a priority over his relationship with Tom, improve his relationship with Bob, and continue recognizing Bob as an equal.

In the beginning, there was little sign that anything was going to change. Fred's intention of using the mediation as a way of forcing Bob to admit that he was right and follow the terms of the contract was clearly inconsistent with his deeper desire to make the partnership work. But once Bob spoke up and told him how he felt, Fred was able to drop his initial ego position and negotiate collaboratively. Both had to be encouraged, gently but inexorably, to clarify what they really wanted, speak directly to each other about their feelings, and negotiate—not just the division of their administrative tasks and financial remuneration, but the heart of their entire relationship.

Throughout the mediation, both partners were given full permission to say that they wanted to dissolve the partnership, or needed more time to think about it, or really did not like or respect one another. Their recognition of the real possibility of their dissolution helped focus the process, made them more open and honest, and gave them the feeling their choices mattered.

Most importantly, they were able to address the underlying emotional, systemic, and attitudinal elements that were aggravating their dispute and might have been ignored in a superficial effort to stop their fighting or settle their financial issues. As a result, they arrived at a full, lasting resolution of the underlying source of their conflict, transformed their communications and relationship, and evolved to a true partnership and higher level of relationship based on emotional completion, forgiveness, and reconciliation.

Chapter 5 Transforming Conflict Stories

Children, only animals live entirely in the Here and Now. Only nature knows neither memory nor history. But man—let me offer you a definition—is this story-telling animal. Wherever he goes to he wants to leave behind not a chaotic wake, not an empty space, but the comforting marker-buoys and trail-signs of stories. He has to go on telling stories, he has to keep on making them up. As long as there's a story, it's all right. Even in his last moments, it's said, in the split second of a fatal fall—or when he's about to drown—he sees, passing rapidly before him, the story of his whole life.
–Graham Swift

It is not only in our last moments, but in every conflict—subtly, indirectly, and in miniature—that we can see passing before us the story of our lives. In the stories we tell about our conflicts, every word we select, every fact we recite, every transgression we recount indirectly chronicles our life choices. Every detail in our stories provides a clue to who we are, what we think, how we feel about ourselves and others, what we have done and failed to do, what we fear and hope will happen to us, why we remain stuck, and what we might be willing to do to transform and transcend them.

If listened to correctly, every conflict story allows a mediator to reach deeply into the subconscious mind of the storyteller. A single story, properly understood, holographically reveals the facts about what happened and their emotional meaning to the storyteller, and the reasons it remains unresolved, the emotions and assumptions that lie at its core, and a set of instructions for how the parties might live happily ever after. How is this possible?

As people describe with great anger, fear, or sadness how they came to be in conflict with each other, they indirectly reveal their innermost anxieties, expectations, hopes, and desires. Their stories are signposts, maps, and directions that lead backward into their subconscious minds, emotions, hearts, and spirits. They are revelations and confessions that, even as they falsify or camouflage the truth, like all good fiction, reveal deeper truths in the process.

The Aim of Conflict Stories

When we listen to conflict stories told about some terrible person, we may be aghast—especially when we realize that this terrible person is or could be us. Even if we enter the conversation with a serene and empathetic heart, we can rapidly be reduced to outrage, defensiveness, and counterattack, culminating in our refusal to listen any further to lies and falsehoods. Yet responding defensively only hinders us from recognizing the deeper implications of the story and responding in ways that might steer the conversation toward resolution.

People tell stories about their conflicts principally to alleviate the shock and pain of their experiences, reweave the fabric of perceived reality, and tell themselves everything will be all right. But there is more to conflict stories than a desire for emotional comfort. Every conflict story identifies, for anyone willing to listen, what the storyteller most needs to learn, understand, do, and become. This is why stories are used by cultures around the world to transmit critical life lessons. As African novelist Chinua Achebe put it, bluntly but poetically, "It is only the story...that saves our progeny from blundering like blind beggars into the spikes of the cactus fence."

All conflicts consist, in the first place, of actual experiences, and in the second, of their recapitulation in the form of stories that routinely deny, discount, and disparage the possibility of resolution. As Walter Benjamin wrote, the meaning of a story is not the same as its "way of meaning." The way of meaning of conflict stories is the storyteller's desire to elicit sympathy, invite alliance against undeserving opponents, or request coaching on how to respond to a troublesome situation. Their purpose is to sum up not merely an upsetting event, but the person whose perfidy authored it, and the storyteller who unjustly suffered from it. At a deeper level, they are rationalizations for engaging in behaviors that might otherwise appear illogical or reprehensible to the listener. For this reason, the relationships they describe are presented as closed, unalterable, and complete, when in life, they are open, malleable, and unfinished.

While conflict stories are usually heard as assertions of facts or feelings, they can also be heard as confessions of vulnerability or requests to the listener to do something, if only by offering sympathy, alliance, or advice. The accusation that forms the core of the story is intended to

- draw the listener into a close, sympathetic relationship with the storyteller, and into a distanced, antagonistic one with the opponent;

- describe, rationalize, and reinforce the tensions that separate them; and

- counterbalance or equalize the perceived power of the opponent while justifying the storyteller in failing to communicate more effectively or working harder to resolve the dispute. In these ways, conflict stories indirectly discourage their own resolution.

Conflict stories are also acknowledgments of feeling discouraged, cries for help, confessions of powerlessness, and requests for forgiveness. The cunning or depravity of the opponent is simply the flip side of the storyteller's own powerlessness, pain, sadness, and frustration. Because people feel powerless in conflict, they seek comforting explanations, justifications for their failure to do more, and rationalizations for their adversarial reactions. When they experience pain at the hands of others, they are drawn to ask what could possibly motivate someone to harm them. If they want others to respect them as decent people who do not deserve this kind of treatment, they are drawn to characterize their opponents as wicked, malicious people who intend harm for no good reason, which explains why the storyteller could do nothing to prevent or resolve it.

In these ways, conflict stories dress up the facts regarding upsetting events, yet in so doing they create signposts pointing inward to the hidden sources of conflict within the storyteller. Each story directs the listener's attention outward toward what the perpetrator did, partly out of a desire to minimize or deny the storyteller's own complicity, fear of confrontation, or wish to prevent future attacks through the deterrent of a well-timed counterattack. The perpetrator's perfidy is magnified in proportion to the storyteller's desire to appear innocent. In these ways, conflict stories protest too much.

Yet conflict stories can also be heard as invitations to resolution, as calls for storytellers to

- develop a more constructive attitude toward their opponent,

- confront and overcome their own inner demons,

- take collaborative responsibility for resolving the dispute,

- transform the antagonistic elements in their relationship, and

- transcend the conditions that made the issues irresolvable in the first place.

Nonetheless, people use conflict stories to paint themselves into corners, justify their antagonistic behaviors, and let themselves off the hook from seeking mutually acceptable solutions.

Conflict stories are parables in which storytellers describe how someone broke their heart or caused an emotional or spiritual crisis in their life. These stories are communicated both to listeners and to themselves, not simply to ameliorate the crisis, but to disguise its significance, demands, and potential consequences. The tone, metaphor, and symbolism of the story are shaped by the needs of the storyteller, who uses the music, rhythm, and dramatic tension of the story to evoke and excite resonant emotions in others and soothe their own anxieties.

Conflict stories are also fairy tales, in which the storyteller becomes a princess (victim) describing the actions of a dragon (perpetrator) to someone they hope will become their prince (rescuer). In the fairy tale, the princess is primarily responsible for expressing feelings and being emotionally vulnerable, the prince is responsible for coming up with solutions, and the dragon is responsible for directing attention toward problems that might otherwise be unnoticed. In order to elicit sympathy and support from the listener, the storyteller must be seen as powerless in the face of evil. The action of every conflict story is therefore to trade power for sympathy. Instead, the mediator offers empathy and empowerment and shows each person how they play all three roles. This means refusing to become a rescuer, asking the princess to accept responsibility for part of the problem, helping the dragon become more open and vulnerable, and encouraging both to participate in solving the problem. [For a more detailed discussion of the narrative structure of conflict stories, see Kenneth Cloke and Joan Goldsmith, *Resolving Personal and Organizational Conflicts: Stories of Transformation and Forgiveness*, Jossey Bass / Wiley Publishers, Inc., 2000.]

Every conflict story is, at its core, a cry of the heart and a protest against the absence of other, infinitely more desirable stories, not about the pain of conflict, but about the desire for resolution, intimacy, compassion, forgiveness, and reconciliation. Each story is a hypothesis hoping to be disproved, a child's plea for comfort and mutual affection, a wish for the world to be different, a list of what most needs changing.

Truth and Lies in Conflict Stories

Oscar Wilde wrote in *De Profundis* "...to speak the truth is a painful thing. To be forced to tell lies is much worse." Wilde's observation is especially apt in conflict stories, where lying is a sign not so much of dishonesty as of distrust, fear, and emotional vulnerability. Everyone wants their story to communicate the hard logical facts, but also the soft emotional truths of what they experienced, the heartfelt desires their story was designed to conceal. For these reasons, the best way to listen to conflict stories is to be deeply empathetic without being pitying or sentimental, deeply honest without being harsh or judgmental, and to walk side-by-side with the storyteller without accepting the *literal* truth of what they are saying.

Every conflict story falsifies and distorts the events it describes, if only by insinuating emotionally charged information into ostensibly unbiased depictions of the facts. Yet if every conflict story is false, it is also an effort to communicate a deeper, more powerful truth. As a result, it is important for mediators to recognize that it is impossible to tell a *false lie*, since even the lie someone tells originated in a subconscious desire to alter or shave the truth, which itself reveals a deeper truth. D. H. Lawrence wrote, "Never trust the artist. Trust the tale." Ernest Hemingway echoed, "All good stories have one thing in common: they are truer than if they had actually happened."

At a deeper level, *all* conflict stories are false, not merely because they are factually and emotionally distorted, but because they ignore the humanity and prior victimization of the perpetrator, minimize responsibility for what the storyteller did and did not do, and fail to adequately recognize the possibility of resolution, forgiveness, and reconciliation. At the same time, all conflict stories are true because they contain verifiable facts and because their exaggerations allow a careful listener to intuit the perpetrator's humanity and prior victimization, what the storyteller did or failed to do, and genuine desire for resolution, forgiveness, and reconciliation.

Every conflict story reveals the metaphoric emotional and spiritual truths of what happened—directly and externally regarding the perpetrator, and indirectly and internally regarding the storyteller. In this way, every conflict story is a kind of autobiography, which, as Mark Twain wrote:

> ...is the truest of all books, for while it inevitably consists mainly of extinctions of the truth, shirkings of the truth, partial revealments of the truth, with hardly an instance of plain straight truth, the remorseless truth is there, between the lines.

While all good storytellers have a stronger desire to be emotionally compelling than to be factually correct, at a deep, heartfelt level, they would rather their stories end in resolution, forgiveness, and reconciliation than in enmity, impasse, and recrimination. They can be supported in achieving these ends by mediators who do not desert or silence them, but pay close attention to the emotional subtexts of their story, patiently elicit its deeper meanings, and interpret facts as metaphors rather than scientific truths.

This does not mean there is no such thing as factual truth in conflict, even rigorous mathematical truth, but rather that the truth of any conflict experience is inherently subjective and uncertain. Conflict truths are composites, defined partly by

- distorted sensory perceptions;

- faulty intellectual frameworks;

- biased lenses;

- imprecise memories;

- untested ideas;

- fluctuating moods;

- contradictory feelings and desires;

- inconsistent attitudes;

- false expectations, complex systems, and relationships; and

- a constantly shifting balance between these elements.

Just as there can be more than one truth about anyone, there can be more than one truth about conflict. There is, for example, the truth that people want to communicate their pain, not by talking about it directly, which might make them feel vulnerable in the presence of someone they do not trust, but by telling a story that hurts their opponent in exactly the way they feel hurt. If someone insults us, we can either tell them how painful it feels to be insulted or insult them right back, communicating more safely, powerfully, and pleasurably the experience of what it felt like to be insulted by them.

Yet by doing so, conflict stories provoke irrational responses and escalating actions, including defensiveness and rationalization, aggression and counterattack, cynicism and distrust, desensitization and withdrawal, prejudice and stereotyping, escalation and revenge. These responses and effects stimulate counter-stories that cascade until every anecdote becomes a self-fulfilling prophecy calling forth the very behaviors it was intended to prevent.

Invitations to Battle and Resolution

Every conflict story simultaneously invites those it demonizes to participate in a mutual exchange, either of defensiveness, competition, escalation, and battle or of vulnerability, collaboration, empathy, and resolution. Consider, for example, the following conflict story told by A, with two equally possible responses by B and the agreements that are likely to result from each.

A's Conflict Story:	You never want to spend any time with me.
B's Response 1: *Invitation to Battle:*	Yeah, well that's because you're always yelling at me.
A's Agreement to Battle:	Well, if you didn't act like such a jerk I wouldn't have to yell at you!
B's Response 2: *Invitation to Resolution:*	I would love to spend time with you, what would you like to do?
A's Agreement to Resolution:	I would love to be with you too, what would you like to do?

To understand A's story, B needs to be able to hear it at a deeper level, not merely as an *accusation* and call to combat, but as a *request* and call to intimacy and relationship. For A, this took the form of a small lie that exaggerated the facts but was designed to communicate a deeper emotional truth that would hopefully (yet improbably) shame B into listening and somehow result in improving a relationship that is not working for either of them.

A's story can therefore be heard not only as an accusation, but as a confession of vulnerability and a request for direct, open, honest communication and a more intimate relationship with B. Were it not for A's distrust, injured feelings, and vulnerability, it would have been far more honest, encouraging, and effective to skip the demonizing parts of the story and just say, "I would love to spend time with you, what would you like to do?" Yet doing so requires trust and vulnerability, which A's response simultaneously spurns and intensely desires.

Most conflict stories can be interpreted in these two opposite ways. In the end, ignoring the provocations contained in the conflict story and interpreting them as an invitation to resolution and relationship allows the listener to recognize the subjective truth of the story without attributing evil intentions. Doing so automatically transforms the story, encouraging both sides to become more empathetic, envision a different future, and realize that it is possible to get what they want by asking and negotiating for it.

Goals in Listening to Conflict Stories

Conflict stories, like dreams, consist of ciphers and symbols, desires and fears, honesty and deceit, passion and surrender, and a myriad secret constituents, most of which lie hidden beneath their surface yet can be revealed in mediation through skillful questioning. Our goals as mediators in listening to conflict stories are therefore complex, multilayered, time sequenced, and difficult to achieve.

Our first goal is to *open and enlarge* the story by listening to it with an empathetic, unguarded heart and an honest, curious mind in an effort to extract its deeper meanings. This requires empathy to locate the story within ourselves; honesty to explore the parts of the story that seem unclear, confused, illogical, or incompatible; and insight to reveal its hidden narrative structure.

Our second goal is to *defuse and destabilize* the story by revealing it as one of many in a field of possible stories. If we imagine all the facts regarding what happened as a random array of dots, each person's story will connect some but not all of the dots, yet not come close to exhausting all of the possible ways of connecting them. This idea is illustrated in the diagram on the following page, adapted from John Winslade and Gerald Monk.

Each set of consistent connections represents a "true" story about what happened, but also a "false" story, in the sense that it ignores or minimizes other stories that are equally true. Every conflict story, then, is an arrangement or connection of facts in a pattern that reveals the storyteller's deeper meanings and communicates to the listener how the storyteller would like them interpreted.

For example, as Monk and Winslade show in *Narrative Mediation*, in addition to negative, harmful stories about conflict, there are

- positive, acknowledging stories people can tell regarding what their relationship was like before the conflict began;

- what they did to try to resolve it;

- what they might have done differently;

- what they still respect or admire about each other;

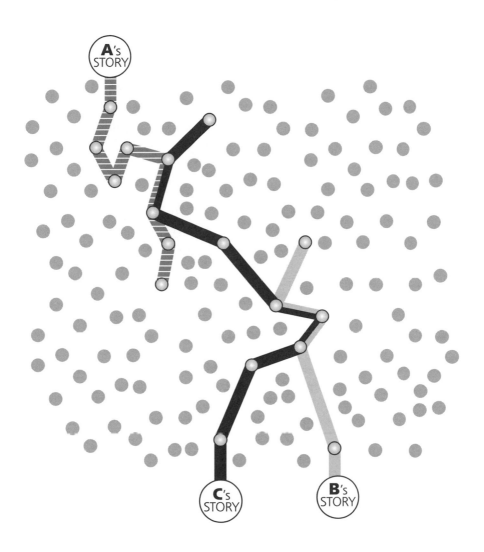

- how they tried to reach out and communicate; and

- how they tamed their desire to escalate or strike back.

People can tell stories not only about their pain, heartbreak, disappointment, and loss, but how they survived these difficulties, how they remained committed to achieving common goals, how they did not succumb to evil intentions, and how they might yet engage in problem solving, collaborative negotiation, and dialogue to achieve a resolution.

Our third goal in listening is to discover ways of *recontextualizing* the story and expanding the storyteller's awareness of its meaning so the conflict can be seen as a choice, rather than as bad luck, fate, or the result of their opponent's pernicious intentions. Recontextualization makes the earlier story increasingly unnecessary, allowing it to be discarded in favor of a resolution story that emphasizes problem solving, collaborative negotiation, dialogue, and resolution.

There are many ways of recontextualizing conflict stories and leading them in constructive directions. We can ask questions, such as, "What do you hope will happen as a result of this conversation?" "What kind of relationship would you *like* to have with each other?" and "Why?" We can pose questions that redefine conflict as a relationship, as opposed to a personal flaw, or ask what each person might have done differently. We can ask questions that identify the systemic sources of the disagreement, or challenge assumptions and ask them to find out what their opponent really experienced, thinks, feels, or intends. We can ask questions about the parts of the story that present each person as different from who they think they are, or that shift their focus from disagreements to commonalities, from egoistic to relational forms of thinking, and from external blaming to internal responsibility.

Our fourth goal is to *design a third story* that supports the storyteller in creating fresh, positive experiences, telling encouraging, acknowledging stories, and planning specific actions to bring them into existence. We can ask parties if they would be willing to meet on an ongoing basis, or create a joint announcement to co-workers that their conflict is over, or appear at a staff meeting to discuss what they learned from the conflict, or meet once a week over breakfast to review recent communications and give each other regular feedback on what could be done to improve their relationship.

Once we shift our attention from assessing the truth or falsity of the story, we can recognize that it was designed to communicate the storyteller's subjective interpretation, emotional response, mental confusion, fear of vulnerability, and desire for assistance in understanding what happened. Recognizing these elements in conflict stories makes it possible to transform the story and invent new ones that end in resolution, forgiveness, and reconciliation.

Transforming Conflict Stories

There are undoubtedly hundreds of interventions and techniques we can use to encourage parties to transform their conflict stories, subtly alter their emotional messages, and create movement in the direction of resolution, forgiveness, and reconciliation. Here are a few drawn from my experience, which a mediator or either party might decide to use.

- *Summarize what is useful or true in the story and reframe it, leaving out the parts that demonize or victimize others.* Summarizing helps people feel their stories have been heard, though simply summarizing accusations can make them worse. Instead, it is better to reframe accusations as confessions or as requests. For example, if A describes B as brutal and uncaring, we can ask A whether his feelings were hurt by B, whether he would like B to be more polite or caring, and, if so, if he would be willing to ask B to do so. Or, we can ask A if he feels he is being successful in getting through to B and, if not, why not. We can then ask B to coach A on how to communicate with him more successfully. Or we can reverse the *hot* adjectives A used and ask what it would take to make their conversation more respectful and caring.

- *Ask the storyteller to clarify the context in which the conflict occurred* or what might have led their opponent to behave that way. Most conflict stories reveal vast areas of ignorance and negative judgments about opponents. For example, several years ago I mediated a divorce in which the husband admitted having numerous affairs during their engagement, cheating continuously throughout the marriage, and giving his wife a sexually transmitted disease. Instead of slipping into judgments about his behavior, I became curious and asked questions that revealed deeply troubled family histories on both sides. It turned out that both their fathers had engaged in similar behaviors and both parties had been sexually molested as children. His way of coping was to have affairs, while hers was to become frightened of sexual contact and withdraw, allowing each behavior to reinforce the other. In the end, their stories became one, revealing experiences of extreme perpetration matched by equally extreme victimization. Their conflict stories made no sense until they were merged in a single, integrated whole that could contain both, revealing a still deeper story that needed to be told.

- *Offer a contrary, positive, empowering interpretation.* Conflict stories generally describe the storyteller as a disempowered victim, yet they can often be reinterpreted using positive terms. For example, in a mediation I conducted, a woman said "I was so frightened when he yelled at me." Instead of reinforcing her fear, I said, "You must have been very courageous to have stood there while he yelled at you," and her entire demeanor changed. In another mediation, a son yelled at his father, "I am so angry at the way you treat people." Again, instead of reinforcing his story, I responded, "You must care a lot about your father and other people to be so angry about how he treats them." And later, "Is that because of how he treated you?" "Why don't you tell him right now how it felt?" And still later, "Were you trying to show him through your anger how you wanted him to treat you?" "Why couldn't you just tell him directly?" These reversals had a powerful impact on their understanding and self-esteem, and dramatically changed the way they were communicating.

- *Identify the cultural influences on the storyteller.* Many conflicts reflect differing cultural assumptions, particularly if we consider culture as including not only race, gender, age, disability, sexual orientation, and national origin, but also birth order, political and religious beliefs, years of education, work experience, and similar factors. I may ask, for example, "What does that mean to you?" Or, "What life experiences have you had that have led you to feel so strongly about this issue?" Or, "Where did you first learn that?" Or simply, "Are there any cultural influences that have led you to think that way?" In cross-cultural or interracial conflicts, I may ask "What role would you like me to play?" Or in marital disputes, "What do the words 'wife,' 'husband,' or 'marriage' mean to you?" Or "Tell a story about yourself, your culture, or your family that illustrates what you mean when you use those words."

- *Identify the ghost roles in the story.* Many conflicts between husbands and wives, for example, may indirectly involve their in-laws, who are conspicuously absent from the stories told by their children. In response, I may surface these ghost roles by asking the husband what effect his mother may have had on his conflict with his wife, or help the wife trace her demeaning stories back to her family of origin. I often find in disputes between co-workers that the actual conflict is not with each other, but with a manager who is not a party but gives conflicting work assignments, plays favorites, creates excessively competitive, hierarchical, or authoritarian work environments, or fails to provide clear leadership and direction.

- *Point out the gaps in the story.* Every conflict story highlights whichever facts support the storyteller and minimizes the importance of others that do not. It is often useful to ask people to identify what they think was left out of the other person's story, then ask the storyteller why these elements were omitted and how the story might change if these gaps were filled.

- *Jointly or separately investigate the factual assumptions behind the story.* When people disagree about what happened, it is often useful to ask them to find out whether their factual assumptions are correct, perhaps by jointly interviewing witnesses, checking documents, getting outside opinions, researching past practices, or visiting other locations to find the answers to an agreed-upon set of questions. Whenever they jointly investigate, they discover that they can act together to solve their problems. For example, I sometimes ask, "What evidence or information, if you discovered it, would cause you to feel differently about what happened?"

- *Separate facts from interpretations in the story.* Every conflict story confuses fact with interpretation, making the storyteller's interpretation appear indistinguishable from the facts they recount. I often separate and tease these differences apart, for example, by using a flip chart, taking a fact, asking the storyteller and the listener how they each interpreted it, and writing down their answers. I then ask them to brainstorm alternative interpretations, listing all, until it becomes clear that every interpretation is subjective. For example:

Fact	Interpretations
X yelled at Y	X hates Y.
	Y pushed X's buttons by going behind his back and complaining to his boss.
	X is responding defensively to Y's earlier insult.
	X is suffering from personal problems and simply taking it out on Y.
	X is really mad at himself for not having said earlier what he really wanted from Y.
	X cares deeply about Y and yelled only to motivate her to do better.
	X just discovered he has cancer and is in a lot of physical pain.

Any or all of these interpretations could be true. What matters is that they reveal the futility of single, subjective, unilateral interpretations, that X really doesn't want to be yelled at, that yelling is a cover for some deeper problem, and that they can easily negotiate an agreement not to yell at each other in the future.

- *Correct false assumptions about causation and intention.* In conflict stories, the perpetrator is usually portrayed as causing or intending something harmful to happen, yet in many cases, they either caused but did not intend it, or it happened accidentally, or it was caused by someone else, or neither party caused or intended it. I may ask, "What did you intend to happen?" "I understand that was what you intended, but what effect do you think your actions had?" "Was the effect you described the one that B actually experienced?" "Would you like to find out what the actual effect was on B?" "If so, why don't you ask her right now?" Afterward, "Would you be willing to acknowledge that you caused the harm B experienced and tell her how you feel about having caused it?" "If you did not intend to cause it, could you tell her what you did intend and why?"

- *Clarify the false expectations in the story.* Many conflicts occur as a result of false expectations that neither party clarified nor negotiated. For example, in partnerships and marital mediations, I may ask each person to identify their expectations that the other person has not met; whether they clearly communicated their expectations, and if not, to take responsibility for failing to do so; to tell the other person honestly what they want or expect from them in the future; and to negotiate new understandings. People in conflict often have interlocking, interdependent, and conditional false expectations in which each waits for the other to meet their expectations before they are willing to reciprocate. In marital mediations, if the wife indicates disappointment in what her husband said, I may ask, "Was that what you wanted him to say?" When she says "No," I ask, "Would you be willing to tell him right now what you wanted him to say?" And "Why was it so important to you that he say that?" I then ask him to respond, then tell her what he wanted her to say.

- *Identify the hidden judgments in the story.* Most conflict stories contain hidden judgments about opponents that are not expressly communicated or openly acknowledged. For example, I mediated a dispute in which a manager accused an employee of poor performance. When I asked him what standard he was using to judge her performance, he realized that his accusation was based on an unspoken judgment that only hard-working people (like himself) were responsible, and that her arrival at work and departure on time meant that she was not motivated. This led to a deeper story that revealed where, how, and why he had formed this opinion, which originated with his father and had nothing to do with her. He was then able to confess how miserable and jealous he was, how he hated being a workaholic, and how much he wanted to change.

- *Create a conflict map to outline how the conflict occurred.* Conflict stories evolve over time and can be mapped in ways that reveal the precise places where communication went awry. For example, I asked an embattled teacher and principal to map what happened in their conflict, step by step. As they did, they could see that Step 5 consisted of the principal falsely assuming that the teacher did not want to resolve the dispute. They mapped that step into smaller steps to identify where, when, and how this false assumption occurred, discovering that it originated in a minor misunderstanding, which they quickly resolved.

- *Correct the conflict story step by step.* It is helpful, with or without conflict mapping, to correct the conflict story minutely and thoroughly. For example, in a parent-child mediation, the mother said, "He never thanks me for what I do for him," and her son answered, "She never listens to me." I asked him whether he appreciated what she had done for him and he said he did. I then asked him if he would be willing to thank her and tell her what he appreciated and why. Afterward, I asked her whether she had really listened to him, how it felt to hear him say that, whether that was what she wanted to hear, and, if not, what she did want to hear. She said he sounded insincere, so I asked him, "On a scale of 1 to 10, 10 being highest, how would you rank your 'thank you'?" He said he thought it was a 7, while she felt it was a 5. I ask him to try again, and this time try to make it a 10, which he did.

- *Ask the storyteller to change the pronoun in the story and discuss what happens as a result.* There is a vast difference in the meaning of conflict stories based on the pronoun people use to describe the problem. By changing the pronoun, we can change the form of the communication, with predictably different results.

- *Clarify the deeper metaphoric meanings in the story.* The mediator can reveal the hidden meanings in the conflict story by asking what key words mean, including power words that convey strong emotions and words that hold special meaning for the storyteller based on culture, background, and experience. For example, in a mediation involving a mother and her teenage son, I asked her, "What do you think his story means?" She said, "I think it means he doesn't appreciate me." I asked, "What do you think it means to him?" She said she didn't know, so I asked her if she would like to know, and if so would she ask him. She did, and he said, "It means you don't have any idea who I am and don't even want to find out." Finally, she knew what the conflict was about and how she could start to resolve it.

Pronouns and Conflict Resolution

Pronoun		Form of Communication	Predictable Result
They	[Example: They are lazy and irresponsible.]	Stereotype	Prejudice
You	[Example: You are lazy and irresponsible.]	Accusation	Counteraccusation/ Denial
He, She	[Example: He/She is lazy and irresponsible.]	Demonization/ Victimization	Blame and Shame/ Disempowerment
It	[Example: There is a lot of work here. How shall we divide it so we pull our own weight?]	Objectification	Problem Solving
I	[Example: I feel overworked and would like to take time off but won't let myself and am jealous when you do. / Could you give me a hand with this?]	Confession/ Request	Listening/ Responsiveness
We	[Example: We haven't been clear about how to share our joint responsibilities. How would you suggest we share them? / How can we work together to complete them?]	Partnership/ Collaboration	Consensus/ Ownership

[Drawn from Kenneth Cloke, *Mediating Dangerously*, Jossey Bass / Wiley, 2001]

- *Ask each party to tell a story about their opponent that is positive and acknowledging.* Everyone in conflict feels underacknowledged and unrecognized, and hearing their opponent say something positive about them undermines their negative assumptions and defensiveness. For example, I mediated a dispute involving an employee who complained about his manager's negative, hypercritical, micromanaging style. When I asked the manager to say something positive about him, he was reluctant at first but quickly got into the spirit of it. As the employee began to soften he realized his manager did not hate him, but was merely frustrated because his efforts to communicate had been blocked by the employee's defensiveness. The manager agreed to stop micromanaging in exchange for the employee agreeing to produce the results that were required.

- *Elicit alternative stories about the ability to communicate or collaborate.* It is often useful to ask questions that highlight the efforts each person made to control their negative emotions or behave fairly in spite of their temptation to retaliate. For example, I sometimes ask divorcing couples: "Have you been able to reach agreements regarding your kids?" "Why didn't your anger and hurt feelings prevent you from doing so?" Or I may ask what they did to reach out to each other, focusing not on their failures, but on their good intentions, or ask whether they meant to cause each other harm, and if not, why not.

- *Ask each person to write a conflict story. Then ask them to write the other person's story. Then to write a third story that combines them.* Each person's story is different, each is partially true, and each is more true when merged with its opposite than when standing alone. In a recent mediation, I asked a woman who complained about her sister's angry, insulting, critical demeanor to write her story, which she enjoyed. Later, when I asked her to write her sister's story, she was forced to reflect on how her parents had treated her sister unequally and how resentful she must have felt as a result. When she combined them in a third story, she realized that the only solution that made sense was for her to call her sister, apologize, and invite her to mediation. Afterward, they agreed to call a family meeting and ask their parents to stop playing favorites.

- *Identify the larger systems, processes, and conditions that impact the story.* Many interpersonal conflicts are actually a result of dysfunctional systems, including family systems distorted by dishonesty, addiction, and abusive behavior; organizational systems made impersonal by hierarchy, bureaucracy, and autocracy; and social systems characterized by inequality, discrimination, and powerlessness. Yet these conflict-generating systems are rarely referenced in conflict stories. Nonetheless, they generate chronic conflicts in which people mistakenly assume that their opponent is motivated by personal animosity. I may ask questions to identify the roles these systems played in triggering a dispute. For example, in organizational conflicts, I may ask others if they have experienced similar conflicts, or to brainstorm the sources of their conflict, or to make joint recommendations regarding what could be done to prevent similar disputes, or to communicate their recommendations to senior management. Or I may seek permission to broaden the mediation to include those who can correct systemic dysfunctions or consider how to redesign the systems that triggered the dispute.

- *Contrast the conflict story with what the storyteller most deeply wants to do, learn, have, or be.* Every conflict story describes a failure of communication, understanding, relationship, or process in which the storyteller may genuinely want to succeed. For example, I asked a parent who described serious conflicts with her daughter, "What is your most important goal in communicating with your daughter?" "What do you most want for her in life?" Then, "Is the story you just told going to help her achieve those goals?" "What was it about your story that could prevent her from achieving those goals?" "What kind of story could help her become more successful?" "What could you do together that would allow you to begin telling that kind of story?" And, "Would you be willing to start laying the foundations for that story right now?"

- *Help the storyteller create a third story leading to resolution.* It is often possible to combine antagonistic stories and create a third story that omits the distortions created by demonization and victimization and expresses a mutual desire for resolution. For example, in a divorce mediation, I asked each person to write down, as homework, the story of their relationship, starting with the words "Once upon a time...," cover all of the facts regarding the history of their conflict, and find a way of ending with the words "...and they lived happily ever after." At the next session, they read their stories aloud to each other. Both began sobbing as they saw how much they cared for each other, and that their solutions were nearly identical. Their conflict disappeared and these implacable enemies again became friends.

Marina Warner wrote regarding fairy tales that "In the kingdom of fiction, the tension between speaking out and staying silent never eases." The same can be said of conflict stories, which walk a delicate line between what people desperately want to say and what they are afraid to hear, and therefore try to ignore, suppress, or disguise. The mediator's objective in using these techniques is to locate that line, take both storytellers by the hand, and formulate questions that will encourage them to cross it, only to discover that on the other side is who they really are and what they really want.

No Chance For Resolution—A Case Study

Before we began, several representatives for the Company and the Union told me they agreed there was no point mediating Barbara's grievance as she had been fired and there was no chance that they would reach a resolution. The Company was insistent on termination and the Union was equally insistent on reinstatement. Each side made it clear that they were attending the session only on instructions from higher-ups, and were ready to call it quits.

Neither side wanted to sit through an introductory explanation of mediation and how it works, or agree on ground rules, or offer opening statements of what their positions were, or discuss what was needed to reach a final agreement. They considered all this a waste of time and said they thought they might as well leave. I agreed that it certainly seemed there was little chance of settlement, but asked them to stay for just a few moments so I could satisfy myself there was nothing else we could do and they agreed.

I moved quickly past preliminaries and statements of position to a request for clarification of the bottom line for each side. I asked them to briefly tell me their stories so I could see whether any further discussion might be fruitful. Though they clearly wanted to leave, they also wanted to tell their stories, but insisted I hear each side's story separately. They already knew each other's positions and thought it would needlessly undermine their already strained relationship to listen to adversarial stories, as the issues were not going to be resolved anyway.

I met first with the Company representatives because they chose to fire Barbara and could give me their reasons, which would allow me to speak more directly with her afterward. Also, the Company had the power to reinstate her or offer options that might satisfy the Union's interests short of reinstatement, whereas Barbara could only argue that her termination had not been for just cause and hope to obtain a favorable award if the case proceeded to arbitration. Her situation gave her somewhat less flexibility in negotiating than was available to the Company.

In caucus, the Company representatives argued they had treated Barbara fairly. She was "an unpleasant and vulgar person" who had been involved in drug use and been so argumentative that the other employees in her unit strongly objected to bringing her back. I asked what she had been fired for, and they indicated it was for chronic tardiness rather than drug use, which they agreed they would not be able to raise in arbitration.

Barbara had worked for the Company for more than 16 years and was satisfactory in work performance, but had been late over 100 times in the last year of her employment. She had offered many reasons for her tardiness, but none were persuasive. She had given reasons such as traffic, her car not working, and so on, none of which were sufficient to prevent her from getting to work on time if she had genuinely wanted to do so. She had been seeing a Company Employee Assistance Program officer for drug addiction, but had not shown any improvement.

I asked the Company representatives if, while I met with Barbara and the Union, they would write down every reason they could think of for *not* taking Barbara back. They were reluctant at first to perform what they saw as a useless task, but agreed to do so, partly because I had not asked them to change their position regarding reinstatement.

I then met with Barbara and the Union. The Union representative spoke for her and told the following story. Barbara had initially worked at a location closer to her home and had only had a few tardiness problems. She had been reassigned to a new office that was farther away and, while she had worked out a swap with another employee, the Company would not allow her to transfer back. She had proposed numerous alternatives, but none had been accepted. She had been under a great deal of stress and pressure in her work group as a result, had been suspended twice for tardiness in two successive months, had received a final warning, and finally was given a notice of termination. The Union's position was that her tardiness was minor and the Company should give her a second chance.

I carried Barbara's story back to the Company with the Union's permission. The Company representative responded that the reasons for her termination went beyond lateness. Once she had claimed her windshield wipers didn't work on a day when it hadn't been raining, the Company had received employee complaints about her "foul mouth," and there were technical deficiencies in her work in which accuracy was an important factor.

The Company representative then read the list they had created of all the reasons for Barbara's termination. After they finished, I asked them if they would be willing to convert every reason for terminating her into a *condition* for reinstatement, based on the idea that if Barbara could successfully overcome every reason that had led to her termination, the Company would be willing to consider reinstating her. I asked them not to decide now whether they would eventually offer reinstatement, or whether Barbara would agree to their conditions, but to make sure they listed as many conditions as required. They agreed to go through their list again and implement my suggestion.

When I took the Company's comments back to the Union, Barbara responded that her last evaluation had given her high marks in quality and a more than acceptable rating in quantity of work, and that her emotional and psychological problems had been due to her drug addiction. She told a very personal story about feeling she was sliding out of control, becoming obsessed and suicidal, and eventually recovering through therapy and a twelve-step program. She was confident she could prove she had fully recovered.

The Company representatives reiterated their concerns regarding the allegations of tardiness, difficulties with co-workers, and production problems, and indicated they were still unwilling to move off their original position and offer reinstatement. They said that if they were willing to reinstate her, she would have to agree to the following conditions.

• Barbara would return to one of two locations picked by the Company.

• She would receive no back pay.

• She would receive no seniority, but return as a new hire, thereby giving up her right to arbitrate any future termination for six months.

• She would return to work at a final warning stage.

• She would meet *all* job standards (including work performance), conduct (including attitude and language), attendance, and punctuality.

• She would be placed on one year's probation.

• She would get psychological assistance and go into a Company-paid therapy program for her problems.

I felt the Company had not fully heard Barbara's emotional story and, as a result, could not empathize or believe in her intense commitment and determination to prove herself. I asked them to return to a brief joint meeting so each side could make their intentions clear, and ask the questions that needed answering before considering changing their position.

In the joint session, I asked Barbara to tell her *personal* story about her addiction, and how she had struggled to reclaim her life. At first she was reluctant to speak, so I asked her some difficult questions I would have wanted answered if I were a Company representative, but might not be willing to ask, including: "Why did you start using drugs?" "What did this do to your performance?" "How did drugs cause you to be habitually late?" "Why did you make up false reasons for being late?" "Why did your relationships with your co-workers go sour?" "What did it feel like for you emotionally?" and "How did you kick your addiction?"

For the first time, Barbara told the full story of what had happened to her, and what it was like to be addicted to drugs. She said she knew she had been out of control and felt like she was going crazy. She said it felt like she was "going downhill without brakes." She could not plan or be anywhere on time, and constantly felt suicidal. She became obsessive about unimportant slights at work and felt herself falling apart. After her termination, she asked for help and thought her therapist and Alcoholics Anonymous had helped her immensely. She had gone back to school at night and was currently in the top 10% of her class. She was holding down three part-time jobs, had not been tardy or absent once, and had no conflicts with her co-workers. She felt much better now and thought she was capable of handling her work assignments and being a successful employee. Her present jobs, though only part-time, put her under a lot of stress, yet she had been able to deal with the public and co-workers without any complaints.

Barbara's answers were deeply honest and personally compelling and helped convince the Company representatives that she wanted to perform according to their expectations, though they were still not convinced that they would offer her reinstatement. I moved them back into separate caucuses and asked the Company representatives to identify some areas where there might be room for give and take, and consider what they would need from Barbara as a bottom line in order to be willing to reinstate her.

I met next with Barbara and the Union representative and we developed the following counteroffer.

- Barbara would be reinstated to one of several offices of her choice.

- She would receive seniority retroactive to the date of her termination.

- She would receive back pay less wages and unemployment benefits earned in the interim in the sum of $42,000.

- She must agree to meet all the usual and customary standards for employees regarding job performance.

- She must agree to continue seeing her own therapist at Company expense.

- She could preserve her right to arbitrate if she were fired in the future.

- She would return to a final warning status for three months for tardiness only, as that had been the sole ground for her discharge.

I presented the Union's proposal to the Company's representatives, who were upset that the Union was asking for too much and began to retreat from their prior feelings of sympathy for Barbara's story and willingness to consider her reinstatement. In response, I asked the Company representatives to make a counteroffer and indicate what they would require *if* they were willing to agree to reinstatement. Together, we developed the following counteroffer.

- Reinstatement only to the location from which Barbara had been terminated.

- Conversion of the termination to a ninety-day suspension.

- Agreement to reinstate lost seniority and benefits.

- No back pay.

- Barbara would agree to meet all the usual and customary standards for employees.

- Barbara would pay for her own therapist or receive insurance compensation through the Company's plan.

- Barbara would be given a final warning on tardiness and attendance that would be in effect for three months, so that any tardiness or absence during the probationary period would be grounds for immediate termination.

The Company representatives agreed to drop their previous demand that Barbara waive her right to arbitrate her termination, since she would be going back with a three-month suspension and a final warning in her file. Again, they asked me to make it clear that they had not yet agreed to take her back.

I met with Barbara and the Union and told them that if they wanted reinstatement they would need to show that they were willing to satisfy the Company's interests. Barbara said she didn't care that much about back pay and the other issues, and the Union agreed to accept the Company's terms, provided the Company agree to reinstatement.

At this point, I recognized that we were at a turning point, and asked Barbara if she really wanted her job back, giving her full permission to say no. She said she did, I asked her why, and she spoke convincingly about how much she enjoyed working there. I told her that the Company representatives still believed a story about Barbara that made them doubt that she was capable of changing her behavior. I asked if she would be willing to take a big risk in an effort to change their story. She said she would. I asked her what gesture she thought she might make that could convince the Company she meant what she said and was serious about her recovery and determination to succeed. Working together, we came up with a proposal I thought had a chance, and called the parties back together so Barbara could present it personally.

I told the Company representatives that Barbara had something she wanted to say to them. Barbara told them she completely understood their reluctance to believe in her because she had not deserved their trust in the past. In order to prove that she meant what she said, she was willing to accept all their terms and conditions, except that where they had offered three months probation, she proposed to *double* it to six.

The Company representatives were bowled over by her willingness to do more than they had demanded, and agreed to reinstatement along the lines she offered. Because of her generosity, they voluntarily modified their offer, without a Union demand, and agreed to pay her $5,000 in back wages so she could pay her therapy bills. They also agreed to return to mediation if there were any problems enforcing or interpreting their agreement.

I congratulated everyone on having reached an agreement, and asked them to compare their feelings now with how they felt at the beginning when they had thought there was no possibility of resolution. Everyone expressed satisfaction with the process and wishes for Barbara's successful return to work. I told Barbara this proposal would only work if she really wanted it to, and that the ability to make it work was completely in her hands. She said she understood, wanted it to work, and was confident she could meet all the Company's expectations. Six months later, I called the Company representatives, who told me that Barbara had not received a single complaint. She had been consistently on time, was getting along well with all her co-workers, and had become a model employee.

What allowed these entrenched, adversarial, conflict stories to dissolve and give way to a single, open-ended, collaborative story about the possibility of redemption and resolution? Several elements contributed to achieving a positive outcome, including the parties' willingness to continue meeting in spite of their certainty that resolution was impossible, entertain fresh options for resolution that went beyond what they initially wanted, acknowledge key elements in each other's stories, and finally drop their core stories of demonization and victimization.

Perhaps most important was Barbara's willingness to take three important steps: first, to include in her story an honest acceptance of personal responsibility for her mistakes; second, to relate with compelling vulnerability the story of her addiction, emotional suffering, and arduous recovery; and third, to communicate her deep commitment to re-earning their trust in a way that was authentic, obviously heartfelt, and could not be encompassed or made consistent with the Company's earlier story about her dishonest, undeserving, irresponsible character.

By the end of the mediation, both sides' stories had been transformed and, for Barbara at least, the conflict had been transcended, regardless of what the Company decided to do. She had learned from her conflict what the story of the rest of her life had to become. A third story could then be created, not only about her commitment to succeed, but about the willingness of both sides to work together without requiring conflict stories to reinforce their negative judgments about each other, or predict futures that were already foregone conclusions.

Instead, the stories that described their conflicted relationship, dubious intentions, and inevitable failures were opened up, made malleable, and transformed into mere preambles and indications of what each side needed to do to transmute them into collaborative, heartfelt stories of redemption and resolution.

As novelist Margaret Atwood wrote in *The Blind Assassin*: "In paradise there are no stories, because there are no journeys. It's loss and regret and misery and yearning that drive the story forward, along its twisted road." To transform our conflict stories, we need to move off this twisted road and recognize that the paradise of resolution already lies within, requiring no journey to reach other than the journey we are all on to increased our wisdom, our skill, and our understanding.

All we have to do to transform our conflict stories and reach these higher levels is drop the simplistic stories we have fashioned out of our own needs—about good and evil, fairy tale relationships, predictable endings, and safe outcomes. We have to reach out to touch the human heart of our opponent with stories that are raw and vulnerable, that draw us into collaboration and resolution, that describe who we authentically are. Doing so is a path to transcendence.

Chapter 6 Getting to Completion,
Closure, and Disappearance

He suddenly felt that the very thing that had once been the source
of his suffering had become the source of his spiritual joy, that what
had seemed insoluble when he condemned, reproached and hated,
became simple and clear when he forgave and loved.
–Leo Tolstoy

T olstoy's description of the conversion of suffering into joy is not mere hyperbole or literary contrivance. While it is difficult for anyone in conflict to even imagine ending it—let alone forgiving or reconciling with their opponents—forgiveness and reconciliation emerge naturally from the resolution process when parties move beyond ending their disputes to completing them, reaching closure, and making them disappear. With complete disappearance, it sometimes happens that their suffering is suddenly converted into joy.

From Ending to Disappearance

There is, of course, an immense difference between ending a conflict, completing it, reaching closure, and making it completely disappear. When we end a conflict, we settle or compromise it and abandon the field, generally without obtaining a clear victory or suffering an irreparable loss. When we complete a conflict, we move beyond victory and loss to resolve the underlying reasons for the dispute. When we reach closure, we move beyond completion to forgiveness and the simplicity and clarity that reveal a true change of heart, as described by Tolstoy. Beyond closure lies the total disappearance of the conflict through reconciliation, redemption, and transcendence. And beyond disappearance lies prevention, through the redesign of systems, cultures, and environments so as to discourage similar conflicts in the future. These degrees of closure can be charted as follows:

Order of Resolution	Degree of Closure
Stopping the fighting	De-escalation
Settling the issues	Ending
Resolving the underlying reasons for the dispute	Completion
Forgiveness	Closure
Reconciliation	Disappearance
Systems design	Prevention

Ending a conflict can result simply from physical exhaustion or a logical decision that it is time to cut one's losses or to compromise and move on. Completion, on the other hand, requires emotional release and a satisfaction of interests, even if only in the form of venting and collaborative negotiation over minor issues. For closure to occur, it is necessary for people to discover the sources of the dispute within themselves, forgive each other, and transform the ways they interact and communicate, for which no amount of logical reasoning or emotional venting will suffice.

For a conflict to completely disappear, people must reopen their hearts, transcend what caused it, evolve to a higher level of conflict and resolution, and become fully reconciled with their opponent. For prevention to occur, the system, context, culture, and environment that created or sustained the conflict must be collaboratively redesigned. Each successive level is exponentially more difficult to achieve than the one beneath it. Each requires greater time, commitment, and willingness to fundamentally change oneself.

Power, Contempt, Compromise, and Humility

Many people end their conflicts simply by deciding it is time to walk away, by compromising, by using their power to force their opponent to surrender, or by asking a judge, arbitrator, manager, or other third party to impose a solution in their favor. These power- and rights-based processes are called zero-sum games because they result in win/lose outcomes that allot victory to one side and defeat to the other, fostering pride and contempt in the victor and shame and resentment in the vanquished. None of these approaches complete the conflict, repair relationships, or improve communications, but instead they invite injured feelings to fester, encouraging future conflicts.

To end a conflict, both sides must at least agree to settle the issues over which they are actively struggling. But settlement requires consent, which entails compromise, and involves each side getting at least part of what they want. Settling conflicts often creates a perception on both sides that they have lost, producing lose/lose, rather than win/win outcomes. Compromise is not always an inferior result, and it may represent the best that can be achieved under the circumstances. It has a limited feel of balance and fairness about it, since no one completely wins, and both sides can walk away feeling that they at least were not defeated.

While it is a solution, a process, and a relationship, compromise allows conflicts to continue in their original form, along with the possibility that minor future slips will trigger fresh rounds of fighting. These defects led Mary Parker Follett, one of the early founders of mediation in the US during the 1920s, to argue eloquently against resorting to compromise:

> Compromise...is temporary and futile. It usually means merely a postponement of the issue. The truth does not lie "between" the two sides. We must be ever on our guard against sham reconciliation. Many, unfortunately, still glorify compromise. I have just read that the spirit of compromise shows the humble heart. What nonsense. In the first place it doesn't, as you will find if you watch compromise; in the second place that kind of humility, if it existed, would not be worth much. Humility needs to be defined: it is merely never claiming any more than belongs to me in any way whatever; it rests on the ability to see clearly what does belong to me. Thus do we maintain our integrity.

Humility, integrity, and the refusal to claim any more than what actually belongs to us clearly extend to how we participate in conflict, achieve resolution, and end our disputes. These, in turn, require and actively create deeper levels of integrity, flowing from our unwillingness to use power or rights to achieve ends that impact other people's interests and our recognition that our conflicts do not belong exclusively to us.

For this reason, the more *substantively unequal* the distribution of power between people in conflict, and the more positional and power-oriented they behave, the more likely they will be to hold their opponents in contempt, resist recognizing even their fair and legitimate interests, claim a unilateral right to decide how the conflict will be resolved, and end it by imposing their will on others or simply by stopping the fighting and walking away.

On the other hand, the more *formally equal* the distribution of power between the parties, and the more rights-oriented they behave, the more likely they will be to recognize the fair and legitimate interests of their opponents, seek compromise through adversarial negotiation as the best possible solution, and end their conflicts through settlement, without necessarily reaching completion or closure.

Beyond these is a third distribution. The more *substantively equal* the distribution of power between the parties, and the more collaborative and interest-oriented they become, the more likely they will be to listen and respect each other's interests, work toward mutual satisfaction, seek ways of moving from compromise to partnership, act with humility and integrity, and resolve the underlying reasons for their dispute through completion, closure, disappearance, or prevention.

Power, inequality, contempt, and incompletion thus travel together. Each significantly affects the extent of reconciliation and the quality of resolution that are possible in any conflict. As the brilliant Hungarian novelist Sandor Marai noticed:

> Every exercise of power incorporates a faint, almost imperceptible, element of contempt for those over whom the power is exercised. One can only dominate another human soul if one knows, understands, and with the utmost tact despises the person one is subjugating.

Power evokes contempt in those who use it because they understand, at least subconsciously, that it allows them to act dishonestly, immorally, and unfairly. It divides them not only from the powerless, but from powerless parts of themselves, generating a fear that others may someday use it in retribution against them. Power evokes contempt because it is addictive, and like all addictions is both desired and feared. It evokes contempt because people respect *it* rather than those who wield it; because it undermines self-esteem, both in its users and its victims; and because it proposes a Faustian bargain, inviting anyone who uses it to sacrifice their compassion, humanity, and integrity to do its bidding.

The contempt of the powerful is not confined to those over and against whom their power is exerted, but extends to anyone who is or appears powerless. Their contempt includes punishing anyone who aids or sides with the powerless; conquering animals, nature, space, and the environment; dismissing "soft" ideas such as peace, collaboration, conflict resolution, and non-violence; ridiculing heartfelt, compassionate, "touchy-feely" communications; suppressing love, pleasure, and sensuality; and repressing whatever they perceive to be weak within themselves, all of which create conflicts that, in turn, justify these responses.

What is more difficult and important to understand is that *every* exercise of power over or against others automatically communicates contempt, whether the communication is express or implied, intended or unintended, and whether the exercise of power is great or small. This includes even the petty forms of power people use every day, especially in conflict—and not only physical power, but intellectual, emotional, and spiritual power as well. Sociologist Mihaly Csikzentmihalyi writes:

> One feature that distinguishes humans from other animals—perhaps as characteristic as speech or upright posture—is the fact that we find so many ways to oppress and exploit one another. Distinctions of wealth, status, and knowledge make it possible for some individuals to live off the psychic energy expended by others. "Power" is the generic term to describe the ability of a person to have others expend their lives to satisfy his or her goals.

For these reasons, power always triggers resentment, along with a desire for its equalization, and a demand that it be shared or transferred. These inspire power to defend itself and counterattack, recycling the conflict, justifying its escalation, and discouraging completion and closure. What is more important, these dynamics occur in all conflicts regardless of scale, allowing purely personal conflicts to fuel social ones, and vice versa.

Thus, petty, interpersonal brutalities lay the foundation for large-scale dictatorships, torture, and the systematic organization of social hatreds. Even the smallest bully creates a space and an archetype for larger ones, making bullying socially acceptable and encouraging it to spread. In this way, every small-scale demeaning or diminishing behavior, every refusal to listen or negotiate, every exercise of power or contempt, every effort to repress or curb one's opponents, magnifies the social and political power of tyranny and makes completion and closure more difficult on every scale.

There is, of course a fundamental distinction between power *against*, which instills fear; power *over*, which triggers resentment; power *for*, which encourages participation; and power *with*, which builds collaboration and trust. Power is a relationship rather than a thing. Through its diverse forms, one can distinguish debate from dialogue, adversarial from collaborative negotiation, and moralizing from consensus over shared values.

Power arises in every human interaction, and is invariably present in conflict. Yet power is fluid rather than fixed, allowing one kind of power to be transformed into another. In this way, changing the nature of people's discourse and moving from debate to dialogue, or from lecturing to listening, fundamentally alters their power relationships, increases genuine humility and collaboration, and encourages resolution, forgiveness, and reconciliation through interest-based processes that lead naturally to completion, closure, and disappearance.

As rights are based on power, they are similarly impermanent and dependent on society's willingness to limit abuses of power and stabilize the ways it will be shared, balanced, and manifested. In a muted way, everything that can be said of power can also be said of rights, except that rights rely on technical distinctions, bureaucracy, and institutionalization, which power simply ignores. For this reason, while power encourages contempt, resistance, and rebellion, rights encourage alienation, cynicism, and purely procedural reforms. [For a more detailed discussion, see Kenneth Cloke and Joan Goldsmith, *Resolving Conflicts at Work: Eight Strategies for Everyone on the Job* (Second Edition) Jossey Bass / Wiley Publishers Inc., 2005.]

In the end, power and rights are *both* inconsistent with affection, collaboration, and integrity, partly because they generate contempt and indifference, while affection, collaboration, and integrity dismantle them. Carl Jung also found these to be mutually exclusive, writing, "Where love lives there is no will to power; and where power predominates, there love is lacking. The one is the shadow of the other." Interests, on the other hand, discourage resort to power and rights and enable parties to work toward completion and closure in their conflicts.

Interests and Completion, Forgiveness and Closure

When people use power or rights in conflict, they become positional or rights oriented in all of their communications, problem solving, negotiations, and relationships, and it becomes difficult for them to imagine doing more than stopping their fighting or settling their disputes through compromise. But when they shift from using power or rights to satisfying interests, they automatically transform their conflicts in ways that make it possible for them to reach completion.

Interests are commonly elicited by asking "why" questions, which are simply ways of revealing what is uniquely important to each person. When people identify their interests, they indirectly communicate to their opponents that they are willing to act with integrity and claim no more than actually belongs to them. Doing so automatically transforms arrogant, *power*-based acts of aggression and alienated, *rights*-based acts of coercion into interdependent, *interest*-based acts of collaboration, and invites others to follow suit.

By identifying and satisfying interests, mediators encourage synergistic combinations, allowing solutions to arise that result not merely in win/lose or 50/50 outcomes, but in win/win outcomes up to 100/100. These are not compromises that carve out a middle ground between two truths and end up eliminating both, but higher truths that consist of mutually affirming combinations, amalgamations, and syntheses of apparently separate, hostile, and contradictory truths.

It is possible, in any conflict, to move beyond ending or completion and reach closure. Closure in conflict simply means that the parties have said and done whatever they needed to say or do for the conflict to be finally and completely over, allowing them to let it go. While this may sound easy, it requires them to forgive their opponents for the harm they did and themselves for the harm they did in return. For this reason, mediators should be careful not to pressure anyone into reaching forgiveness prematurely, before they are genuinely ready for the conflict to be over.

Forgiveness should not be reserved for the most serious conflicts and catastrophes, but can be introduced even in the most miniscule everyday difficulties we face living and working with people who are different from us. Indeed, these minor acts of forgiveness allow us to live together in diversity, tolerance, and creative interaction. As the German romantic poet Rainer Maria Rilke wrote:

> Once the realization is accepted that even between the closest people infinite distances exist, a marvelous living side-by-side can grow up for them, if they succeed in loving the expanse between them, which gives them the possibility of always seeing each other as a whole and before an immense sky.

There are hundreds of ways of reaching closure, but all of them require forgiveness. In its simplest form, forgiveness is a willingness to let the conflict go and release ourselves from the burden of our own false expectations. Mediators can encourage closure by asking, for example, "What do you need to say or do for this conflict to be completely over?" "What would you most like to hear the other person to say before ending?" "This may be the last time you have an opportunity to talk with each other. What is the last thing you want to say?" "Is there anything you would like to apologize or request forgiveness for?" "Is there anything you would like to forgive yourself for?" "What do you wish for each other, or for your relationship in the future?"

Choosing to forgive our opponents requires us to be clear about the reasons for *not* forgiving them and to abandon all of the expectations we had of them that they did not meet. We can then decide to release ourselves, one by one, from each reason and expectation. If we are unable to do so, we must then calculate the price we are going to pay for our inability by identifying what it will cost us to hold on to each reason and expectation. Only then will our choice become clear and invite us to reach closure in our conflicts.

In the end, people need to forgive *themselves* for not having done better, or been better people, or lived more successful lives. Whenever anyone commits suicide, their friends inevitably feel guilty and wonder whether they could not have done more to support them. Similarly, even when conflicts are beyond our capacity to avoid, we berate ourselves over whether there wasn't *something* we could or should have done to avert them. Even the smallest failures to forgive ourselves accumulate over time, creating mountains of self-doubt that block us from being open and able to experience joy.

Disappearance, Trust, and Integrity

For conflict to completely disappear, it is necessary for the parties to go one step further and engage in openhearted communications with each other, perhaps including acknowledging their opponents—not only for whatever they may have said or done that encouraged collaboration and joint problem solving, but for entering into the conflict in the first place, thereby making it possible for them to learn from each other, develop new skills, invent better solutions, and improve their integrity, communication, and relationship.

Even if people feel ready, willing, and able to open their hearts to each other, it is not easy to become reconciled with a former opponent after participating in adversarial conflict. This is partly because reconciliation requires trust, which resolution and forgiveness do not, and it is difficult to repair trust after it has been broken. Nonetheless, it is possible for former adversaries to gradually rebuild trust by

- treating each other with unconditional respect;

- listening deeply and sincerely, especially to criticisms;

- expressing empathy for each other, even if they do not listen or empathize in return;

- speaking openly and honestly about problems and failures, especially one's own;

- being as sincere and unlimited with apologies as with criticisms;

- negotiating clear boundaries and respecting those established by others, even when others do not respect them in return;

- supporting participation and teamwork, empowering others, and making decisions collaboratively;

- agreeing on vision, shared values, and goals, and acting on them;

- acknowledging interests and being flexible regarding solutions;

- being willing to sacrifice something important to aid a former opponent or achieve a higher goal;

- participating in social interactions and sharing information about each other's personal lives; and

- being consistent and dependable in crises and hard times.

None of these actions guarantee that trust will be restored or that reconciliation will occur, but each gradually diminishes trust-breaking behaviors and makes it more difficult to maintain distrust and hostility. Trust is rebuilt by focusing not on what the other person did or did not do, but on improving one's own behaviors, increasing one's trustworthiness, and being congruent—not just in words and promises, but in actions, attitudes, and character.

Rebuilding trust therefore depends on integrity and authenticity, which reflect who people actually are beneath their egos, masks, and poses, and how much of themselves they are able to bring to their most difficult conversations and relationships. When people consider whether to reach completion, give up their conflicts, and proceed with reconciliation, part of what they consider is their opponent's integrity and authenticity, yet what finally determines the choice is their *own* integrity and authenticity.

When people act in ways that lack integrity or consciously harm others, as often occurs in conflict, it is difficult for them to admit their errors. As a result, they may become incapable of reaching closure and completion, and may become counterfeit and unbalanced. Only by admitting their errors can they develop a clear sense of who they are, act with integrity and authenticity, reach closure through restitution, redemption, and reconciliation, and ask their opponents to do the same.

While mediators can invite people to act with integrity and authenticity and work toward closure, completion, and disappearance, we cannot force them, or tell them how to achieve it. Everyone needs to find their own way by honestly examining their innermost selves and releasing whatever does not belong there. The more difficult the conflict and the more damaging the catastrophe created by the conflict, the harder this is to achieve.

Transcending Catastrophe

A catastrophe can occur in any conflict. It can happen to anyone, anytime, anywhere. In a twinkling, we turn an invisible corner that was always there, though we never noticed. The change is profound. It *strips* us. It is simpler than ideas, deeper than identity, more profound than imagination. The loss of control is complete, even over our own bodies and minds. Our lives are no longer the same.

Even the smallest dispute can slip out of control and trigger chaotic, unpredictable, unimaginably destructive results. A series of gradual, uniform, quantitative changes reach a critical value, then suddenly, qualitatively, they dramatically shift. In nature, a mountain collapses, liquid turns into gas, predictability gives way to chaos. In conflicts, trust is broken, cruel words are spoken, friendships dissolve, love turns into hate, and hate into revenge. The simplicity of this description belies the complexity of its experience. To truly understand, we have to *become* the mountain that collapses, the liquid that turns into gas, the predictable event that is broken into pieces by chaos.

What do we, as mediators, do with the memory of catastrophic experience? How do we help people who only want to return to who they were before it happened? We have to begin by recognizing that the road back is forever closed, and that there is no alternative other than to forge a new road forward. This is the creative power of catastrophe that is contained in miniature in every conflict. It allows us to embrace our suffering and use it as a beacon to find a path forward that has integrity and balance. Only in this way can people transcend what happened, heal their wounds, and reach completion, closure, and disappearance. The deeper the catastrophe, the longer it takes to heal and bring their conflict to an end.

In the beginning, there is always denial. No matter what proof is presented, no matter how convincing the loss, its unacceptability simply overwhelms rational thought. Denial springs eternal from a subterranean pool of hope. The only real hope, the only stable place from which anything can be measured, comes from an unconditional acceptance of what has happened and a complete surrender to its truth. With the relinquishment of denial comes the beginning of peace of mind and a modest, calibrated strategy for moment-by-moment improvement.

Yet conflict is a world of illusions, false priorities, stories about a past that never was the way people recall it, and expectations of a future that will never happen the way they imagine it. Only the present produces meaning, and catastrophe instantly redefines the present as beyond both past and future. In this way, catastrophe shatters the illusion that what people think is important actually is. Yet denial, along with stories about the past, false expectations about the future, and a desire to fix responsibility for loss on someone other than ourselves, continues to cause damage, prevent healing, and block closure, completion, the disappearance of conflict, and systemic prevention.

Catastrophe reminds people of the importance of relationships and simple pleasures, principally by threatening to take them away. As the catastrophe recedes, these things may gradually return, but it is not altogether certain that their return is a good thing. In the tedium of daily life, relationships and simple pleasures are taken for granted, which comforts people and shapes their lives and relationships, yet doing so distracts attention from their fragility and the magnitude of what really matters.

The discourse and chatter with which people surround themselves, especially the alienated, adversarial discourse of conflict, causes them to focus on events, on doing and having, rather than on relating and being. None of this is wrong; it just ends up being terribly unimportant when viewed from the perspective of catastrophe. What *is* important is their capacity for empathetic and honest communication, collaborative relationships, and love for themselves and others, including their opponents. These, in turn, depend on their ability to escape catastrophe and reach completion, closure, and disappearance in their conflicts.

The common experience of catastrophe draws people together at a depth they are rarely able to achieve without it, and the experience and memory of that connection remains, both as memory and as lure. The part of each person that is without pretense or show, without distance or time, is somehow able to touch and be touched by that same part in others, creating heart connections and a desire for completion and closure. Suffering gives people humility, resets their priorities in a more human domain, and helps them connect with and feel compassion for others who have suffered. Of course, they can do these things without suffering if they can learn to use their heartfelt awareness to transform small, everyday, microscopic sufferings into moments of compassion and self-realization.

Oscar Wilde wrote that suffering is a gift, meaning that the experience of suffering makes us more authentic, sensitive to others, aware of what is really important, able to enjoy the small things in life, and desirous of resolution, forgiveness, and reconciliation. While suffering is a gift no one asks to receive, few, if asked in retrospect, would choose to avoid it if doing so meant they would also have to surrender the learning, openheartedness, and transcendence that came with it.

Here is why. When catastrophe occurs, we are forced to choose between three fundamental responses. First, we can focus on the tragedy of what happened, allow ourselves to sink into pain, self-pity, long for a past that can never return, and adopt a passive, victim mentality that ultimately ends in our continued victimization. Second, we can focus on the cruelty and evil of what the other person did, allow ourselves to become consumed by anger and self-loathing, become locked in a past that can never disappear, and adopt an aggressive, perpetrator's mentality that ultimately ends in a willingness to do to others what was done to us. Third, we can dedicate part of our lives, which are already forfeit and can never be restored, to making certain that no one will ever again have to suffer as we did, consecrate our suffering to this higher good, and transcend the pain and anger that flow from what happened to us by transforming it into prevention, learning, compassion, and love. By so doing, we beat our swords into plowshares, transcend catastrophe, and force the suffering to end with us.

An illustration of this last response can be found in an anecdote concerning Mahatma Gandhi, captured in the film about his life. While fasting to end a civil war between Muslims and Hindus, Gandhi was approached by Hindu man who said that a Muslim had killed his son and he had, in retaliation, killed a Muslim and would burn in hell for eternity. Gandhi told him there was only one thing he could do: he had to find a Muslim child whose parents had been killed, adopt him, and raise him as a Muslim.

What is most important about this story is the feeling one experiences on hearing Gandhi's pronouncement, which reflects our intuitive understanding of what must be done to achieve transcendence. This feeling can be used to guide people to their own forms of poetic justice. It can tell them what they need to do to reach forgiveness and reconciliation. It can lead them to learning, compassion, and love. It can help them decide to dedicate some part of their lives to making sure that others will not suffer as they did.

Paradoxically, for suffering to completely disappear, it is necessary for us to be willing to experience its pain forever. This is because suffering partly consists of wanting our lives to be different or wishing the catastrophe had never happened, neither of which is possible. We may not be able to make our *pain* disappear, but we can end our *suffering* by embracing what happened to us and transforming it into something positive. To do so, we need our conflict to end so we can heal and return to strength, after which we can seek release through completion, closure, and disappearance, using the redemptive power of ritual.

Designing Rituals of Release, Completion, and Closure

When people repeatedly engage in conflict, their behaviors, distrust, and suffering create ruts that become deeper and more difficult to escape. The purpose of these ruts is to lead them back to the systemic attitudes, ideas, and intentions from which their conflicts began, so that they can start all over again. How can mediators help people lift themselves out of these ruts and chart a fresh course?

Perhaps the only thing more powerful than a rut is a ritual. Rituals assist people in reaching release, completion, closure, disappearance, and prevention by helping them let go of the past, escape their ruts, and solidify their intention to catalyze a change or transformation in their communications and relationships. A well-designed ritual can help people end their enmity, transcend their suffering, and return to constructive interactions. Indeed, it is healing to perform rituals, even as a way of ending minor disputes, and many couples instinctively invent rituals to help them reconcile following their conflicts.

A simple conflict resolution ritual, for example, consists of shaking hands as a way of symbolizing that the conflict is over. In workplace disputes, a simple ritual might consist of agreeing to speak at the next staff meeting, apologizing for being unable to end the conflict, announcing that it is over, indicating what each person learned from the conflict, and asking the group to support them in improving their communications and relationships.

With separating couples, a ritual might consist of finding a caring way of saying goodbye, or in buying a present for the other person that represents what each person values in the other that the other does not see or value in themselves. For more catastrophic conflicts, greater efforts are required, and mediators need to work closely with the parties to design rituals that match their level of loss. Timing is extremely important, and each conflict and combination of parties will require a different ritual with a different timing. Therefore, mediators need to make sure that people are ready for release, completion, or closure, and place emphasis on the design process, rather than on the ritual itself.

In Mediating Dangerously: The Frontiers of Conflict Resolution, I described several ways of designing rituals and gave examples of rituals to encourage forgiveness and reconciliation. Here are some additional questions mediators can ask to assist people in designing their own rituals:

- *Name What Needs to Change:* What do you want to release, affirm, or celebrate now that you have resolved your conflict?

- *Symbolize the Transformation:* What physical symbols or objects can you find, create, or purchase to represent what you most want to end or bring into existence?

- *Symbolize the Action:* What will you do to symbolize and make the shift real? What represents the new person you want to become or the relationship you want to have? What represents the old?

- *Choose Time and Place:* What special time and environment do you want to select for the ritual?

- *Witnessing:* Who will personally witness, participate in it, or be told about it?

- *Opening:* How can you begin in a purposeful, consecrated, meaningful way?

- *Intent:* What might you say about what you intend to change in your life or symbolize about what you want to release or affirm?

- *Stories:* What led you to this ritual and what gives it meaning?

- *Creating the Transformation:* What symbolic act of release, passage, or affirmation might you perform to express the transformation or transcendence you want?

- *Acknowledgement:* Is there anyone you want to thank for contributing to your learning, including your opponent?

- *Affirmation/Commitment:* What might you do or say to express your commitment?

- *Celebration:* How will you celebrate the change?

- *Renewal:* What do you need to do to remind yourself and reinforce your commitment to change?

(Based partly on work by Lynda S. Paladin and Evan Imber-Black)

Designing Rituals for Catastrophic Loss

When injuries are catastrophic and suffering is profound, it is more difficult for the parties to release their pain and anger, even through ritual, because their identities have merged with their suffering and they are unclear who they will be without the conflict. In these cases, life itself is the best ritual for inducing them to relinquish their anger, pain, fear, or shame. To do so, they require immense courage, support, and affection from their friends, and sometimes therapy to help unravel their suffering.

For many reasons, some originating in a fear of death, there are few fitting ceremonies for catastrophic loss. Even funerals fall short because people cannot comprehend, communicate, or cope with the full disaster for the living, and may focus instead on meaningless rituals, pitying homilies, and misleadingly laudatory eulogies. At the same time, the very *magnitude* of grief can make it impossible to express. As Dante wrote in *The Inferno*:

> At grief so deep the tongue must wag in vain;
> the language of our sense and memory
> lacks the vocabulary of such pain.

Perhaps for this reason, rituals help people acknowledge, articulate, and release their grief, not only with regard to small-scale losses, but to large-scale catastrophes like divorce, disability, and death. Grief-releasing rituals connect people in non-trivial ways, focus their priorities, and give them strength by releasing their pain and by giving it *meaning*. They are based on a recognition that whatever parts of the past people carry with them make them less attentive to what is happening in their present, or may happen in their future, and that whatever they cannot see within themselves will blind them to what is within others, allowing their conflicts to happen again.

Effective rituals for reaching completion in conflict or catastrophe might invite people to

- choose for themselves how they will express their suffering;

- tell stories about what happened as a way of acknowledging
  and expressing, as completely as possible, the pain it produced;

- express regret and forgiveness for whatever they did or did not do that contributed to the suffering of others, or themselves;

- celebrate the lives and sacrifices of those who have suffered;

- clarify the meaning of their suffering;

- say or do whatever remains unspoken or undone;

- reaffirm the continuation of love, life, humor, joy, and hope;

- choose to let the suffering stop with them;

- identify something that can be done to reduce suffering;

- dedicate some part of their life to making sure others suffer less; and

- concentrate all the suffering in words, rituals, and actions, and let the rest go.

Memory, Closure, and Forgiveness

Over time, rituals turn into habits, teachings into dogmas, ceremonies into empty forms, and values into moral strictures that no longer lead people to profound or poignant truths, or challenge and sustain them in transforming and transcending the inescapable, unforeseeable obstacles and suffering they face in life. It is therefore necessary to continually reinvest them with meaning, through memory, closure, and the redemptive power of forgiveness.

The poet T. S. Eliot famously asked, after the catastrophic horror of World War II, "After such crimes, what forgiveness?" Closure ultimately requires people to recall exactly what happened to them, rather than forget it, and to forgive—not the *acts* that were committed, but the *people* who committed them. As Dr. Martin Luther King, Jr. described it:

> Forgiveness does not mean ignoring what has been done or putting a false label on an evil act. It means, rather, that the evil act no longer remains as a barrier to the relationship. Forgiveness is a catalyst creat-

ing the atmosphere necessary for a fresh start and a new beginning. It is the lifting of a burden or the cancellation of a debt...The degree to which we are able to forgive determines the degree to which we are able to love our enemies.

Forgiveness requires a deliberate combination of struggle *against* and surrender *to*. It requires struggle against the systems, forces, and behaviors that created or sustained the conflict or catastrophe and surrender to the inevitability of human frailty and error, to chance and fate, to the inalienable weaknesses of those who did it, to our own empathy and compassion, and to the incontestable hunger of the heart for reconciliation.

In South Africa, it was necessary first to *end* apartheid. Only then was it possible to tell the truth about the crimes committed by both sides, and only then did forgiveness and reconciliation become possible. To reach genuine forgiveness, as opposed to what Algerian novelist Albert Camus called "sentimental confusion," it is necessary to recall precisely and in detail what was done and how it felt—not in isolation, but in combination with understanding what happened to one's opponent and how they might have felt. In short, it asks people to become merciful and compassionate toward others and themselves, while at the same time being *merciless* and unforgiving about what was done and the pain it caused.

There are many ways of forgetting about conflicts and catastrophes, including repression, denial, compartmentalization, defensiveness, blame, diversion, and compulsive repetition. Daniel L. Schacter has identified seven discrete forms of forgetting.

1. Forgetting facts over time (*transience*).

2. Forgetting details due to preoccupation (*absent-mindedness*).

3. Forgetting information for emotional reasons (*blocking*).

4. Forgetting the real because of the ideal (*misattribution*).

5. Forgetting due to suggestibility (*implanted memory*).

6. Forgetting based on ideas or beliefs about what is true (*bias*).

7. Forgetting the present based on past trauma (*persistence*).

Each of these ways or forms of forgetting can keep people locked in conflict and prevent them from reaching forgiveness and reconciliation. In each, the parties create distance between who they are and what happened to them, rather than using their identity and memories as sources of information, learning to become better people than they were before and transforming what happened in the past into reasons for being more aware and less forgetful in the present.

More subtly, the Czech novelist Milan Kundera wrote that there is a secret bond between slowness and memory, speed and forgetting. For example, if we are walking and want to recall something, we slow down, but if we want to forget it, we unconsciously speed up. Thus, in existential mathematics, "the degree of slowness is directly proportional to the intensity of memory; the degree of speed is directly proportional to the intensity of forgetting."

When couples divorce, one commonly wants the relationship to end and tries to speed up their separation, while the other wants it to continue and tries to slow it down. When people have important issues to discuss and their conversations remain at the periphery, they try to speed them up. When they are addressing issues that deeply matter to them, they feel time slowing and coming to a halt. Often simply slowing the pace of conversation allows their conflict to catch up with them so they can complete it and move on.

In *The Ethics of Memory*, Avishai Margalit argues that we have a duty to recall the painful things that happened to us, and to forgive those who harmed us in order to free ourselves from "poisonous attitudes and states of mind." The negative emotions we experience in conflict are stored in our brains as memories, producing harmful chemicals when we recall them. These toxins transform the physical structures of our bodies and deplete us of the energy we need to live. Yet disregarding these memories and toxins can lead to a repetition of the events that created the suffering. For this reason, forgiveness is not something we do solely for others, but for ourselves. It is reclaiming our energy, memory, and awareness, and therefore our selves, so as not to forfeit our lives to the past or repeat it in a different guise.

Reclaiming the past allows us to convert anger, pain, and suffering into sources of learning. Only by combining a clear recollection of the past with a determination to create a different future can we bring these forces into the present, transform them into a commitment to change, and transcend them. Forgiveness becomes possible once we leave the prison of our wounded egos, reach closure regarding painful events and the people who caused them, and release ourselves from reliving the past.

In the end, release, completion, closure, disappearance, and prevention teach us how to evolve to higher levels of conflict and resolution, how to end our suffering by transforming it into learning and change, and how to bring about a new, higher level of conflict and resolution. While our lives move along vectors or trajectories largely defined by our pasts, we can decide at any moment to change directions and create an entirely different future. The Sufi poet Rumi tells us how:

> Inside this new love, die.
> Your way begins on the other side.
> Become the sky.
> Take an axe to the prison wall.
> Escape.
> Walk out like someone suddenly born into color.
> Do it now.

The Door to Closure—A Case Study

Jim and Frances were married in the Midwest in 1953 and moved to Los Angeles, where they raised three children and purchased a home. Frances worked as a secretary at a local college and Jim worked as an engineer at an aerospace company. Jim was a quiet man, uncomfortable with emotional communication, yet proud. His first response to confrontation was sullen withdrawal, which angered Frances and made her more shrew-like and bitter, resulting in his further sullen withdrawal, and so on. As the kids grew older, Jim and Frances moved further and further apart.

Their silences grew deeper and their separations longer, until Jim withdrew into the garage not just to work, but to sleep, watch TV, and drink himself into a silent, morose, resentful cocoon, waiting for the chrysalis of reconciliation that never came. Years went by, thirteen of them. The chasm between them widened and the silence grew louder. When the youngest child began college, though still living at home, Frances declared the marriage over and asked for a divorce. Jim was angry and uncooperative, as he had been for years, but Frances persisted and forced him to come to mediation rather than face an expensive court battle.

At the first session, Jim was still trying desperately to resist making any changes in his life. He had grown accustomed to living in the garage and maintaining a distant relationship with his family. He was happy to continue dying by degrees, rather than face what he feared would be certain death through separation. Sensing his resistance, I asked Frances to confirm her intention regarding their marriage. She said there was a huge discrepancy between what Jim preached and what he practiced, that she no longer trusted him, that he was an alcoholic who had been arrested twice for driving under the influence, and was clear that she wanted a divorce.

Jim countered that the arrests had occurred three or four years earlier and he no longer drank and drove. I asked him if he was happy in the marriage. He answered emphatically "No!" I asked him, since he was unhappy, whether he also wanted a divorce. He said that for him to move out and separate from Frances, he needed to overcome his fear of suicide and death, and felt unable to look positively on his future as a single man. He said he was now nearly sixty and living completely without joy.

Responding to his apathy, intransigence, and fear of suicide, I asked him whether there was anything he enjoyed doing. He said: "Nothing really." Where did he like to go? "Nowhere in particular." Any hobbies? "No." Any special interests? "No." Where did he go on vacation? "Just stayed at home." These passive responses encouraged me to use a more direct approach. I said that this year, since they would probably be separating, it would be unlikely that he would remain in the home. Of all the places in the world where he could go, which would be his favorite? He answered clearly, and with the first glimmer of positive feelings: "Oregon." "What do you like about Oregon?" I asked. "The trees, the air, the quiet." His whole expression and demeanor began to change as he spoke about his experience of being in Oregon during the one time he had visited. I continued to expand this heart opening, and discovered an additional source of enjoyment in woodworking. He agreed in the end that it would make sense for him to move to Oregon where he could get a house and garage and develop his woodworking skills.

Jim seemed to respond well to visual imagery, so I incorporated visual metaphors into my questions, for example, by periodically asking him if he could "see" himself living separately, or "envision" the possibility that he could be happier than he had been in years. I also used visual imagery to positively reinforce his acceptance of the separation, create a life of his own, and affirm it as *his* solution rather than Frances'.

During the time I spent discussing these issues with Jim, Frances began to change as well. She stopped offering cynical, biting assessments of his character that revealed a sense of frustration and anger that had been smoldering for thirteen years. She shifted to being amazed at the disappearance of his resistance to separating, and his open, honest, interest in self-analysis and self-discovery. She became much more engaged and empathetic, and expressed a positive hope that he would find something that would make him happy.

At this point, I asked them if they would now be willing to discuss the issues they needed to resolve in order to separate and they agreed. The first of these, Frances said, was for Jim to find another place to live and move out. Jim again became resistant and did not understand why Frances wanted him to move out so quickly. I asked him if he would like to find out why she wanted him out of the house so quickly. He said he would. I asked him to ask her directly. He turned, asked her, and she answered with great bitterness and anger, "Because you're driving me crazy! I just want to get on with my life, like you do, and I can't do it with you holding me back. I want to reorganize the house, and I want you and your things out. It's time, Jim, for us to move on. You have to let me go."

Jim softened, and began to tear up. I asked him if he now understood, and he said he did. I asked him to tell Frances what it was he understood. He told her he heard her, that she needed to move on, and that he was willing to move out. I told him the longer he stayed in the house the more their relationship would deteriorate, and that he had a choice, which was to do it quickly and easily or take longer, increase the amount of anger and frustration between them, and make any future relationship between them more difficult.

Jim said he would start looking for a place, but had no idea where he would go. I asked him concretely how he would go about deciding, who he might consult to help him decide, whether he was going to speak to real estate agents or look in the newspapers, would he rent or buy, did he want to be close to work or his kids, how long did he think he needed to look, and when did he think he could move out, all in order to make the move feel real and draw him step by step into actions that would reinforce his commitment to move. He agreed that he would start looking immediately and would call a real estate agent he knew for help right after the mediation ended.

At our second meeting, Jim had still not moved out or located a place to live, and Frances was furious. I let her vent her anger, acknowledged her feelings, and allowed Jim to do the same. I reaffirmed that the longer it took for them to separate the more they could expect to get angry at each other and that their relationship, poor as it was, might deteriorate even further. I asked Jim what efforts he had made to find a new home. He spoke of several meetings with real estate agents, ads placed in newspapers, and visits to houses, and of being unable to find anything that was suitable.

I acknowledged and appreciated his efforts, asked Frances to do the same, and asked what he planned to do next. He said he would continue looking as hard as he could. I asked him if he felt he could set a firm deadline for moving out, which he did, in two weeks' time. I asked Frances whether that would work for her, and she said it would. Since Jim had not met his earlier commitment, I asked him to turn to Frances and tell her what he planned to do and why he felt it was important to move out soon.

Before discussing the division of their assets and provisions for support, I asked them what goals or values they wanted to guide them in making these decisions, what they wanted to achieve, and where they wanted to be at the end of the divorcing process. They identified and reached consensus on the following goals and values.

- We will behave respectfully toward each other and end the process amicably without bad feelings.

- Frances will get the house.

- We will both get to retire comfortably.

- We will divide our assets equally without bankrupting anyone.

- We will each have enough money to live modestly, but no more.

- Jim will work three more years and then retire.

- Jim will be able to move to Oregon.

- We will resolve everything quickly and complete the divorce by the end of the year.

- We will continue to work together to support our children.

We discussed their financial issues in detail and reached a number of agreements regarding their assets and debts. At the end of the session, I assigned them to each write, as homework, a proposal for settlement with at least three outcomes they thought might be acceptable to the other person, and to meet and agree on final figures for several of the financial items, including the fair market value of the house.

When they returned two weeks later, Jim had still not moved out and Frances' anger had increasing markedly. Frances again vented and I acknowledged her increasing frustration and anger, and again turned to Jim for an explanation. He said he had actually made an offer on a house, but that it had been taken off the market. He recognized that his living in the house was becoming a serious problem and that Frances was more angry than he had ever seen her. After some discussion, he agreed to move into a motel for a few days until he could find something more permanent, and would do so that weekend without fail. I asked him if he would be willing to name a penalty that would encourage him meet his commitment, and he said he would pay Frances a thousand dollars if he failed. I asked Frances if that was acceptable to her, and she said it was.

I felt a deeper, more heartfelt discussion of the reasons for their impasse was needed, and asked them what life must have been like for them during a marriage in which they had lived apart for so many years, with only the door between the kitchen and the garage in common. They spoke about the door as a kind of metaphor for their relationship, which was squeaky and had not worked for years, for either of them. They agreed that the door kept them separate—not only from each other, but from their own true selves. They started their divorce thirteen years ago, but without the positive elements that came from completing their relationship and starting a new one. Now they wanted to complete what they had begun and make it positive by creating new lives for themselves. They spoke openheartedly of the good times they had had together, of their love for their children, and of the opportunity they each now had to establish newer and closer relationships with them.

Because their hearts had been opened by this conversation, they were able to quickly put the finishing touches on their agreement. Final figures were put in place and a plan was worked out under which Frances kept the house, they each kept their own retirement plan, each had some cash available, Jim would pay off the mortgage, and alimony would be paid by a money market account that would accumulate with employer contributions over the next three years while Jim continued on payroll, after which he would retire and they would cease. On review, they each felt the agreement incorporated their goals and values, and they had gotten 100% of what they wanted.

They signed the agreement and I congratulated them on the way they had handled the difficult issue of their physical separation, on their willingness to compromise and satisfy each others' interests, on their courage in facing an unknown future, and on their honesty and cooperation throughout the process. I then worked with them to design a ceremony with their children that would mark the end of their marriage.

After much discussion, they agreed to meet at the house with their children and conduct a ritual of closure in which they would announce that their divorce was final, talk about the lives they now wanted to live, and how they wanted their children to share in their future lives. They agreed to acknowledge that they had loved each other, but now needed to separate and live their new lives apart, and wish each other well. Afterward, they agreed to take down the door to the garage, build a bonfire in the back yard, and burn it. At the end of the session they laughed, shook hands, hugged, cried, and left in good spirits.

When I spoke to them a week later, Jim had moved out and this final ritual had allowed them to move beyond ending or completion to closure and an ability to walk away from their conflict feeling good about themselves and each other. Their earlier heartfelt conversation had set the stage for a collaborative closure and ritual design process that encouraged them to transcend the dysfunctional issues in their relationship, separate amicably, and move on with their lives.

SECTION III:
FROM RESOLUTION TO
TRANSFORMATION AND TRANSCENDENCE

You must be able
to do three things:
to love what is mortal,
to hold it
against your bones knowing
your own life depends on it
and when the time comes to let it go,
to let it go.
–Mary Oliver

Chapter 7   The Music of Conflict

How strange the change
From major to minor,
Every time we say goodbye.
–Cole Porter

C ole Porter clearly got it right. But what exactly is it that changes from major to minor when we say goodbye? What allows music to express and stimulate our moods so precisely? How does it ignite or dampen our spirits, make us feel romantic or cynical, lighthearted or blue? Why do simple sequences of musical notes or complex symphonic strains cause us to weep with sorrow, waltz with elegance, march in disciplined military formations, or swirl sensuously across a dance floor? And what does any of this have to do with conflict?

The Music of Conflict

In a brilliant comedic sketch on the 1950's "Your Show of Shows," Sid Caesar and Nanette Fabray pantomimed a marital spat to the strains of the Overture to Beethoven's 5th Symphony. Words were unnecessary, as the music gave the audience everything it needed to recognize the flow and commiserate with the futility of their argument.

It has since occurred to me, sometimes in the middle of a mediation, that even the most prosaic conflicts have a subtle musical quality about them. In the first place, there is the explicit music of the parties, reflected in their contrasting tempos, pitches, inflections, timbres, and tones of voice. There are solos as individuals hold forth, duets as they discuss, and dissonance as they argue and interrupt each other. There is fortissimo, pianissimo, diminuendo, and crescendo, mirroring the stages of their dialogue and transporting them from fear and rage to forgiveness and reconciliation.

Second, there is the mediator's calming, measured, propitiating, yet hopeful tone, using tone of voice to draw people together. There is the refusing of invited counterpoint, the offering to each side of a solo or aria, and the prompting of a duet or chorus. There is the soprano of injury and distress, the baritone of bitterness and injustice, the bass of hopelessness and depression, and the tenor of optimism and resolution. There is the interplay of score and libretto, moving toward a single harmonious and satisfying finale. Throughout, there is the mediator, trying to orchestrate and harmonize the diverse instruments and tones and blend them into a single symphonic whole.

Third, there is the emotional attunement of the listener to the music that transmits, more accurately than words, the emotional experience of the storyteller, allowing the listener to resonate, and thereby empathize and approximate the experience of another. Empathetic resonance allows the music to vibrate *inside* the listener, who experiences secondhand what the speaker experienced and discovers internally what it might have felt like to experience it firsthand.

It has long been recognized that music stimulates intense emotions. Plato distrusted the emotional power of sensuous music and saw it as dangerous enough to justify censorship. Schopenhauer recognized the deep connection between human feeling and music, which "restores to us all the emotions of our innermost nature, but entirely without reality and far removed from their pain." Nietzsche described an Apollonian-Dionysian dichotomy in music, representing form and rationality versus drunkenness and ecstasy. For Nietzsche, music was the sensual, Dionysian art form *par excellence,* which could be used to convey all the emotions for which words would never be enough. Russian poet Marina Tsvetaeva declared that "The heart: it is a musical, rather than a physical organ," and Austrian philosopher Ludwig Wittgenstein maintained that "Every word strikes an emotional tone."

These observations help us recognize that every emotion, attitude, and mood in conflict possesses a signature frequency and amplitude, a unique rhythm that is communicated as much through tone of voice, pitch, pace, and timing as through verbal description. These unique emotional frequencies are also communicated through body language and gestures, choice of words, and the narrative structure of conflict stories, to listeners who are asked to resonate, empathize, evoke, and experience within themselves what happened to the speaker. The mediator or facilitator in this scenario can be thought of as a tuning fork, grounding the conversation in a tone or musical theme with which everyone is asked to resonate, and, if possible, combine in a single all-encompassing, harmonizing melodic strain.

It is clear that different musical rhythms evoke radically different moods. There are rhythms of control as with marching music, rhythms of exploration as with jazz, rhythms of sadness as with blues, and rhythms of devotion as with gospel. Each style of music evokes a different set of emotions, memories, and spiritual or energetic responses.

Can we then use rhythms of speech to *elicit* sadness, anger, or fear? Can we counter these dusky tempos with lighter, upbeat rhythms in order to draw forth joy, affection, or courage? What are the qualities of vibration that impart these special, *substantive* meanings? What, for example, is the vibratory quality of a sincere apology as opposed to an insincere one? And how do we know the difference between them?

We appear to combine sensitive, even subliminal information from multiple resonating sources, including inflection, body language, eye contact, auditory signals of stress, and other signs that are often too faint to distinguish consciously, yet are perceived subliminally. Much of what we think, feel, and do in conflict is grounded in these microscopic, subliminal, nearly unconscious messages that are often beneath the level of conscious awareness. In one experiment, for example, volunteers were shown a video with peaceful visual images punctuated by a car crash that produced a characteristic stressful response in the brain. Researchers then sped up the video so that none of the subjects could recognize that there had been a car crash, yet their brains continued to respond as though they had, indicating that something had been communicated beneath the level of conscious attention.

The vibrations we receive from others tremble, sway, and oscillate subtly inside us. The consequence of this internalization is that all our conflict responses, from rage to reconciliation, take place *within* us, yet do so at a level that is beneath that of conscious attention. We routinely make subtle assessments, such as whether we feel respected or discounted by other people based on the vibratory quality of their speech, their posture, attitude, or quality of presence, as these resonate within us. We make these assessments by paying attention to how *we* feel when we are with them. As the Sufi poet Rumi wrote:

> What if a man cannot be made to say anything?
> How do you learn his hidden nature?
> I sit in front of him in silence,
> and set up a ladder made of patience,
> and if in his presence a language from beyond joy
> and beyond grief begins to pour from my chest,
> I know that his soul is as deep and bright
> as the star Canopus rising over Yemen.
> And so when I start speaking a powerful right arm
> of words sweeping down, I know him from what I say,
> and how I say it, because there's a window open
> between us, mixing the night air of our beings.

Indeed, there is rhythm and refrain, euphony and cacophony, not only in music, but in sight, touch, smell, taste, and thought, which are subtly present in every conversation. Unfortunately, we spend so much time and energy focusing on the relatively superficial literal meanings of what people say that we miss much of what they really mean beneath the surface of what they are saying. If we discount the words and simply focus on facial expressions, body language, tone of voice, and the ways their conversation affects us, we may gain a far better understanding of what they actually intend.

We know that music strikes people in different ways, so while these effects may be experienced and encouraged, they cannot be precisely predicted or calculated. For this reason, among others, it makes no sense to think of conflict as being created by one side without our other sides' active participation. When we describe conflict as taking "two to tango," we suggest not only that a dance partner has selected us, but that we have selected them and agreed to sway in unison to an agreed-upon piece of music. Yet this fact also implies that we can change the music or the dance whenever we decide to do so.

Science, Waves, and Vibration

Once we recognize that every conflict has emotional, energetic, and spiritual overtones, we can go deeper, and explore the subtle, invisible, vibratory lines along which it and much of reality runs. By paying attention to the music of ordinary communication we can discover a hidden fulcrum that can be used to nudge a conflict from impasse toward resolution. We can use scientific understanding as a metaphor to locate this fulcrum, and consider, for a moment, the role scientists believe may be played by vibration in the universe as a whole.

Since Einstein, physicists have been clear that our universe consists of matter and energy that translate directly into each other and are therefore simply different expressions of the same thing. Matter, which consists of energy moving very slowly, behaves at a quantum level like a wave. Energy, which consists of matter moving very rapidly, takes the form of a field whose invisible lines of force are revealed, for example, through patterns that can be seen in iron filings sprinkled on a sheet of paper covering a magnet.

Without digressing too far from our topic, it is useful to recognize that many physicists believe all matter is composed of vibrating 10 or 11 dimensional strings, or *branes*, that oscillate at different frequencies to produce all known elementary particles. A grand unification of all known forces and particles within a single vibrational framework would tell us that the universe does not consist simply of lumps of matter separated by vast reaches of empty space, but of varying energies, vibrations, waves, and fields, producing spin and similar qualities that may have no discrete physical existence. Ordinary particles, which we generally think of as matter, are now thought to comprise only a tiny part of the universe, and are themselves composed principally of empty space. To illustrate, if a proton in the nucleus of an atom were the size of a tennis ball, its electron would be circling two miles away, and the strings that make it up, scientists theorize, would be the same size in relation to an atom as an atom is to our solar system. Yet our focus and attention are attracted to particles or, by analogy, to substantive issues in conflict, with little focus dedicated to the energetic, vibrational fields created by polarization.

If these speculations by physicists are correct and we live in a world that consists not only of particles of fixed matter, but of waves of vibrating energy—if we ourselves unavoidably express that world—and if our emotions and spirits can partly be explained by thinking of them as wave-like, vibrational, and energetic, we need to consider how our views of conflict and efforts at resolution might shift by treating them as vibrations or waves, rather than as static particles.

There are many deep and profound issues related to the physical nature of the universe that have had a significant impact as metaphors on how we think about and respond to conflict. It is useful, for example, to recognize that we cannot pin down someone's position and at the same time be precise about their momentum, that our uncertainty about them imparts a kind of fuzziness to the entire resolution process, or that there is a complementarity to underlying interests in conflict that allow them to feel both fixed or particle-like, and flowing or wave-like.

We can go further and hypothesize that *anything* that vibrates or resonates can be tuned to a different, less adversarial or destructive frequency. There is no absolute or fixed frame of reference for people's perceptions, and we can imagine that when we open heart-to-heart communications between previously hostile combatants, they merge to form a new, unified, collaborative state, similar to a Bose-Einstein condensate, which, at temperatures near absolute zero, causes individual atoms to lose their distinctness and form a single integrated whole from thousands of otherwise discrete parts.

I sometimes find it useful to adopt a geometric analogy that views people's perceptions of time and space as relative, elastic, and warped by their gravitational attraction to some emotionally massive invisible black hole of pain around which they are rotating at rapid speeds. It is similarly useful to think of impasse as a vacuum in conflict space and not empty, but seething with polarizing energy that I can borrow from for an instant to create something new. These diverse, seemingly inapt physical metaphors have improved my ability to think about and articulate what I do and, in the process, led me to develop new techniques that draw on these understandings.

While these physical examples are purely metaphoric, they point to underlying unities and relationships. If we begin with Einstein's proof that space and time can be described in a single simple equation—that mass bends the shape of space-time, and that the elastic curved geometry of space-time tells matter how to move—we can hypothesize that the greater the density or mass of emotion surrounding a conflict, the greater the distortion it will create in the relational space-time geometry that connects and separates people. The greater the distortion, the greater the gravitational tug, which may result in the parties going into synchronous orbit around each other, moving away, or falling toward its center.

Using these metaphors also allows our understanding of conflict to shift from linear, particle-like, mechanical theories of causation to complex, subtle, wave-like, relativistic field theories, with multiple tensors and interacting causes and effects. Developing a unified field theory of conflict, as discussed in the next to last chapter, will allow us to recognize its complex movements and energetic fluctuations at different points in conflict space. Similar changes in our understanding occur when we shift from seeing conflict as regular and predictable to seeing it as chaotic, self-organizing, and sensitively dependent on initial conditions.

Geometry can also be used to enhance our understanding of relationships, since conflict is after all a relationship—not only with others, but with ourselves, with the past and future, and with the ecological system, environment, or context in which it occurs. Space, then, translates into relative qualities of distance, angle, and trajectory, while time translates into relative qualities of speed, frequency, and direction, and the angle by which we approach or examine the issues. Assessing the angle of our speed and position relative to others, or to the system or environment in which conflict occurs, can help define the meaning of our dispute and locate the vector of resolution.

Similarly, we can extract from evolutionary biology the competing and collaborating elements that are responsible for the evolution of conflict as a complex self-organizing system. Just as Einstein reduced gravity to the flexible geometry of space-time, so Darwin and Wallace reduced species differentiation to the adaptive process of evolution, in which birth and death, competition and collaboration, change and conservation, combine in a continually fluctuating natural selection process.

Computer simulations are now being used to model evolutionary processes and generate solutions to problems through artificial Darwinian experimentation. In the 1950s, mathematician John von Neumann developed a theory of cellular automata that described how computer programs could reproduce themselves and create non-repeating patterns by applying simple rules or algorithms. Subsequent researchers have developed algorithms that allow information to evolve in a computer-simulated environment of conflict and resolution, birth and death, change and conservation, using a combination of random mutation, reproduction, competition, and cooperation to simulate natural selection processes. The most successful cells are then allowed to reproduce and pass their genetic advantages on to future generations, while diversity and innovation are encouraged through cross-breeding and mutation.

Using evolution as a metaphor, as discussed in Chapter 2, allows us to see that people in conflict face environmental pressures from their families, spouses, workplaces, cultures, and societies that subject them to unpredictable non-equilibrium conditions and require them to learn and adapt in order to survive. Every conflict can be seen to generate a small-scale Darwinian environment that can be intentionally redesigned, as in computer modeling, to favor constructive outcomes and encourage evolution to more advanced levels of skill and collaboration.

In these ways, nature provides us with useful metaphors for recognizing hidden symmetries, forms, and patterns that allow us to analyze and influence conflict behaviors. It teaches us that nature is not "out there" but "in here," and that we *are* nature—possibly constituted out of vibrating ten-dimensional strings, but certainly made up of wave-like quarks, gluons, protons, neutrons, and electrons, all obeying the laws of physics. We are living, evolving organisms composed of interdependent organic compounds, bacteria, and diverse collaborating cells. We are primates with a capacity not only for rational thought, self-awareness, and strategic thinking, but irrationality, blinding emotion, and self-destruction. Every part of nature is manifested through us in ways that can help us understand how and why we behave as we do when we are in conflict and lead us to newer, more powerful methods of resolution, transformation, transcendence, and prevention.

Orchestrating the Music of Conflict

Adopting a vibrational metaphor for conflict also allows us to improve our skills by treating communications and emotions as though they were waves rather than particles and by working with their elements at a more subtle level. For example, waves possess both amplitude and frequency and can be cancelled by equal and opposite waves, or amplified and increased by adding waves of similar frequency. Therefore, we should be able to use tone of voice to stimulate others to increase their empathy, communicate emotion at a deep level of authenticity, acknowledge a willingness to resolve a dispute, or let go of grief and rage. All this can be done by using words that convey precise meanings, and by tone, pitch, frequency, and modulation.

We can also stimulate awareness through a variety of physical acts and rituals, such as

- shaking hands,

- shifting body movements,

- moving closer,

- nodding,

- altering our tone of voice,

- whispering,

- using repetitive phrasing or summarizing,

- interrupting negative interactions through process interventions,

- using a poignant or heart-based tone of voice, and

- the vibrational quality of character or who we *are.*

Each of these, if used with the right person at the right time, can create a sense of sympathetic vibration or emotional resonance, spiritual or heart connection, and relational synergy, all without words. As the Sufi poet Rumi observed:

> There is a way between voice and presence
> where information flows.

Similarly, by thinking of emotions as waves or vibrations, we can consciously de-escalate our conflicts by

- lowering or deepening our tone of voice,

- slowing the pace or frequency of our comments,

- softening our pitch,

- using repetitive or modulated phrasing, and

- emphasizing vowel sounds as opposed to harsher sounding consonants.

We can release pent-up emotion by

- leaning forward,

- nodding rhythmically and repetitively,

- taking a deep breath and releasing it slowly,

- using caressing gestures that do not actually touch the other person, and

- using a gentle physical touch or pat to produce a calming effect.

All of these vibratory acts can profoundly influence, resonate with, and direct the attribution of meaning within a listener.

At a deeper level, it is possible to alter the rhythmic patterns of our words. We can significantly change the meaning of our communications, for example, by repeating key words or phrases, slowing down, or using rhythmic emphasis, as was done to great effect by Dr. Martin Luther King, Jr. At a deeper level still, it is possible to make peace and tranquility so powerful within ourselves that, without using any of these interventions, others intuitively understand that it is unnecessary to act aggressively.

I often use musical or vibrational qualities of voice, body language, metaphor, pacing, liturgical repetition, and my own clear, committed, heart-based intention to calm people in conflict and induce a sense of trust and comfort in the process. To do so, I expand my awareness of what is happening in the present moment and do not get stuck in the past or future, or worry about what I am going to say next. Sometimes, as in deep meditation,

I experience a subtle, affirming background vibration that is extremely calming. This vibration does not occur as thought or emotion or body sensation, but as something distinct. The phrase that best describes this state of mind is an ancient Zen definition of enlightenment, which is "being available for anything at every moment." When I am in this state, people in conflict often become calm effortlessly.

In truth, conflict is inherently chaotic and so sensitively dependent on initial conditions as to be unpredictable, making it impossible to plan in advance how I will respond. It has been my experience that when I have a preset plan it often goes awry because I am unable to move naturally, in concert with what someone just said or did. On the other hand, when I am able to sense the vibratory wave-like quality of what is happening in the conversation and be completely open, present, and available for whatever others say or do, I can respond in creative, unimaginable ways that are far more effective than the best prepared strategies. This does not render strategy and planning irrelevant, but provisional and secondary to intuition and experience.

How We Attribute Meaning

The more closely we listen to our inner voice, the more clearly we are able to hear the voices of others. Indeed, when we consider how sense impressions are processed, the entire distinction between self and others begins to unravel and dissolve. All our sensory perceptions are based on a combination of largely unreliable factors, including external objects that produce or reflect waves or vibrations, which strike specialized sensory detectors, which transmit electrical signals through neurons to the brain, which trigger synapses, which create patterns that are recognized as matching previously experienced patterns, which have been stored in memory, all of which culminate in awareness and attribution of meaning. Minor errors in any of these maneuvers can result in radically different meanings.

Vision, for example, is a coordinated, even collaborative relationship between an object, light, the eye, nerve cells, the brain, and patterns of meaning that have been stored from prior experiences. What we see is therefore not actually something outside us, but a relationship between what is inside and what is outside. Light waves of a specific frequency and amplitude are reflected off objects at angles that render them perceivable by the eye, but perception necessarily includes the angle of perception, translation into electrical and chemical signals, matching, and attribution of meaning, much of which takes place inside us.

This does not mean that the things we see are not also seen by others, and can therefore be said to exist "objectively." It means that attributing meaning is highly personal, based on individual prior experiences, and dependent on multiple variable inputs, interpretations, and *choices* that can be altered to create different or opposite meanings. Thus, love and hate are complex externally triggered internal vibrations that we have imbued with special meaning based on past experiences, but these meanings exist only inside us as a result of our unique histories.

Consequently, every attribution of meaning is a combination of sensory perceptions and individual experiences, intentions, personalities, and innermost nature, all of which are communicated through wave-like interactions. As a result, we can choose at any time to interpret our perceptions differently, to recall and amplify a set of experiences we previously ignored, or to interpret events differently.

We can therefore recall or design fresh experiences that cancel previous wave patterns, or recognize that we have selected from a mass of perceptions only those that fit a predetermined emotional pattern, then discover the source of this pattern within ourselves and consciously dismantle it. Attribution of meaning is not fixed or static, but open to change and constantly evolving. It is, like our conflicts, a mutable music that makes us who we are.

In these ways, we can see that conflict possesses a vital, largely unexamined musical quality that, if recognized and developed as a skill, might allow us to understand the deeper meanings we otherwise ascribe only to language. For example, consider how this might have been done more effectively in the following case study.

The Language of Conflict—A Case Study

Exploring our failures is as important as exploring our successes in becoming skillful in conflict resolution. This is *more* critical in connection with transcendence, because it is here that conflict resolution reaches its scientific and artistic frontiers. What follows is a case study of a mediation that both succeeded and failed, for reasons that can improve our understanding of the dangers and difficulties in speaking from the heart and encouraging transcendence.

For over eleven years, two language professors at a community college had been stuck in a bitter personal quarrel. Hamid was a Middle Eastern Muslim in his late sixties, while Michele was a strictly Orthodox Jew in her midthirties. Their dispute came to a head when Hamid wrote a letter to the chair of the department complaining about his treatment by the chair, and referring to Michele, whose last name was Wein, as "Weinstein." The letter was circulated to every member of the department and an uproar ensued, resulting in my being asked to co-mediate with the entire department, but for scheduling reasons, without any advance interviews.

I opened the session by asking each faculty member to express in a word or phrase the qualities they would like to characterize their relationship with each other. I did so in order to reorient their attention toward the future and what they wanted, and to create a positive context from within which I might surface the negativity of their dispute without overwhelming what was actually working in their relationship. All of their words and phrases centered on words like respect, professionalism, and collegiality. I asked if anyone disagreed with any of these words, and when they did not, I asked them to reflect on the fact that they were able to reach consensus over what they wanted for the future, but not over what had happened in the past. I asked if they would be willing to start implementing these words immediately and using them to guide our discussion as we returned to the past, and they readily agreed.

I next asked them to identify the main issues they were facing that were preventing them from achieving these goals. After a brief moment of silence, Hamid described Michele's angry, hostile behavior toward him. I asked him if he knew why she was acting this way and he said he did not. I asked if he wanted to find out, and he said he did. I asked him if he would address his question directly to Michele and ask her why she was acting angrily toward him. He did, and she responded, not by referring to the twisting of her name, but by unexpectedly dropping a bombshell.

Michele said that eleven years ago, Hamid had come on to her sexually, and that she had been deeply offended by his behavior. Everyone was shocked and silenced by the revelation. In an effort to minimize the damage created by raising this issue publicly, I asked her if she had ever spoken to Hamid about this incident, and she said she had not because she felt too upset about it. She added that he was Muslim and might have thought what he did was acceptable, but she had communicated non-verbally through her anger toward him that his behavior was unwelcome.

I asked her if she felt her efforts had been successful in communicating what she wanted to communicate, and whether she thought Hamid had understood what her angry behavior meant. She agreed on both counts that he probably had not. I asked her if she would be willing to meet with him privately and tell him directly how she felt about what happened. She said she would be frightened to do so alone, but would gladly tell him now.

I turned to Hamid and said that this was really a private matter between the two of them that might be better handled in a separate mediation session rather than in front of the group. Hamid said that talking about it now was fine with him, and that he had nothing to hide. Without further ado, Michele turned to him and with the force of eleven years of holding back, shouted, "I do *not* want to have sexual conversations with you. It is extremely painful to me. Please *stop* it."

Realizing that Hamid needed my assistance in responding to the emotional intensity of her accusation and the fact that it had taken place in front of his colleagues, I asked if he would prefer to respond to Michele now or later in a private session, and he said he wanted to respond now. To give him an opportunity to reflect and calm down so he would not respond in anger, I asked if he recalled the incident, and whether he had intended to cause Michele this kind of pain. He said he neither recalled it nor wished her any harm. I asked him if he would say that to her directly, and he did so in a very clear and gentle tone of voice. He also said that he was happily married, and in his mind, he had never come on to her.

I again asked if he would be willing to meet Michele later to ask for more details about the incident and try to understand what she was talking about. He agreed to do so, but proceeded to ask her directly how she could accuse him of something he had not done. Michele responded that he had talked to her about sexual problems in his marriage and about her son masturbating. Hamid said he recalled these conversations, but did not consider them sexual overtures. I asked him why, if he knew Michele was angry at him, he had not gone to her to find out what she was upset about. He said he had tried to do so, but that she had refused to talk to him, which Michele confirmed, because she was extremely upset over what had happened and did not think he would listen.

It now became clear that, in addition to their other difficulties, they had a problem of cultural miscommunication: Hamid's insensitivity to what Michele was feeling regarding the topics of their conversation and inability to interpret her hostility as meaning no, and Michele's heightened sensitivity to the topic, unwillingness to say how she felt about the conversation to Hamid, and inability to say the word no explicitly so he could hear it.

I asked them what meanings their different cultures attached to the topics they had discussed. Hamid said that, in his family and culture, talking about these issues was not considered a sexual overture, but a discussion of important human problems, whereas in Michele's family and culture, cross-gender discussions of these topics were considered inappropriate.

I pointed out what they had each contributed to their miscommunication and opened a broader discussion of cross-cultural communication to broaden the discussion and get input from other faculty members. At the end, Hamid and Michele agreed that neither of them had acted skillfully or successfully in their communications with each other, and agreed to speak more respectfully to each other in the future.

The group now felt it was possible to move on and consider how they would all relate to each other in the future. They quickly reached consensus that they all wanted to have respectful, professional, collegial relationships with each other. During the discussion, Michele said she felt collegial meant being cordial and saying hello to each other, which she agreed she had not done for years following the incident. I asked her if she would be willing to say hello to Hamid, and how she would like him to respond if she did. She said she would be willing to do so and would like him to say hello back. To solidify her commitment and help her reach closure, I asked her if she would be willing to do so right now, and she turned to him and said hello, and he said hello back. I asked them how that felt, and they both said it felt good, and they again agreed to say hello to each other in the future. I congratulated them on taking this first step and told them that the more they practiced being cordial and collegial with each other, the easier it would become.

I then asked the rest of the group how they might support Michele and Hamid in resolving their conflicts, improving their communications, and creating more professional and collegial relationships, and a number of excellent suggestions were made and adopted by the group. I then broke the session up into small, randomly assigned teams in order to shift the focus back to the faculty as a whole, and asked each team to brainstorm all the ways they could support each other in creating more successful collegial relationships. They rapidly reached consensus on a number of actions they could implement, and the mood in the room felt quite positive.

As our time had run out, I ended the session by asking each person to say one word or phrase that expressed how they felt about the session, as a quick way of getting feedback and evaluating the process. All the words used, even by Hamid and Michele, were positive and hopeful. Everyone agreed they had achieved the goals they had identified at the beginning of the session. I congratulated them on moving from the language of hatred to the language of collegiality, wished them well, and ended the session.

Within a week of the mediation, Hamid became angry and refused to speak with either Michele or me, or to return to mediation. He later told me he felt he had been led into the mediation thinking there was only a small issue having to do with distorting Michele's name and had no idea it would turn into an attack on him as a sexual harasser. I agreed and empathized, but when I reminded him that he had given permission to continue the conversation, he told me he felt I should have stopped it anyway.

On one level, Hamid was right, because the issue of sexual harassment had been unexpected both for him and for me, and as a result, took place in front of the entire group rather than privately where it might have led in a different, less humiliating direction. On the other hand, Hamid and Michele continued to engage in the conversation, and in spite of my invitation to talk privately, clearly wanted to discuss and resolve their differences, even in front of their colleagues, because they had waited so long for someone to intervene.

While each step I took was calculated to repair their relationship, the shame Hamid felt as a result of the attack could not be assuaged, or even identified as needing to be assuaged, since that would have required him to expose his injured feelings in front of his colleagues, which his pride and culture precluded. The same was true for Michele, whose deep sense of shame had kept her from even saying hello to him for years, yet she burst into a personal attack in public.

What I learned from this mediation was that it is critically important to understand the cultural differences between people in conflict, as well as to explore the underlying sources of the dispute more fully in advance of the mediation. In this case, once the real issue had surfaced in the middle of the session, I did all I could to get them to talk to each other and improve their relationship, but was unable, in spite of using everything I knew at the time, to reach or resolve the shame that formed the hidden heart of their dispute. In retrospect, which is always the best teacher, I might have stopped and caucused with each of them during the session without asking their permission, and tested to see whether my impression that I was making progress was correct. I did not do so because Michele and Hamid rejected the idea of meeting separately, everything seemed to be going well, thirty faculty members would have been required to wait while I met with Michele and Hamid separately, time was limited, and no one said anything to indicate that the issue was not being successfully handled. None of these reasons, however, was as important as what happened as a result.

Had I been more culturally sensitive to Hamid's background, I might have guessed at the truth, that he was deeply shocked by these revelations and merely feigning a willingness to improve his relationship with Michele. Had I realized this was the case, I would have taken him aside, even canceled the remainder of the session, explored what needed to be said in caucus and subsequent sessions between the two of them, and followed up with a meeting with the faculty, though I knew the college had a fixed budget and timetable for the mediation and was unwilling to pay for additional sessions. Michele's culture provided her with an offensive interpretation of Hamid's remarks that might have been cleared up if she had been able to tell him they bothered her. It also made it difficult for her to speak after the event until she finally blew up during the joint session, subconsciously humiliating Hamid as she felt he had humiliated her. In addition, the academic culture of the college had prevented them and the rest of the faculty from discussing their hostile relationship for eleven years, or from bringing them together to discuss these issues, though everyone knew about their enmity.

This experience also suggests that resolving conflicts should not be thought of or described to participants as taking place in a single discussion, but as requiring a number of conversations over several weeks or months, permitting multiple opportunities to surface issues that have been hidden, hoarded, or not fully resolved in prior sessions. It then becomes possible to assess whether interim agreements worked, transform the organizational systems and cultures that reinforced the conflict, and have ample time to revise and continue improving communications and relationships over a prolonged period.

Having said this, it is important to add that it is not finally up to the mediator to prevent people from talking about their problems or to direct them to transcend their conflicts. Instead, we invite them to do so as skillfully as possible, respecting their choices should they decide not to settle or resolve their disputes, or even return to fighting. Their hearts, minds, and conflicts do not belong to us, and it is critical that we respect their choices, while at the same time making sure we have offered them a choice between real alternatives, with as much skill as possible, and learn from what happens.

Chapter 8 Conflict as a Spiritual Crisis

The price of anything is the amount of life you pay for it.
–Henry David Thoreau

We all pay an incalculable price for conflict. We pay a *financial* price in wasted time, attorney fees, and lost productivity; a *physical* price in stress-related illnesses, injuries, and accidents; an *intellectual* price in adversarial assumptions, distrust, false expectations, and failures; and an *emotional* price in suffering caused by anger, fear, jealousy, guilt, shame, and grief.

In addition to these, we pay an unseen *spiritual* price in stress, imbalance, blindness, and loss of energy, life force, or chi, that is aggravated by worry over what already happened, or fear over what might yet happen; a *heart* price in destroyed relationships, silence over things that matter, and loss of family, joy, and affection; and a *systemic* price in dysfunctional relationships, false polarizations, lost opportunities, and chronic, preventable conflicts. In these ways, even if only on a small scale, each conflict confronts us with a spiritual crisis, breaks our hearts, and keeps us trapped in a dysfunctional system. At the same time, it reveals a path to spiritual transformation, heartfelt transcendence, and systemic change.

These last costs of conflict are less commented on than the first, yet they can be far more costly, measured by the amount of life we end up paying for them. Think of it this way. Each of us has a 100% supply of energy to invest in living our lives. Of this 100%, we invest part in worrying about events that happened in the past or contemplating events that might take place in the future. Since most conflicts result from past events that will never change and future expectations that will never be realized, these efforts divert energy from our ability to live in the present. Even if we could recover 99% of this energy, leaving only a fraction of our life force wrapped up in unresolved conflict, that last, insignificant, unresolved 1% would leave us less able to live in the present. To estimate the true human cost of conflict, we would need to subtract the energy and attention we give it from the total available to us to live our lives.

The deeper the resolution, the smaller the percentage of our life energy remains invested in conflict. When we stop fighting, we reclaim some of this energy, but leave perhaps 90% in fear and rancor. When we settle the issues, we reclaim more of our energy, but may leave 40% of the dispute untouched. Resolution, which eliminates the underlying reasons for the conflict, leaves 5 or 10% unresolved. Forgiveness, which eliminates nearly all the rest, still leaves a tiny residue, which accumulates over time. Only reconciliation allows us to reclaim every ounce of energy we have siphoned into conflict.

Conflicts between spouses, intimate partners, and family members often arise, settle, resolve, and end in a matter of moments, hours, or days. But if there is not a full and complete reconciliation, the remaining parts can coalesce and accrue over time, creating what meditation teacher Shinzen Young calls *waxy buildup*. This residue of unresolved issues gradually clogs our communications, undermines our capacity for deep levels of intimacy, and makes us less willing to be open and honest with ourselves and with others. Over time, this residue congeals into coldness, withdrawal, exhaustion, alienation, distrust, petty personal animosities, chronic pain, and fractured relationships.

What percentage of your life is invested in conflict right now? How much energy and attention have you squandered in low-level anxieties due to incomplete or unresolved conflicts with children, parents, siblings, ex-spouses, significant others, managers, employees, neighbors, or others? How has this investment affected your ability to be wholly present? How many of your remaining days, weeks, months, and years are you prepared to invest in issues that are over, expectations that will never be met, discussions that will go nowhere, and people you do not like or trust? How much of what poet Mary Oliver calls your "one wild and precious life" are you prepared to waste on unresolved conflict?

From Price to Value

Given the enormity of this expenditure of life energy, it is important to identify the costs of conflict in two fundamentally opposite ways. First, we can portray the amounts of our lives we have invested in conflict as losses, by describing their *price,* or what they have cost us. Yet we can also portray these same amounts as gains, by describing their *value,* or what they have taught us.

When we focus on the value of our conflicts, we release ourselves from the burden of feeling forced to pay their costs, and we reveal a fundamental truth: that every conflict can teach us how to reclaim our energy and become better human beings. Thus, every conflict contains at its core a *spiritual* crossroads leading beyond impasse and resolution toward learning, forgiveness, reconciliation, and transcendence.

When we recognize that every conflict has the capacity to teach us unique and important lessons—that it contains secrets that can transform our lives; that it is not only a place where we get stuck, but an opportunity to free ourselves from impasse; and that it can show us how to become better human beings—all of a sudden the price of conflict turns into an *immense* source of value. We can then learn to transform its destructiveness into cleansing, its suffering into rites of passage, and its investments of life energy into gifts, not just to ourselves, but to our opponents, society, and anyone suffering from similar conflicts.

We cannot choose whether we will experience conflicts. We can only choose whether we will pay their price or invest our life energy in learning from them, evolving, and making certain they do not happen again. When we *live* our conflicts this way, even if we pay their price, we free ourselves from their icy grip, open our hearts, minds, and spirits, and discover within them paths leading to transformation, transcendence, and systemic prevention.

Defining the Indefinable

Every conflict communication is an effort against enormous odds to bridge the nearly unbridgeable gap that separates one person from another. It can be argued that conflict communications are actually *impossible* because everyone has a unique set of perceptions, experiences, cultural frameworks, and accumulated meanings and associations that distort the meaning of even the simplest words. As playwright George Bernard Shaw quipped, "The biggest problem with communication is the illusion that it has been accomplished."

Not only do personal attitudes, moods, and diverse social and cultural backgrounds subtly alter the content of conflict communications, they dramatically impact what we are *capable* of thinking, saying, or hearing, including what we *think* we said and heard, especially when someone we do not trust is yelling at us.

In order to communicate anything accurately, we need to step outside the thing we are describing, look at it objectively, and analyze it dispassionately. But how do we step outside *ourselves*, examine our antagonism objectively, or analyze our anguish dispassionately? Our inability to do so makes it more difficult to see our opponents without distortion or explain our conflict objectively. And whatever we cannot see or appreciate in ourselves, we will find it difficult to see or appreciate in others. Thus, who we *are* impacts what we see, just as what we see impacts who we are. As diarist Anais Nin wrote, "We do not see things as *they* are. We see things as *we* are."

Finally, there is something inherently indescribable about the relationship between conflict and resolution, transformation and transcendence, spirit and heart. Each has been extensively examined and elegantly described, yet each shuns a precise, practical, predictable, scientific definition. Ultimately, it is impossible to be exact, except perhaps through art or poetry, about how we find our way into conflicts or out of them, reach forgiveness, open or shut our hearts, or free ourselves from what kept us stuck. Partly, this is because, as in Zen, the resolution we seek is *already* inside us, and is the very thing doing the seeking.

Every conflict is defined by a crossroads consisting, on the one hand, of what we most need to do, learn, have, or be, and on the other, of our inability to do, learn, have, or be those things. Thus, three-year-olds do not experience conflicts over romantic love because they are not yet ready to do so. Nor do fifty-year-olds experience conflicts with their parents over curfew, because they have already learned to make these decisions themselves. In other words, conflicts occur when we are almost, but not *quite* ready to solve a problem connected with our growth and evolution, or transcendence.

In this sense, conflict resolution, transformation, and transcendence are simply conversations leading to the center of *ourselves*, our relationships, and our capacity for learning and evolution. These conversations allow us to experience our conflicts directly, as the Greek philosopher Empedocles wrote, as circles whose "circumference is nowhere, and whose center is everywhere," as grains of sand in which it is possible to discover the entire universe.

How Deep is the Ocean, How High is the Sky?

Henry David Thoreau asked, "With all your science can you tell how it is, and whence it is, that light comes into the soul?" Countless efforts have been made to define spirit, all of which seem woefully inadequate. Partly, this is because definitions consist of words, which are inevitably self-referential, circular, and elusive. Partly it is because every definition is a limit, and no limit can explain something that is, by its nature, limitless. Definition means to make finite, which automatically places anything non-finite beyond definition. Moreover, language is a way of pointing attention at things, feelings, and ideas. But who or what is doing the pointing? Is it possible to point at what is pointing? And what is the nature of attention that is not pointed at anything?

On the other hand, we can try to define spirit by what it is *not* and distinguish it from other things. But if spirit is related to energy, as I believe it is, it is impossible to find anything that does not possess energy, and we again find ourselves unable to separate it from everything else. We can try to define spirit by comparing it to something to which it is similar, but if it is part of everything, how do we create a unique or meaningful contrast? How do we compare something that is *not* comparable to something that *is*? Against what background does it appear as foreground?

A number of plausible scientific justifications might be offered to explain this definitional difficulty. If we draw on scientific ideas currently being advanced to explain equally bizarre aspects of the physical universe, we can see that several might help explain spiritual experiences. A complete scientific explanation of spirit is beyond my expertise and the scope of this book, but having thought about this issue for some time, I am drawn to several intriguing possibilities.

For example, it *might* be that what we are trying to measure extends throughout the entire universe and is larger than any existing unit of measurement. It might be, as in quantum physics, that what is being measured is so small that the act of measurement substantially alters it or is antithetical to its operation. It might be, as with quarks inside subatomic particles, that it is impossible to separate pieces of it because the gluonic forces holding them together increase in strength as they are pulled apart. It might be that what is being measured is itself a quality of space or time from which everything is formed and by which it is measured, so that it is indistinguishable from everything else. It might be, as with Minkowski's description of Einstein's four-dimensional space-time, that the addition of an imaginary number based on the square root of minus 1 creates a complex world line, a path through space-time that allows for such phenomena. It might be, as with quantum entanglement, that the wave-like nature of spirit allows information to be shared instantly across physical distances. It might be that what we want to measure cannot presently be detected because it is the size of the smallest Planck unit of space-time at 10^{-33} centimeters and either wrapped up or extended throughout the universe like one of the ten or eleven dimensional strings some physicists think may constitute all matter. It might be that what we are defining is not a thing at all, but a wave that collapses when we try to measure it. It might be that the left brain cannot know what the right brain is doing. It might be that the piece we are examining is holographically organized, indivisible, and therefore indistinguishable from a much larger whole. It might be that it is a four-dimensional quality beneath the three-dimensional surface of a membrane, or D-brane. It might be that it is the by-product of a compactified or infinitely large, warped fifth dimension. It might be, according to physicist David Bohm, that it is a quality of wholeness or implicate order that has been enfolded into the structure of the universe and cannot be detected.

The point of these speculations is that there are a number of plausible scientific explanations for the existence of spirit that do not require divine intervention, mystical beliefs, moralizing attitudes, or unclear thinking. Spirit is not the same as religion, morality, or ethics. It does not require belief in any kind of supernatural deity. While spirit forms the basis for much religious experience, religious beliefs have little in common with spiritual experience, which precede and transcend them. Religious beliefs have often led to the silencing of spirit and the suppression of doubt and curiosity, which led psychologist Carl Jung to define religion as "a defense against the religious experience."

Moreover, certain qualities seem to disappear the moment we try to analyze, quantify, distinguish, measure, or enumerate them. For example, what happens to the feeling of love when we undertake to scientifically define its nature? Is it possible to reason from a list of objective characteristics of love to a complete description of what it feels like to be in love? Can the idea of love ever be satisfactorily explained to someone who has never experienced it? What is in common between the experience of happiness or joy and the five or ten elements a scientist may cite as making them up? Who is unable to recognize the fragrance of a rose, or the sound of raindrops, or the feel of a lover's touch? But who can accurately describe them to someone who has never experienced them? The English writer G. K. Chesterton observed:

> The real trouble with this world of ours is not that it is an unreasonable world, nor even that it is a reasonable one. The commonest kind of trouble is that it is nearly reasonable, but not quite...It looks just a little more mathematical and regular than it is; its exactitude is obvious, but its inexactitude is hidden; its wildness lies in wait...Everywhere in things there is this element of the quiet and incalculable.

Creativity and counting do not mix, Eros and logos are non-translatable, and calculating a bottom line to love is as absurd as employing the pleasure principle in accounting, or judging a work of poetry, music, or art by strictly scientific standards. This difficulty led poet John Keats to define negative capability as a state of mind in which a person "is capable of being in uncertainties, doubts, without any irritable reaching after fact and reason." Or, as Timothy Leary famously remarked, "You have to lose your mind to come to your senses."

Even at a physical level, it is not possible to use quantitative reductions to define qualities that are holistic, or entirely different, or emanate from everywhere. Where, for example, in the schematic diagram of a television set's electronic circuitry is there anything that could predict MTV or Star Trek? Can one take apart the engine of a car and discover the thrill of racing, or locate the single organ responsible for sustaining life in the human body? As Antoine de Saint-Exupery wrote, "How could the drops of water know themselves to be a river? Yet the river flows on."

These scientific and philosophical ideas suggest that there is something in nature, conflict, and spirit that is finite and infinite, simple and complex, predictable and chaotic. While there may appear to be nothing in common between complexity, chaos, and predictability, or between infinities and seemingly normal, finite equations in mathematics, unpredictability routinely arises from conditions that are determined and in equilibrium and infinite results appear unexpectedly even in simple, finite mathematical calculations. Chaos and disorder are continuing sources of complexity, innovation, and higher levels of order, both in natural and human conflict.

Consequently, it is important to recognize that conflict and spirit are intrinsic, indispensable, creative properties of the universe as a whole, and that the more deeply we understand the subtle, complex, chaotic, infinite, and contradictory elements of conflict, the closer we come to understanding and being able to use spirit, not as a belief, wish, or imaginary construct, but as a source of practical technique, and an integral, holistic component of the art and science of resolution.

Which One is Moving?

In defining spirit, it is customary to begin by associating it with mind and contrasting it with body, following philosopher Rene Descartes' famous declaration, "I think, therefore I am." Yet as the Buddhist monk Katagiri Roshi humorously pointed out:

> I have been reading your Descartes. Very interesting. "I think, therefore I am." He forgot to mention the other part. I'm sure he knew, he just forgot: "I don't think, therefore I'm not."

Descartes considered the mind, which he associated with the soul, to be a separate, distinct, disembodied, non-physical entity:

> A substance, the whole essence or nature of which is to think, and that for its existence there is no need of any place, nor does it depend on any material thing; so that this "me," that is to say, the soul by which I am what I am, is entirely distinct from body, and is even more easy to know than is the latter; and even if body were not, the soul would not cease to be what it is.

Considerable scientific research, however, has demonstrated that Descartes' soul and the body are inseparable, integrated parts of a whole organism that is, in turn, an inseparable, integrated part of its entire physical and social environment. Neurologist Antonio R. Damasio has summarized this research, finding, in opposition to Descartes, that

> ...love and hate and anguish, the qualities of kindness and cruelty, the planned solution of a scientific problem, or the creation of a new artifact are all based on neural events within a brain...The soul breathes through the body, and suffering, whether it starts in the skin or in a mental image, happens in the flesh.

Whether we regard the brain or the spirit as primary, or the soul as the thing that connects them, together they form an undifferentiated whole, containing the entire movement of each into the other, their integration, and ultimate harmonization on a higher level, which we can analogize to spirit. In this sense, spirit is what transcends the effort to separate wholeness into categories, thereby lying beyond categorization.

At the risk of making this perplexing point more confusing, consider the ancient Zen problem of "which one is moving," in which two monks are avidly debating which is moving, the flag or the wind. They ask the Sixth Patriarch, who answers that it is their minds that are moving. In the language of physics, we can only know what is moving by comparing its change in location to something that is not moving. However, as Einstein explained, if our point of reference is the universe as a whole, everything is in motion relative to everything else and we cannot know which is moving because there is no fixed or absolute point of reference we can use for comparison.

Accordingly, if there is one object, we can only measure its movement against the background of space, which is itself in motion. Black ink is noticeable only against a white page, the page against a book, the book against a scenic background, the background against a horizon, and the horizon against the whole of space. But against what do we contrast the whole? If spirit is a quality of the whole, we will be unable to distinguish it by comparing its motion against a moving background of which it forms a part.

Or consider a movie projected onto a screen. We lose ourselves in the movie by ignoring the screen on which it is projected. If the screen is bent, moving, or has its own color or shape, it distorts the movie. Spirit can be thought of as the screen on which our sensations, thoughts, and feelings are projected, the space in which they move, the background of everything. Ultimately, however, the screen is no different from the movie that is playing on it, space from the objects moving in it, or background from foreground.

Spirit is therefore described in Zen as not one, not two. It is neither the whole nor any of its parts, neither unity nor diversity, but greater than both. As Lao Tze wrote in the Tao Te Ching, "The Tao that can be spoken is not the true Tao." In relation to conflict resolution, this can be thought of as the undifferentiated unity that precedes conflict and follows its transcendence. It is the truth of who we are when we are one, two, and one again, but at a higher level, and therefore not exclusively either, both, or neither. This indivisible, holistic quality transcends all opposing categories, and is the energy and animating principle that unites and divides them. The arising of sensation is concurrent with the separation of opposite forms, while its cessation is their coming together, transcendence, and disappearance.

Differentiation into categories for the purpose of analysis does not imply actual separation. Thus, while waves can be subdivided into peaks and troughs, there are no naturally occurring waves that can be said to possess peaks in the absence of troughs. Similarly, what is material cannot be distinguished from what is spiritual, just as matter cannot be contemplated separate from energy and, as Einstein famously demonstrated, they are fundamentally the same.

We can therefore analogize spirit to the movement, rhythm, and unimpeded flow of the energy of life within, around, and between us, the backdrop or screen against which our physical sensations, mind, and emotions are projected. Spirit is anything left over after our physical, mental, and emotional sensations become silent, a combination of intense awareness and unfocused concentration, and undifferentiated direct experience, as in the Zen adage, "The sound of the rain needs no translation."

Experiencing Spirit Through Mindfulness

Even if we find it difficult to define spirit, we nonetheless experience it directly and materially in countless ways. We may experience spirit whenever our energy shifts as we interact with different people; or as we shift from being focused to distracted, angry, or frightened; or when someone withdraws or decides without physical or verbal signaling that it is time to leave. We may experience it as our conversations grow shallower or deeper, or our attention is diverted from the past or future into the present. We may experience it intentionally by moving closer to someone, starting from four or five feet away, and sensing how the quality and depth of our energy, communications, and relationship shift as we approach the invisible boundary that defines their space. We may experience it unexpectedly at the moment of death of someone we love, allowing us to sense the difference between a living, even comatose being, and lifeless flesh, as what it was that disappeared.

Whether we call it spirit, soul, life force, energy, awareness, or chi, we may feel it any time, all the time, as it arrives, increases, declines, and leaves. We may experience it as open and joyful, or closed and sad, or compressed and fearful, or expanded and courageous. We may experience it in silent meditation by finding a still, soundless space inside that is neither body sensation, thought, nor emotion, but an undirected energy of awareness and equanimity, a state of being that is empty yet full, stable yet constantly changing, a nowhere that feels like home. We may experience it by tracking our breath or body sensations, or shifting attention, say, from our feet to our hands, and considering what exactly it was that moved from one to the other. We may experience it by observing physical, mental, or emotional sensations and watching as they interact and flow. We can consider: Who is the one watching, and who is being watched? And who is now watching the watcher?

As Leonard Riskin has written, mediators can use mindfulness meditation to break up conflict-hardened physical responses, ideas, and emotions, and form a clear, self-reflecting awareness of conflict experiences, become conscious of their impermanence, accept their emotions with ease and equanimity, watch as they move toward completion and closure, and learn to respond more skillfully as they arise and disappear.

Meditation can also help parties in conflict dissolve the grasping, aggressive and defensive behaviors that have kept them locked in impasse by noticing these qualities silently and peacefully within themselves and disarming them through empathetic listening, collaborative negotiation, and open-hearted communications. They can do so by finding a place of stillness, like the calm in the eye of a hurricane, and becoming more focused, calm, and present, even in the midst of raging, adversarial arguments.

Spirit has a quality of timelessness to it, allowing mediators to slow the pace of conflict communications and move the parties' awareness into the present, as happens in moments of intense love or joy, in the presence of great art, in meditation, in nature, in danger, in moments of deep awareness and realization, and in heartfelt moments. We can create a sense of timelessness in mediation by

- listening without aim or intention to each person;

- observing moment by moment what is happening inside ourselves and others, especially in moments of intense emotion;

- expanding empathy and compassion toward others;

- encouraging them to speak honestly from their hearts, and act with unconditional integrity and skill;

- recognizing that their conflicts have something important to teach them; and

- working collaboratively in a committed way to transform and transcend what got them stuck.

In each stage of resolution and location of conflict, it is possible to reduce the amount of conflict or friction by calming or slowing its energy. We can stop people from fighting and de-escalate their confrontations using physical calming techniques, as by sitting down with them, slowing the pace of their speech, and listening peacefully. We can settle issues using intellectual calming, as by brainstorming creative ideas, caucusing, and open-mindedly exploring options. We can resolve underlying issues using emotional calming, as by acknowledging feelings, empathizing, and satisfying interests. We can encourage forgiveness using spiritual calming, as by encouraging them to learn from their conflicts, apologize, design rituals of closure, and let them go. We can reach reconciliation through heart calming, as by opening heart-to-heart communications, rebuilding trust, and encouraging acknowledgement and expressions of affection. And we can help prevent future disputes using systemic or environmental calming, as by identifying the systemic sources of chronic conflict and designing systems that prevent or respond more effectively to them.

There are three main reasons for mediators to learn how to directly experience spirit. First, in doing so, we become increasingly aware of the quality of our energy, and notice what happens to it when we do, think, say, or experience anything. We become aware at a sensitive level of how it shifts as conversations move from conflict to resolution, from lies to telling the truth, from anger to compassion, from defensiveness to openheartedness, and the reverse. This allows us to notice more readily when the parties we are working with do the same.

Second, directly experiencing spirit, energy, or life force can make us more skillful in directing or channeling it. We can discover how to make it stronger, clearer, and brighter, and avoid what makes it weaker, blurrier, and darker. We can more quickly reconsider the insulting remark we are about to make and speak respectfully, even to someone who does not do the same to us. We can watch angry judgments form and choose to listen with an open heart, even to people who are upset with us.

Third, the experience of spirit can help us recognize that conflicts exist partly to teach people who they are and might become by helping us identify and resolve the underlying issues that are dissipating their life energy. Every conflict is simply a place where people are stuck and unable to be authentic in the presence of others. By learning to become unstuck and authentic, they can discover how to transcend that particular conflict, and all similar conflicts, liberating themselves from the confused ways of thinking and inauthentic ways of being that got them stuck in the first place. In this sense, every conflict is fundamentally a spiritual path leading to higher levels of conflict and resolution.

Conflict and the Art of Waking Up

Even adversarial conflicts wake people up and give them energy, but it is often negative energy that is ego oriented and either turned outward against others as anger and fear or inward against themselves as guilt and shame. Most of this energy gets short circuited, drawn into destructive channels, and prevented from flowing freely and being converted into growth, learning, and change. If impasse and adversarial conflicts are the damming, diverting, and decaying of this energy, then resolution, transformation, and transcendence are its release, redirection, and rejuvenation.

Conflicts tie people's personal and relational energies in a knot, causing a loss of the positive flow associated with trust, love, collaboration, and unguarded, compassionate communication, and a gain in negative flow associated with distrust, alienated affections, competition, and pointless, self-centered bickering. In either case, conflicts wake them up, allowing them to observe how its energy flows within, between, and around them.

In *The Art of Waking People Up: Cultivating Awareness and Authenticity at Work*, Joan Goldsmith and I cited a number of life circumstances and events that can wake us up and release our spirits. While anything can wake us up at any time, we are most often aroused by painful events that shock us out of complacency, as when we experience a sudden awareness of death, a horrible humiliation, a personal failure, a lover's rejection, a loss of employment, or an unresolved conflict. We can also wake up as a result of pleasurable events that enchant or delight us, as when we experience a moment of intense joy, a perception of beauty, a deep meditation, a recognition of absurdity, a spectacular success, or a gift of honest feedback. Painful experiences sap our energy, while pleasurable ones increase it.

We wake up and increase our energy when we

- participate in open, authentic, profound conversations with our opponents;

- honestly address the sources of our disagreements;

- speak directly from our hearts;

- say what we most want to say;

- listen compassionately;

- discover what we can learn from what happened;

- cease being hostile, artificial, and divided by differences; and

- become affectionate, authentic, and undivided in the presence of others.

Every opening to real awakening can be painful because it is accompanied by fear, associated with the death of a false idea of who we are. But it can also be pleasurable, since it is accompanied by the birth of a truer, more integrated, authentic sense of self and others. Often, the very thing we are holding onto with all our might out of fear of loss ends up being the thing we most need to let go of if we want to live more fully and without fear. Awareness, waking up, and letting go are, in this way, intertwined and inseparable. As Buddhist nun Pema Chödrön writes:

> Our life's work is to use what we have been given to wake up. If there were two people who were exactly the same—same body, same speech, same mind, same mother, same father, same house, same food, everything the same—one of them could use what he has to wake up and the other could use it to become more resentful, bitter, and sour. It doesn't matter what you're given, whether it's physical deformity or enormous wealth or poverty, beauty or ugliness, mental stability or mental instability, life in the middle of a madhouse or life in the middle of a peaceful, silent desert. Whatever you're given can wake you up or put you to sleep. That's the challenge of now: What are you going to do with what you have already—your body, your speech, your mind?

When we stop wishing our lives were different from what they actually are, we begin to take responsibility, learn, and evolve. When we stop ignoring or resisting our conflicts, we convert them into sources of awareness and compassion. When we stop searching for quick, simple solutions, we learn the art of waking up, discover the wisdom at the center of our conflicts, and embark on a spiritual path leading toward resolution, transformation, and transcendence. As an illustration of how this is possible, consider the following case study.

No More Teachers' Dirty Looks—A Case Study

Several years ago, I mediated a dispute involving Rose, a teacher who was being fired for yelling at three other teachers and using what could be considered world-class swear words in front of children during school hours. Rose had been chair of the union at her school for twenty years and a strong advocate for teachers. The incidents that threatened her job all began six months after she stepped down as head of the union.

At the mediation, the three teachers angrily described what Rose had said and done to them. Rose responded defensively, first by denying that what she had done was so serious, then by attacking the other teachers for having provoked her, and finally by quibbling over details in their descriptions of each event. The mood was one of entrenched animosity, unyielding blame, impasse, and shared recrimination.

Sensing the determination behind her resistance and at the same time being aware of its utter futility, and as the principal had made it clear that without a full resolution Rose would be terminated, I did something I had not planned or thought about in advance. I stopped her in midsentence during one of her defensive counterattacks against her accusers, and said, "Excuse me, Rose. Can I ask you a question?" She said "Yes," and I asked, softening my tone of voice, lowering my posture, and leaning toward her until I was at the edge of her personal space, "Has anyone ever *thanked* you for what you have done for this school?"

Her mouth dropped open and she immediately burst into tears and started sobbing uncontrollably. I decided to deepen the heart opening created by her response, and after a moment of warm, sympathetic silence, I turned to the teachers who had accused her and asked if they would each turn to Rose, tell her one thing they thought she had contributed to the school, and thank her for having done it. Now they all started crying, and as they told their stories about Rose's dedication to the teachers and the school, their accusativeness, her defensiveness, and the atmosphere of impasse were completely transformed.

After the teachers finished and Rose had stopped crying long enough to speak, she apologized profoundly and profusely for what she had done. She said she cared so much about the school and about the teachers and children, but didn't know how to show it and was desperately unhappy about how useless she had become. Her "accusers" supported her by saying they knew she cared about them and about the school, and apologized to her for becoming accusatory rather than reaching out and helping her make what must have been a very difficult transition.

Rose felt she needed to do something more to repair the damage, not just for the teachers who were not in attendance, but for the school as a whole. After a lengthy discussion they decided they would work together to help everyone learn from what happened, discuss how they might work more collaboratively in the future as members of a team, and use Rose's experience to train and support new union leaders.

I asked how they wanted to communicate to people who were not present what they had decided, let others know how they resolved their conflict, and help the school heal. Rose said she felt she needed to apologize to the entire faculty and staff, and would start by asking to be put on the agenda at the next staff meeting. The other teachers said she should not have to do this alone, and felt they should join her so they could also apologize for their role in the conflict.

Everyone started crying all over again, but this time with joy at their new-found, heartfelt connection. I suggested that they immediately go together to report to the principal and ask to be placed on the agenda for the next staff meeting, where they might each describe what they had learned from the conflict and make suggestions about how everyone could do better at listening, acknowledging, teaching, working collaboratively, and solving problems together. They readily agreed.

I again decided to do something I had not planned in order to keep their hearts open just a little longer. Rose said she had gone to one of the complaining teachers after yelling at him, apologized, hugged him, and asked him if she could take him to lunch to make up for what she had done. The teacher said it had shocked him at the time because Rose was not known as someone who hugged people or invited them to lunch.

Riding this wave of collegiality, I asked them if they would agree to hug each other each time they meet and go to lunch as a group at least once a week between now and the end of the semester. They enthusiastically agreed, and I asked Rose whether she would like to invite others who also had experienced difficulties with her to go to lunch and find out what they could do together to improve the school. She agreed.

I later heard from the principal how shocking and transformational it was to see Rose, the tough-talking union advocate, hugging everyone and inviting all her former enemies to lunch. He said the faculty meeting at which she and the other teachers apologized had transformed their culture in the school, triggering a profound conversation about how the faculty and staff needed to care more for each other and teach more collaboratively. He felt this shift had resulted in better teaching and fewer disciplinary problems with students.

In retrospect, it is clear that while Rose was thoroughly defended against insult, isolation, and attack, she was absolutely defenseless against compliment, inclusion, and acknowledgement. Her toughness was a barrier she had raised to protect herself against her own vulnerability, which collapsed at the slightest push in the opposite direction. The gentleness, kindness, and openheartedness that were contained in the question I asked her regarding acknowledgement had spoken directly to her heart and touched a deep chord that released her pent-up emotions.

What allowed me to discover that question was not merely my observation of her physical defensiveness, or feeling of intellectual futility about the way the conversation was going, or sense of her emotional intensity and lack of ownership or real understanding of her accuser's stories, or even my discomfort with the stress-filled accusatory/defensive intentions and energy that filled their arguments, but my sense of the heartfelt attitude that must lay beneath those layers of defensiveness and rationalization.

By going to my heart and asking a question that came directly from the quality I wanted to elicit in her, I was able to touch her heart in ways I could never have done by asking questions from my intellect. Though it all happened very quickly, the question originated in my intuition, empathetic resonance, and willingness to place myself in her shoes. From there, I could ask what might make me do what she did and design a question to reveal whether my intuitive response was correct.

These moments of sublime mediation, or what is sometimes called crazy wisdom, represent a kind of peripheral mind, which, like peripheral vision, consists of paying attention to the background rather than the foreground and empowering intuition. In this state, it is possible to notice the subtle differences between anger and caring, defensiveness and pain, and, within myself, between judgment and empathetic resonance.

Intuition, of course, is fallible, and for this reason should not take the form of an answer, but of a question, particularly one that could be asked by a three-year-old. Because my intention and attitude were clear and I had no judgments, agendas, or stakes in the outcome, I was able to combine innocent curiosity and empathy with dangerous honesty in a simple, disarming, heart-based question that suddenly exposed the nucleus of the conflict and automatically opened a path to resolution.

Chapter 9 Why Every Conflict Breaks Your Heart

The mind creates the abyss and the heart crosses it.
–Sri Nisargadatta

At a simple level, no one gets into conflict over issues they do not care about, even if only symbolically or subconsciously. As a result, every conflict involves an element of caring—sometimes about content, process, or relationship, or about how each person has been perceived or treated—and every conflict includes an element of anger, frustration, anguish, betrayal, and distrust, caused by the destruction or loss of what they care so deeply about. In addition, everyone's deepest desire is to love and be loved, yet this becomes impossible for most people in conflict. Thus, even if only in tiny, subtle, seemingly insignificant ways, every conflict breaks our hearts.

Once our hearts have been broken, we do not readily open them again, especially in the presence of the people who broke them. Yet by hardening our hearts, we justify hard-heartedness in return, allow the damage they caused to live on inside us, and cause others to do the same. Nonetheless, whatever is heartfelt within us endures and continues to seek communion, even in the form of pain. As the Sufi poet Rumi wrote:

> This grief you cry out from
> draws you toward union.
> Your pure sadness
> that wants help
> is the secret cup.
> Listen to the moan of a dog for its master.
> That whining is the connection...

This bedrock desire for heartfelt communications that can end the pain of separation and reconnect those who have cast each other aside is the ultimate defining principle of conflict resolution, its algorithm, singularity, and heart. Nonetheless, mediators have largely ignored the nature of caring and heart, and been unable to explain how it is that distorted, negative, adversarial statements have suddenly been transformed into direct, positive, heartfelt communications, or how intensely conflicted parties have attained forgiveness and reconciliation.

By looking deeply into our own hearts, we can discover profound reasons why others chose to fight, and what makes it so difficult for them to listen empathetically, respond respectfully, act collaboratively, or reach forgiveness and reconciliation. These heart realizations can lead to deep and profound discoveries about conflict that flow inward to the most intimate core of our being and outward to the very nature of our universe.

Discussing the heart of conflict may seem whimsical, maudlin, or romantic. Yet, as I hope to demonstrate, it is possible to dissect the role of heart in conflict resolution without becoming imprecise, sentimental, or romantic, and treat it as a profoundly practical process, based on identifiable methods and techniques, and grounded in broadly replicable experiences. This means learning how to identify a party's desire for heartfelt interactions and design questions and interventions that open and expand them. To do so, we need to understand more clearly what heart is, how to open it, and what to do once it is open.

What is Heart?

Our most intimate relationships are selected, shaped, and shattered at a level far beneath that of conscious attention. No one decides, on the basis of intellectual criteria alone, either to fall in love or terminate a relationship. Neither do we make these decisions only on the basis of isolated intellectual, emotional, or physical inputs. Instead, these seemingly intellectual, emotional, and physical decisions supplement, support, and rationalize choices we have already made in what we euphemistically call our hearts.

It is difficult to define heart or itemize the elements of heart-based communications for the same reasons cited in the previous chapter. Obviously, I do not refer to the actual physical organ contained in our chests, which beats faster and with increased pressure during conflict. Still, the heart plays less of a role in conflict resolution than mirror neurons, which fire when we observe others experiencing pleasure or pain, triggering empathy; or brain-mediated chemicals like oxytocin, which is associated with trust, bonding, and committed relationships; or adrenalin, which is associated with the fight or flight reflex; or endorphins, which are associated with pleasure, including the pleasure of collaboration; and so on.

Instead, we can think of heart as a set of attitudes or qualities, such as loving, kindness, vulnerability, sincerity, compassion, and authenticity, which directly influence our behaviors and relationships in conflict, and exist within, between, and around us. Yet they are difficult to isolate or pin down without freezing and destroying the very thing we are trying to define. For this reason, it is easier to imagine heart than to define it.

We can, for example, imagine heart as a connection with others that is loving, kind, open, honest, compassionate, and authentic, as a synergy created by the collaboration of disparate human beings. We can imagine it as a source of poetry, music, and art, as a seat of wisdom, insight, fellowship, and recognition. We can imagine it as a living, evolving, intimate relationship with someone we know because we are able to recognize them within ourselves. We can imagine it as a willingness to be open, vulnerable, and genuine in the presence of those we think do not like us.

We can imagine heart as a set of challenges, lessons to be learned, or sources of growth; as parts of ourselves we discover by interacting with others; as a sense of well-being that flows from creative, intimate experiences with others. We can imagine it as listening compassionately, not just to the words others speak, but to the words they do not speak, but most want to say. We can imagine it as truths that are so poignant and profound they are understood immediately, without thinking. We can imagine it as deep dedication, crystal clarity, piercing honesty, intense compassion, or absolute commitment.

For example, Arun Gandhi, grandson of Mahatma Gandhi, tells a moving story about a mother and father who came to see his grandfather to ask him to convince their son to stop eating sweets. The boy was addicted and refused to stop, but a doctor had told them it was destroying his health. The elder Gandhi said nothing, but asked them to return in ten days. The parents could not understand why Gandhi did not speak to their son immediately, but returned in ten days nonetheless. Gandhi spoke with their son for only a few minutes. Afterward, the son told his parents he was willing to stop eating sweets. The parents were amazed at Gandhi's success and asked what he had told their son. Gandhi said he had needed the ten days to stop eating sweets himself. He told the boy he loved sweets as well, but had not eaten any for ten days and would not touch another sweet for the rest of his life unless the boy was willing to give them up.

Arun Gandhi tells a similar story about an incident that occurred with his father, Mahatma Gandhi's son. Arun agreed to pick his father up at a certain hour after getting his car fixed, but had gone to a movie and was late. When he arrived, he lied to his father and told him the car had not been ready, but his father had already telephoned the garage and found out that it had been ready for hours. His father said he must have made a mistake in raising Arun if he was willing to tell lies, and insisted on walking the eighteen miles back to their home to meditate on where he had gone wrong. Needless to say, Arun was forced to meditate as well, while following at a snail's pace in the car behind his father and reflecting on his mistakes.

What is common in these stories is the deep commitment both men had to genuine, loving, non-violent, profound, principled relationships in which they were able to make a difference, not by lecturing or preaching, but by living the principles they believed in and being willing to suffer for others. This largely unspoken, poignant, conscientious attitude and way of being illustrates what I believe is meant by heart. What, then, does heart have to do with conflict?

Heart in Conflict Resolution

The extraordinary Chilean poet Pablo Neruda wrote that "Every casual encounter is an appointment." When we take this idea seriously, not only in everyday life, but in all our conflicts, we begin to listen differently, and are led to consider the possibility that we may actually, at a subconscious level, choose our conflicts. This seemingly counterintuitive possibility becomes clearer if we assume that we choose them precisely so that we will be forced to surrender the assumptions, ideas, feelings, and behaviors we need to release in order to learn, grow, and evolve. Merely entertaining this possibility can wake us up, draw our attention into the present, and dramatically increase our willingness to appreciate and learn from our opponents.

After all, if every conflict represents an appointment, who made it? Why with *them*? Why now? And for what conceivable purpose?

When we follow the faint trail of breadcrumbs left by people's conflict stories, communications, and behaviors back into the labyrinth of their subconscious minds, we are ultimately led to the center of what they most need to learn, know, do, or become. Think of it this way: if someone is stuck at a certain place in their lives and cannot grow, evolve, or become who they otherwise might be, would it not make sense for their subconscious mind to find an opponent who can point out where they are stuck, get them unstuck, and clarify what got them stuck in the first place so they can free themselves?

The opponent they choose to assist them may be

- a parent or relative to whom they are so deeply attached that they cannot live their own lives;

- a spouse who represents the parent with whom they have not completed their childhood relationship;

- a boss or co-worker who triggers defensiveness, poor self-esteem, or resentment over how they were treated by siblings or peers;

- a neighbor who does not respect their space or peace and quiet; or

- a rival who triggers primal feelings of shame or rage.

Or there may be a thousand other opponents, each of whom represents an opportunity for learning, growth, and evolution to a higher order of self-understanding, emotional maturity, relationship, and conflict.

Our conflicts intimately connect us with our opponents and, through them, with parts of ourselves that we have silenced, suppressed, or denied. They draw us along deep subterranean channels that usher us into anger, pain, love, and acceptance. Discovering where these channels are located, how they meander, and how to switch from anger and fear to heart-based communications that convey love and acceptance leads us to learn new skills that can resolve that particular conflict and all similar conflicts and conflict in general.

Thus, the heart is a teacher, illuminating what the parties most need to learn, know, do, or be. It is, as Franz Kafka described literature, "an axe to break the frozen sea within." It does so by opening the gates of subtle learning, pointing attention at the unities that underlie opposition. It provides experiences that expand awareness and reset priorities, expose the opponent within the self, and create existential dilemmas that invite people to learn from, transform, and transcend their conflicts.

These ends become possible when the parties decide to move beyond ignoring, denying, and merely settling their conflicts to becoming more aware of their subtle heart lessons and seeing that they can become wiser, more skillful, and freer to develop by learning to overcome the harsh, stupefying insensitivities that adversarial conflict encourages. They do so by heeding Shakespeare's sage advice, "Go to your bosom; knock there, and ask your heart what it doth know."

Yet most people are reluctant to open their hearts to their opponents in conflict, not merely because they are frightened and do not wish to become vulnerable in the presence of those they do not trust, but also because they are confused about what they really want, don't feel strong enough to face all the sadness and pain that have accumulated over the years, find it difficult to say what they really want or feel, are afraid others will reject or laugh at them, or are afraid they will lose their identity if they let go of their conflicts.

Nonetheless, when they do look deeply and clearly into their own hearts, they become more centered within themselves and less fearful of listening, looking into the hearts of others, and willing to take the risks required to resolve their conflicts. As novelist Leo Tolstoy wrote, in *Anna Karenina*:

> Levin had often noticed in arguments between the most intelligent people that after enormous efforts, an enormous number of logical subtleties and words, the arguers would finally come to the awareness that what they had spent so long struggling to prove to each other had been known to them long, long before, from the beginning of the argument, but that they loved different things and therefore did not want to name what they loved, so as not to be challenged. He had often felt that sometimes during an argument you would understand what your opponent loves, and suddenly come to love the same thing yourself, and agree all at once, and then all reasonings would fall away as superfluous; and sometimes it was

the other way round: you would finally say what you yourself love, for the sake of which you are inventing your reasonings, and if you happened to say it well and sincerely, the opponent would suddenly agree and stop arguing. That was the very thing he wanted to say.

Why Bring Heart into Conflict Resolution?

As this passage, common sense, and mediation experience reveal, heart and love can be immensely effective methods of resolving conflict. Yet speaking openly about heart, or proposing to use it as a source of technique in conflict resolution, is often met with derision and resistance. Part of this negative response derives from the assumption that any conversation regarding heart will dissolve into unclear thinking, new age sentiment, anti-intellectualism, and romantic delusion. Yet it is possible to think critically and access heart knowledge at the same time. At a deeper level, it is possible to think with the heart and allow understanding to be augmented by wisdom.

Another reason for resistance to mediating, communicating, or connecting with the heart is that doing so requires us, as mediators, to open our hearts and become more gentle, vulnerable, compassionate, truthful, and kind. This clashes with traditional, patriarchal, professional values of toughness, rationality, invulnerability, distance, safety, and emotional detachment, and suggests the possibility of unacceptable pain to those who have kept their hearts closed for years. Yet, for the following eight reasons, learning to mediate, communicate, and connect with the heart can make us more skillful in resolving even commonplace conflicts.

First, heart is a metaphor for love, which only affection as well as unconditional acceptance of others allows us to see what is good, even in those who behave badly. However, it is not only what we see, but how we see that matters, and how we see is a consequence of who we are, and how we think about ourselves. When we are preoccupied or depressed, even the most sincere apology can pass unnoticed, whereas when we are alert, focused, and happy, even the subtlest hint can seem obvious.

Second, heart encourages empathy, which allows us to recognize others within ourselves. Empathetic listening means wanting to understand who the other person is, discovering within ourselves the reasons we might do or say what they said or did, and turning these insights into questions to find out whether they are accurate. Empathy provides access to a kind of universal shared meaning through which it is possible to understand even the most hateful acts. This does not mean agreeing, condoning, or giving permission to act in hateful ways, but making certain that hatred does not cause us to lose our own humanity or capacity to listen. The true reason for loving our opponents is that, through them, we are able to discover what is opposed inside ourselves and see that self and other are one.

Third, heart signifies honesty. Honesty starts with honesty toward ourselves, which creates a base or platform on which it is easier to be honest with others. Only when we are honest with ourselves will others care what we think or be open to our insights. Being honest with ourselves means recognizing that we are no different from our opponents, except by accidental, adventitious circumstances. In this way, honesty and empathy merge and intertwine, allowing us to look deeper beneath the surface.

Fourth, heart invites intimacy. Intimacy requires vulnerability, which entails a willingness to explore the places where we can be most deeply hurt. We are reluctant to speak openly about our pain because doing so feels like we are providing our opponents with a roadmap and set of instructions on how to hurt us. Yet some degree of willingness to be unguarded, vulnerable, and suffer for others is indispensable to intimate, heart-based relationships.

Fifth, heart demands authenticity and integrity. When we do something that lacks authenticity or integrity, we become false, counterfeit, and unbalanced. When we collapse our identity into a role, or allow our self-worth to be crushed by someone's negative opinion of who we are, or pretend to be someone we are not, we become internally divided and incongruent. We are then less able to listen or give to others because we cannot listen or give to ourselves. An ancient piece of wisdom, attributed to Jesus in the Gnostic Gospel of Thomas, counsels: "If you bring forth what is within you, what you bring forth will save you. If you do not bring forth what is within you, what you do not bring forth will destroy you." Destructive conflict can therefore be understood simply as the inability of the parties to open their hearts and be authentic with each other.

Sixth, heart encourages compassion. While sympathy implies feeling sorry for others, compassion allows us to detect in other people's suffering a representation or mirror into our own. Compassion, as opposed to pity, is grounded in a deep sense of justice, fairness, and identification with the other. Aristotle defined compassion as the product of three sequential thoughts:

1. A serious bad thing has happened to someone.

2. What happened was not, or not entirely, their fault.

3. I am vulnerable to the same thing happening to me.

But Aristotle's definition does not go far enough, as it does not recognize the prior suffering of the one who feels compassion. Our heart memory of unfair treatment at the hands of others can be a powerful prompt to compassion, allowing us to see that the one we are most drawn to protect or support is always ourselves. Compassion is literally "suffering with," but can also be considered a gift of love and kindness to one who suffers, from one who has also suffered. Tibetan Buddhist Chogyam Trungpa offers us a broader definition:

> When a person develops compassion, he is uncertain whether he is being generous to others or to himself, because compassion is environmental generosity...We could say compassion is the ultimate attitude of wealth: an antipoverty attitude, a war on want.

In Tibetan Buddhism, there is an ancient meditation practice known as *tonglen* that is designed to increase compassion. In this exercise, we counterintuitively imagine breathing in all the pain and suffering of the world and breathing out all our own health and well-being for the benefit of others who are suffering. One object of this exercise is to end the fear of pain and suffering that results from grasping after health and well-being, both of which lead to increased suffering. But there is an additional benefit called *maitri*, which means unconditional friendship and compassion for ourselves based on a recognition that punishing, adversarial relationships with others may represent an externalization of punishing, adversarial attitudes toward ourselves.

Seventh, when we engage in heart-to-heart communication, we create a single heart that unites speaking and listening. Listening from the heart means listening without roles, positions, judgments, assumptions, biases, histories, expectations, or preconditions. It means opening ourselves to experiencing who the other person is. Being openhearted is deeply satisfying and it is more effective in the long run, even as an organizational principle, than closed-heartedness.

Eighth, heart means giving ourselves and entering wholly and completely into all of our actions and interactions. I sometimes ask people in conflict, "How much of *you* is present in your conversation right now?" They generally answer, "Not much." Yet the more they open their hearts, the more they become present and able to enjoy life and love those around them, including their opponents. Nobel Prize winning novelist Gabriel Garcia Marquez wrote beautifully about the importance of living an openhearted life, and what he would do if he ever actually woke up and realized he was not a rag doll, but gifted with life:

> I would value things, not for their worth but for what they mean... I would write my hate on ice, and wait for the sun to show...With my tears I would water roses, to feel the pain of their thorns, and the red kiss of their petals...I wouldn't let a single day pass without telling the people I love that I love them. I would convince each woman and each man that they are my favorites, and I would live in love with love...

Communicating with the heart consists of forging, through an alchemy that begins inside ourselves, an openhearted connection with others that is grounded in love, empathy, honesty, intimacy, authenticity, poignancy, and compassion. These moments of heart-based communication are both enjoyable and useful in conflict resolution, helping us clarify intentions, discover what really lies in people's hidden hearts, and find openings to transformation and transcendence that emanate only from the heart.

The Dimension of Transcendence

To clarify the distinction between heart-based techniques and other forms of conflict resolution, recall the discussion of physical dimensions in Chapter 2. Each added dimension transforms conflict by moving it in a direction orthogonal, or at a right angle, to the one it previously occupied, thereby increasing the parties' freedom of movement, deepening and amplifying their communications, expanding their collaboration, improving their skills, broadening their relationship, and allowing them to achieve deeper levels of resolution and closure.

Each new dimension allows them to respond to their conflict in the higher dimension it actually occupies. Yet each higher dimension is unimaginable to someone occupying a lower one. While a transformation can be achieved by interrupting pointless adversarial arguments through 90-degree angle questions that acknowledge underlying emotions or surface interests, transcendence means completing it by moving the conflict 180 degrees to forgiveness, then 360 degrees to disappearance and reconciliation.

Each new dimension moves people's conflict conversations in a radically new direction from the one where they began, drawing them closer to the hidden center of their conflict where its heart is located, inviting them to understand its deeper meaning, and releasing them from the constraints of lower-dimensional thinking. The path to transcendence is therefore invariably a path of the heart that begins for mediators by opening our hearts, and then—slowly, gently, yet inexorably—the hearts of others.

Two Ways, Three Acts, Five Stages, and Ten Steps

Virginia Woolf wrote, "The beauty of the world has two edges, one of laughter, one of anguish, cutting the heart asunder." It is possible to open people's hearts in conflict using either of these approaches: by creating a relaxed, enjoyable, collaborative environment in which conflict recedes into the background and laughter becomes possible; or by creating a poignant, sensitive, truthful environment in which conflict moves into the foreground and the parties become vulnerable enough to communicate their anguish and what they have suffered.

Mediating, communicating, or connecting with the heart in either of these ways can be broken down into three interrelated sequential acts.

1. Understanding that conflicts are organized and need to be resolved not only in bodies, minds, emotions, and spirits, but in hearts as well.

2. Being willing to risk opening our own hearts as mediators.

3. Learning how to ask heartfelt questions and support openhearted communications.

Before beginning, it is important to recognize that closed-heartedness is a choice that mediators need to respect. Conflict can cause suffering so deep and overwhelming that it leaves people unwilling to open their hearts to each other and creates open wounds that have to heal before they can be transcended. As we examine the stages, steps, methods, and techniques of heartfelt conflict communication, it is wise to be sensitive to the slightest signs of resistance and be ready to abandon our quest when the timing, circumstances, or attitudes are unfavorable.

In my experience, there are five distinct stages in mediating, communicating, and connecting with the heart, which are

1. opening our own hearts;

2. reaching out with questions that can open the hearts of others;

3. encouraging and expanding direct heart-to-heart communications;

4. connecting heart awareness to problem solving, collaboration, improved understanding, and creating more satisfying relationships; and

5. designing rituals of release, completion, and closure.

Each of these stages can lead to an unlimited number of practical steps, methods, techniques, and interventions. Among these, I find the following ten stages especially useful as a guide to opening or initiating heart-based conflict communications, which are explored more fully in the next chapter.

1. Center, relax, and balance yourself internally.

2. Release yourself from past recollections, emotions, and judgments.

3. Release yourself from future expectations, goals, plans, and desires.

4. Expand your present awareness of the energy flowing within, around, and between yourself and the parties.

5. Open your heart and use it to search for questions that might open other people's hearts.

6. Clarify and concentrate your energy, spirit, intention, heart, or chi, and expand your capacity for empathy and compassion with everyone.

7. Set the physical stage for intimate, heartfelt conversation.

8. Welcome everyone with an open heart.

9. Begin the conversation with a question, invocation, acknowledgement, apology, or invitation made directly to the hearts of those present.

10. Use silence, pacing, body language, tone of voice, poignant questions, vulnerability, and ritual to communicate your sincerity and heartfelt intention.

It is relatively easy to list these steps, but quite difficult to put them into practice consistently and skillfully in ways that reinforce their underlying purpose and encourage others to free themselves from lower-dimensional conversations and relationships. For mediators, the object is to open our own hearts, use them as sources of information about what might be taking place in the hearts of others, communicate what we discover, and inspire others to do the same. Here are the ten steps again in greater detail.

The first step is to center, relax, and balance yourself internally by focusing your attention inward, rather than outward toward the parties, the conflict, or the world around you. Centering means focusing attention on your core self at its deepest level, beneath ego and the conscious self. This can be done in several ways, including sitting quietly in meditation, sensing and selectively relaxing different parts of your body, concentrating on your breath, repeating a mantra, or simply resting in the center of your self, expanding your awareness, and letting go. Heart-based awareness can help you disentangle complex, chaotic, intermingled emotions and follow your mediation responses moment by moment with precision and equanimity.

The second step is to release yourself from past recollections, emotions, and judgments, particularly if you had a negative experience or interaction with one party, or are feeling frustrated or hostile. The object is not to ignore who the parties are or forget what happened, but to free yourself to respond flexibly in the present and allow yourself to create a different future without being burdened by what already happened, or what you assume to be true.

It is especially important to release yourself from judgments about yourself, as well as the parties, the issues, and what the outcome of your conversation ought to be. Judgments are the end of inquiry. They are answers to rhetorical questions, self-fulfilling prophecies, obstacles to curiosity, and constraints on our ability to find complex, creative, heartfelt answers. They are rationalizations for cynicism, apathy, and distrust; excuses for being unwilling to risk honesty and empathy; and refusals to take responsibility for imagining and implementing collaborative solutions. They are introductions to biases and stereotypes that distort complex circumstances by reducing them to simplistic explanations.

The third step is to release yourself from all future expectations, goals, plans, hopes, and desires, so as to be fully present. Conflict is inherently chaotic, and neither its outcomes nor its processes can be accurately predicted or calculated in advance. Worse, your deepest expectations, finest goals, best-laid plans, and most fervent desires can divert you from discovering a conflict's inner logic, or discerning its natural course of direction, and reduce your ability to listen.

Expectations and anticipations of what will occur in the future, at a subtle level, detract attention from what is happening in the present and define a world different from the one the parties are trying to describe. They are obstacles to empathy and committed listening, rose-colored glasses that filter out what you do not want to see or hear, and barriers to compassion and acceptance. They are mind centered, as opposed to heart centered, and ultimately less interesting or useful in resolving conflict than discovering and appreciating the diversity of what actually exists.

The fourth step is to expand your present awareness of the energy flowing within, around, and between yourself and the parties. This will allow you to follow each delicate twist and turn in their conversation without losing sight of its overall direction, correct miscommunications midstream, move them in a heart-centered direction, and track the flow and quality of energy between you and each of them.

Being present can be achieved by noticing subtle, minute changes in mood, moving your body or chair closer to the parties, subtly mirroring their posture, or slowing down the momentum of experience until it comes to a complete stop. For example, to make sense of any sentence, including this one, it is necessary to focus your attention on the past in order to recall how it began, and on the future in order to anticipate where it is heading. Yet it is also possible to stop a sentence midstream by...pausing...slowing down... a n d . . . c o m i n g . . . t o . . . a . . . c o m p l e t e . . . h a l t ! As you do, past and future will cease to dominate, and everyone's full attention will move into the present.

The fifth step is to open your heart, sense what is taking place at its center and, from your own heart space, search for questions that might open the hearts of others. You might imagine your heart expanding or swinging open like a saloon door, or form a mental picture of some person or animal you deeply love, focus your attention on the feeling of loving, and hold that image and feeling memory throughout the conversation. The only way to locate powerful, heartfelt questions is to feel for them with your own open heart.

The sixth step is to clarify and concentrate your energy, spirit, intention, or chi and increase your capacity for empathy and compassion with everyone in the mediation. This can be done by sensing, summoning, and focusing or circling your energy; renewing your intention and commitment to doing the best you can; taking deep breaths; stretching; doing chi gong or yoga; and making sure the energy inside you is not blocked, but flowing freely and available for use throughout the conversation. Once your energy is concentrated, use it to imagine and "touch" each party vividly, lovingly, and compassionately. Then consider what might have led you to act as they did, and what questions they might like to be asked in mediation. If spirit is life energy or chi, heart is what happens when they touch or become one.

The seventh step is to set the stage for an intimate, heartfelt conversation. This can be done by arranging your physical environment aesthetically to put others at their ease, serving refreshments, and creating an ambiance of amiability, openness, and hospitality. In all but the most risky cases, this means moving tables out of the way so people can see each other fully, facing or triangulating their chairs, or placing them in a circle so you can speak directly to each other. It may mean intermittently adjusting the distance between them and you so you are not so far apart as to make heartfelt connection difficult, nor so close together as to make anyone feel frightened or angry or that their boundaries have been violated.

The eighth step is to welcome the parties with an open heart, greeting them personally, and taking just a split second longer than normal to create eye contact and shake hands to impart a lingering feeling of respect and positive regard. No matter how hostile their attitude or adversarial their prior conversations, higher dimensional solutions can be discovered by opening their conversations in an authentic heart-centered direction, which begins at the first moment of contact.

The ninth step is to set a heartfelt context and begin the conversation with a question, invocation, acknowledgement, apology, or invitation made directly to the hearts of those who are present. In indigenous, aboriginal, Native American, and First Nation mediations, it is common for elders or community leaders to greet disputing parties and offer prayers for successful resolution, pass a peace pipe, sit in silent meditation, or express their wishes for the process. Even the most commonplace conflict conversations can be deepened by a heartfelt request that people communicate what they care deeply about, a reminder of what they have in common, or an acknowledgement of the courage and commitment it took to agree to come together and discuss their common problems.

You may decide to ask questions, such as: "What do you hope to get out of this conversation?" "What is at stake in this discussion for you?" "What is one wish you have for this meeting?" "What is one thing you think I might do to improve your conversation?" "What would you like me to know or understand about you?" You can even conduct a formal invocation, blessing, or supplication, if it is culturally appropriate. The deeper these opening statements go, the more important it is to be cautious and proceed respectfully, or by consensus. For example, instead of unilaterally identifying ground rules, you might ask, "Do you have any suggestions for how we should talk together?" "Are there any requests you would like to make of me or of each other before we begin?" "Are there are any promises you would like to make in response to these requests?" "Is there anything you would like to say to clear the air?" Even, "Is there anything for which you would like to apologize?" Or, "Here is something I would like to apologize to you for."

The tenth step is to use silence, pacing, body language, tone of voice, poignant questions, vulnerability, and ritual to communicate your sincerity and heartfelt intention. You can, for example, use a rhythmic, calming, liturgical recitation of ground rules to lull them into relaxation, or design ritual openings and closings that allow them to open their hearts, or obtain release and closure. You can even ask, "Are you willing to speak to each other from your heart?" "Why not?" and "What would need to happen, or what would s/he need to do, for that to happen?" Even a refusal to answer these questions can move the conversation in a heartfelt direction.

While these steps may seem insignificant, they can initiate enormous shifts if used at the right time with the right people. They are not magic wands, and will not work always, everywhere, or with everyone. Instead, they are a kind of medication, a balm for soothing the wounds of conflict, a way of letting go of all the well-founded reasons for engaging in active hostilities, and an invitation to others to enter into deeper, more authentic communications and relationships.

Once you have opened your heart in these ways, you can proceed with the steps outlined in the next chapter. The choice of which techniques or interventions to use should always be respectful, strategic, appropriate, intuitive, and grounded in cultural and emotional sensitivity. It is better to ask too little at the beginning and intensify the level of intervention later than to ask too much in the beginning and fail.

Every conflict presents the parties and the mediator with a recurrent choice. They can cling to safe territory, keep the conversation focused on relatively superficial issues and avoid mentioning deeper topics, remaining locked in impasse and placing their lives on hold. Or they can take a risk, adopt a more open, honest, empathic approach, and initiate a deeper, more dangerous, heartfelt conversation that could change their lives and result in transformation and transcendence. Which path they take will depend partly on their willingness to engage each other in heartfelt communications, as reflected in the following case study.

Laboring Over Values—A Case Study

I was asked to mediate a labor management dispute for a corporation with about 150 employees, in which nearly a dozen representatives of labor and management had become active participants in a broad, free-ranging, rapidly escalating battle, provoking negative behaviors on both sides. The acrimonious rhetoric and adversarial behaviors escalated and everyone's egos were engaged.

I began by interviewing the leadership teams on both sides of the dispute along with several employees who were not involved. I asked them to identify the behaviors that were undermining their relationship. I then met with all 150 employees and read back to them a list of the behaviors they said they had engaged in during the conflict, including stabbing each other in the back, insulting each other in front of customers, disrespecting each other, making racially and sexually derogatory comments, and telling offensive jokes about each other.

After reading the list, I asked them to raise their hands if they thought any of this represented professional behavior, if they enjoyed engaging in them, and if they wanted them to continue. No hands went up. I then asked them to raise their hands if they wanted these behaviors to stop. Every hand went up. I asked them why they wanted the behaviors to stop, and a rich, energetic discussion followed.

I proposed a plan for eliminating these behaviors and rapidly reached consensus. I divided the group into teams of eight to ten by numbering off so there would be diversity in each group and cliques would be broken up. Each team selected a facilitator and a recorder, discussed the reasons for improving their conflict behaviors, and reached consensus on a set of shared values they wanted to live by. Volunteers from each team combined and consolidated these values into a single list, which was sent back to the teams for fine-tuning, resulting in the following statement of shared values that was unanimously adopted:

We pledge, in our speech and actions, to uphold the following standards, and invite others to remind us of them when we forget so they will become part of our everyday behavior:

1. To put the interests of customers and employees first, and work to make our organization a true learning organization.

2. To respect differences and diversity in race, gender, and culture, and in opinion and personality as well.

3. To listen actively and respectfully to what others are saying, without yelling, blaming, intimidating or gossiping about those we disagree with.

4. To communicate directly, openly and honestly, and tell the truth.

5. To take initiative and encourage teamwork, inclusion, participation, consensus and risk taking.

6. To talk directly to the people with whom we are having problems, focus on issues and interests rather than positions and personalities, and acknowledge work well done.

7. To take responsibility for our speech and actions, to follow the rules, and to be accountable for our behavior.

8. To model the behavior we expect from others and take pride in our work.

After celebrating their accomplishment, I said the list was terrific and would look wonderful decorating a wall in their office, but could easily be forgotten and never implemented. I asked them if they wanted this to happen, or if they wanted to live according to their values. Again, they were unanimous that they did. I asked what they needed to do next to reach that goal, and they said they had to discuss their non-value-based behaviors and agree to stop engaging in them.

I asked them to return to their teams and list the specific behaviors that either supported or undermined their values. They developed with a long list that was rich in detail, especially in the undermining behaviors, which included personal attacks; sabotaging of decisions, rules ,and people; blaming; finger pointing; making excuses; stereotyping; being two-faced; forming cliques; ganging up; favoritism; and whining. They rapidly reached consensus on the behaviors they wanted to encourage and discourage.

I then asked them to raise their hands if they had actually experienced any of the undermining behaviors they just identified while working in their teams. No hands went up. I asked them, "How is it possible, given this long list of negative behaviors, that none of you experienced any of them just now?" One person said, "Because we had a clear goal we were all trying to achieve." I said, "Terrific, so when you have clear common goals you don't engage in undermining behaviors." The group then listed several other processes that discourage undermining behaviors, including working in small teams, having facilitators and recorders, rotating these functions, brainstorming, encouraging participation, and making decisions by consensus, all of which they agreed to adopt in the future.

After celebrating their achievement, I said their list was superb and would look equally attractive posted on a wall next to their shared values. But if they wanted to really stop their undermining behaviors they would need to take additional steps, including deciding what they were going to do if one of them engaged in behaviors that undermined their values. I asked them how they wanted to respond when that occurred. One employee declared passionately that, if that happened, they should all confront the offender, even if it involved public humiliation.

At that point, the head of the employee union, who was one of the people who had engaged in the undermining behaviors, raised his hand and said that while he believed in the shared values and agreed that people should change their behaviors, starting with himself, he did not think they should turn themselves into "values police" or become self-appointed values enforcers.

I asked if other people wanted to speak on this issue and the room exploded. A sea of hands shot up, mostly from people who had never spoken before at a staff meeting. Most of the speakers said they believed in the values and did not want to give anyone permission to violate them or treat them as though they were meaningless. After a great deal of back and forth discussion, someone proposed that letting someone know they were acting inconsistently with their values should be done in ways that were consistent with their values. Ideas on how to do this were brainstormed from the floor and adopted by consensus. They included speaking to the person privately, asking for permission to offer feedback about what they had done, speaking humbly and respectfully, identifying specific behaviors, listening to their explanation, offering support in changing their behaviors, and requesting feedback afterward on whether the feedback had been consistent with their shared values.

The group also decided to form volunteer values teams, which would prepare brief presentations on each of the shared values for monthly staff meetings and facilitate an open discussion about what was involved in each value, how well they had done in meeting it, and what they might do in the future to improve their behaviors. Many people volunteered to serve on these teams. In ending, I asked each person to say one thing they would personally do in the future to support the values. Everyone spoke from their hearts and the meeting ended on an optimistic, enthusiastic note.

Several months later I checked with the labor-management leadership team and was told that nearly all of the ego-based behaviors they had engaged in before the session had stopped and, while there had been occasional slips, these were isolated events that had not undermined their relationship. As a result, they had been able to work more collaboratively and discuss their differences, which had increased their level of trust, honesty, and collaboration, resulting in improved customer service and increased financial success.

Part of the reason for this positive outcome lay in the ameliorative effect produced simply by focusing their awareness on their values rather than on each other. But part also lay in the process used to create them, which drew people out of the confining circle of ego-based, manipulative, negative self-esteem, low integrity, conflict-escalating behaviors, and promoted authenticity, involvement, and collaborative relationships with each other through an intense, positive, self-esteem-promoting, integrity-based dialogue and consensus-building process that proceeded step by step based on informal negotiated agreements.

A key moment in the process occurred when the group considered what it would do when someone engaged in behaviors that undermined their values. Rather than allow anyone to walk away dissatisfied or use manipulation to achieve its ends, the group was able to use dialogue to work through these difficult issues, allowing everyone to feel included, and in the process discovering far better solutions that synthesized the group's divergent interests.

Everyone was so tired of their negative behaviors they were willing to drop their ego-oriented, overcompensating, manipulative behaviors, and engage in I-oriented, collaborative, value-based conversations. This experience lifted their morale, supported their development of positive self-esteem based on integrity, participation, and collective responsibility for results. It reinforced I/thou relationships, and strengthened their ability to work collaboratively. In the end, they realized that the negative behaviors they had engaged in when they were in conflict encouraged behaviors they no longer wanted to experience, and that they had the power, by acting together, to make them disappear.

Chapter 10 Ten Paths to Transcendence

Keep your intelligence white-hot
and your grief glistening,
so your life will stay fresh.
Cry easily like a little child.
Do not seek any rules for worship.
Say whatever your pained heart chooses.
–Jelaluddin Rumi

Resolution can be understood as altering the *content* or substance of conflict, transformation as altering its *contour* or form, and transcendence as altering its *context* or meaning, thereby reducing its overall energy and attractiveness and disabling its underlying causes and cohesiveness. Transcendence occurs when people gain insight into the attitudes, intentions, and perceptions that sustained their conflict, improve their ability to learn from it, work collaboratively to prevent its reoccurrence, and evolve to higher levels of conflict and resolution. Transcendence implies rising above, no longer participating in, overcoming, moving beyond, evolving, growing, leaving behind, and letting go. In conflict, it means releasing ourselves from negative, closed-hearted, antagonistic, withholding, impasse-generating attitudes toward our opponents and ourselves and, as Rumi suggests, crying easily and saying whatever our pained hearts chose.

To achieve transcendence, it is necessary for us to work through the deeper issues in our conflicts and learn the lessons that lie concealed in each of the places they are located. If conflict is present in our bodies, minds, emotions, spirits, hearts, and systems, is it not apparent that the deeper lessons they contain must also be located in these areas, and that each must be identified, resolved, transformed, and transcended in its own unique ways? If our conflict is primarily based on intellectual differences, rational dialogue will likely cure it. But if it is emotional or heart-based, no amount of intellectualizing will succeed in resolving it, let alone transforming or transcending it.

The Dangers in Heartfelt Communications

Because transcendence implies fundamental change, any communication that makes transcendence possible leads into dangerous, uncharted territory. In these exchanges, traditional analytical conflict resolution techniques are of little use, and may even cause emotions to escalate and resistance to harden. Whenever we resort to emotional or heartfelt communications to resolve our conflicts, it is a clear indication that deep-seated issues are at stake.

Every openhearted conflict communication is dangerous, partly because no one ever gives unambiguous permission to fully resolve their conflicts, partly because permission to stop a fight or settle a dispute does not translate into permission to resolve the underlying reasons that gave rise to it or reach forgiveness and reconciliation, partly because every transformation or transcendence represents a breakthrough that could not have been imagined or consented to at the time permission was given, and partly because every genuine breakthrough dramatically transforms people's lives, changing even what is considered acceptable.

Of the many dangers for mediators in initiating open, honest, heartfelt communications between people in conflict, most fall roughly into two categories: those that are readily apparent and could result from any effort to resolve conflict, and those that are more subtle and stem from efforts to create deeper, subtler, more profound understandings. The readily apparent dangers include

- the danger that we could escalate the conflict further;

- the danger that there could be physical violence;

- the danger that we could be subjected to other people's intense emotions;

- the danger that we could have to revisit our own emotionally painful experiences;

- the danger that we could do or say things we do not mean, or become someone we do not like; and

- the danger that we could increase resistance and make resolution less likely.

The deeper, subtler, and more profound dangers include

- the danger that we could discover we are wrong and feel compelled to change our minds and behaviors as a result;

- the danger that we could never resolve the underlying issues for our conflict and be condemned to repeat it;

- the danger that we could continue lying to ourselves about what we have done;

- the danger that we could not tell the truth to someone whose life might change as a result;

- the danger that we could be required to change our own lives and suffer consequences we are not prepared to accept;

- the danger that nothing will ever change;

- the danger of not ever finding out who the other person is;

- the danger of not ever waking up to who we really are;

- the danger that we could have to forgive our enemies or, worse, ourselves; and

- the danger that the conflict will cease, and we will stop growing because there is no more danger and no one asking us to improve.

Openhearted communications are especially dangerous in these latter ways, each of which defines a moment when playing it safe becomes more dangerous than taking risks. When we take risks in conflict, we wake up, face our fears, pay attention to details, drop our egos, become more humble, operate out of the center of who we are, connect more authentically with others, and think creatively. Yet in doing so we transform our conflicts and no longer face the same kind of danger. [For more on this subject, see *Mediating Dangerously: The Frontiers of Conflict Resolution*, Jossey Bass / Wiley Publishers, 2001.]

To encourage dangerous, transcendent, heartfelt conflict communications, we need to navigate a middle passage and simultaneously avoid the twin traps of well-intentioned, hypersensitive, mindlessly sentimental, pop-psychological, superficial, endless emotional processing, and manipulative, insensitive, hardheaded, dispassionate, emotionally disconnected legal or logical analysis. Communicating with the heart is highly intuitive, holistic, sensuous, and circular, and cannot be accessed using techniques or attitudes that are excessively emotional, chaotic, abstract, and sentimental, or exclusively rational, reductive, linear, and insensitive. To avoid these pitfalls, we need to be clear about what we want to communicate, when, how, to whom, and most importantly, why we want to communicate it.

The goal of heart-to-heart communication in conflict resolution is to encourage profound, poignant, authentic, intimate connections that dissipate conflict at its deepest location inside each person—in their heart. Heart-based communications in mediation are less about professing love for others than about recognizing their pain, releasing them from false expectations, and helping them transcend what got them into conflict in the first place. For this reason, the deepest dangers in heartfelt conflict communications lie not in what people say outwardly to their opponents, but what they realize inwardly about themselves.

Transcendence is fundamentally beyond methods, steps, and techniques, since, at its deepest level, *we are* the method, step, and technique. This means that it is possible for us to have every technique down pat, yet if our heart is not in it, the parties will know and remain distant. On the other hand, we can screw up every technique imaginable, but if we communicate with an open heart, the parties will understand and move toward us.

Clues People Drop to Request Heartfelt Conversations

How, then, is it possible for mediators to know which technique to use? Beyond the obvious answer that it is a matter of trial and error, a more profound answer is that the parties will tell us, albeit indirectly, by the clues they leave hidden in their conflict communications, hoping we will detect them. I start by using empathy to locate the internal leverage points within myself where transcendence might begin. These can be identified in every conflict. They can be found, for example, underneath the soft spots in equivocal statements, in the power words that communicate intense emotions, in pointless exaggerations, wounded accusations, energetic denials, and overly defensive attitudes, all of which, if heard correctly, are invitations into deeper, more heartfelt, profound conversations.

For example, the clues that signal someone's desire for a spiritual or heart-based conversation or deeper order of resolution might initially take the form of a seemingly trivial statement that begs to be contradicted. Here are four examples of such statements, followed by my translation, and some initial questions I might use to begin deepening their conversation.

1. *Declaration:*   "He doesn't think I'm a very good person."

   Translation: "I don't think I am a very good person, am vulnerable to what he thinks of me, and am exaggerating what he thinks because I need some reassurance that he doesn't hate me."

   Possible Questions: [To the other person] "Is that right? Do you think she is not a very good person?" [To her] "Why does it matter to you what he thinks?"

2. *Declaration:*   "She did it for no reason."

   Translation: "I really don't know why she did it, but I am afraid to ask because she could have done it because of something I did that I don't want to admit, or for some reason that will force me to stop playing the victim."

   Possible Questions: "Would you like to know why she did it? Why don't you ask her?"

3. *Declaration:*   "He's lying."

   Translation: "What he said does not match my experience, I feel defensive about what he said, and I need him to listen to my experience before I can listen to his."

Possible Questions:	"What truth do you see that is not reflected in his statement?"
	"What do you think is the underlying truth he is trying to communicate to you?"
D. *Declaration*:	"I don't trust her."
Translation:	"I am feeling insecure about what is going to happen, distrustful about her intentions regarding me, and need to hear that she is committed to making this relationship work."
Possible Questions:	"What are you afraid she will do?"
	[To the other person] "Is that what you intend to do? Why not?
	Do you want this relationship to work? Why?"

I have used relatively trivial examples in order to demonstrate that nearly every conflict conversation disguises a hidden, heartfelt concern that mediators can identify, interpret, and turn into questions that invite people into openhearted communications with their opponents, even when they intensely dislike or distrust them. Before asking these questions, it is best to secure permission through empathy, identify the right moment, engage in committed listening, adopt a heartfelt tone of voice, and communicate an accepting intention and attitude that can encourage the parties to do the same with each other. If they can't, or change the subject, or find the question objectionable, apologize and retreat into safer conversation until a better groundwork can be laid.

How to Initiate Heartfelt Conversations

If the parties signal that they are willing to move into deeper, heartfelt conversation, you can ask follow-up questions that invite them, for example, to speak directly to each other from their hearts. Here are some potentially dangerous transformational questions you can use to open such conversations, even with angry, recalcitrant, embittered people.

- Before we begin, can you tell me a little about yourselves?

- What do you hope will happen as a result of this conversation? Why is that important to you?

- Why are you here? Why do you care? What did it take for you to be willing to come here today?

- What kind of relationship would you like to have with each other? Why?

- What is one thing you like or respect about each other? Can you give an example? Another? How does it feel to hear each other say these things? What do you think would happen if you said them more often?

- Is there anything you have in common? Any values you share?

- What life experiences have you had that led you to feel so strongly about this issue?

- What role have you played in this conflict, through action or inaction?

- If you had 20/20 hindsight, what would you do differently?

- Is there anything you would like to apologize for?

- On a scale of 1 to 10, how would each of you rank that apology? What could you do to make it a 10? Are you willing to try right now?

- What is one thing you would like him to acknowledge you for? What is one thing you are willing to acknowledge him for?

- What do you think she was trying to say in that apology/acknowledgment? [To her] Is that accurate? [If not] Would you like to know what is accurate for her? Why don't you ask her?

- How would you evaluate the effectiveness of what you just said in reaching her? How could you make it more effective? Would you like some feedback? Why don't you ask her?

- Is this conversation working? Would you like it to work? *Why* would you like it to work? What is one thing she can do that would make it to work for you? [To her] Are you willing to do that? Would you be willing to start the conversation over and do those things now?

- What is the crossroads you are at right now in your conflict? Where does each road lead?

- Will you *ever* convince him you are right? [If not] When will you stop trying?

- What would you most like to hear her say to you right now?

- What would you have liked him to have said instead?

- What does that mean to you? What other meanings might it have? What do you think it means to her? Would you like to find out? Why don't you ask her?

- Can you imagine what happened to him happening to you? What would it feel like? Would you like to know what it felt like to him? Why don't you ask?

- Would you be willing to take a moment of silence right now to think about that?

- Has anything like this happened to you before? With whom? When?

- What are you *not* talking about that you still need to discuss?

- What issues are you holding onto that the other person still doesn't know about?

- What price have you paid for this conflict? What has it cost you? How much longer are you going to continue paying that price?

- What would it take for you to give this conflict up, let go of what happened, and move on with your life?

- Do you really want this conflict in your life? What would it take to let it go?

- What would change in your life if you reached an agreement?

- If this were the last conversation you were going to have with each other, what would you want to say?

Asking these questions as though they were a prepared script will reduce their power and make the mediator appear less authentic. It is better to design them from scratch based on the clues the parties have concealed in their statements. And remember: none will work always, everywhere, or with everyone.

Seriously Dangerous Questions

In addition to these questions, there are others that are deeper, profoundly personal, and even more dangerous, yet can produce extraordinary insights by drawing people's awareness inward to the secret source of the conflict within themselves. Several of these were contributed by consultant Peter Block, and should be used primarily in caucusing, coaching, or homework.

- What have you done to create the very thing you are most troubled by?

- What have you been clinging to or holding onto that it is now time for you to release?

- What are you responsible for in your conflict that you have not yet acknowledged to the other person?

- What do you most want to hear the other person say to you that you still haven't mentioned?

- What do you long for in your relationship with the other person?

- What is the refusal, or "no," that you have not yet communicated?

- What is the permission, or "yes," you gave in the past that you now want to retract?

- What is the resentment you are still holding onto that the other person doesn't know about?

- What is the promise you gave that you are now betraying?

- What is it they or you did that you are still unwilling to forgive?

- What price are you willing to pay for your refusal to forgive? How long are you prepared to continue paying that price?

- What promise are you willing to make to the other person with no acknowledgement or expectation of return?

- What gift could you give the other person that you continue to withhold? Why?

- What are you prepared to do unconditionally, without any expectation of recognition or reciprocity by the other person?

These are only a few of the hundreds, perhaps thousands, of questions mediators can use to encourage people to deepen their conflict conversations and listen or speak from their hearts. The wording is less important than the questioner's sincerity, desire for real connection, authenticity, honest introspection, and acceptance, communicated primarily by body language, tone of voice, intention, and attitude. Therefore, if it feels uncomfortable or inappropriate to ask them or you encounter resistance, it is better to proceed cautiously or not ask them at all.

Considered together, the questions listed in the last several pages illustrate how mediators can draw attention to the remote, poignant, and profound heartfelt locations where conflicts are principally organized. Doing so allows us to work more subtly, intricately, and successfully, and to invent a richer set of conversations that invite dialogue, nourish dissent, honor differences, and celebrate diversity. The best questions cherish paradox, polarity, and enigma; encourage intellectual and emotional vulnerability; support integrity and commitment; touch people's spirits; release them from continued animosity; inspire wisdom and heart knowledge; and suggest ways of designing systems to prevent future disputes.

Heart and Poignancy

Heart is simply a way of describing whatever is poignant, profound, and touching and moves us deeply. It is, in Thomas Merton's phrase, our "hidden wholeness," our capacity for instinctively recognizing what is true in ourselves and others, the source of our wisdom, insight, and inner peace. It is a way of letting go, a way of no longer holding in, back, or onto our conflicts. It is what we most earnestly want to feel within and between us.

Heartfelt communications have the unique ability to neutralize and overcome the accusations, defenses, trivialities, and smokescreens that fill ordinary conflict speech, allowing people to speak directly to the hearts of those they have hurt or who have hurt them. They allow us to redraw the boundary that separates adversaries, making it smaller, closer, and more porous; and to enlarge the concerns that separate them, reframing their caring as inclusive.

Ludwig Wittgenstein famously wrote, "What we cannot speak about we must pass over in silence." While there are clearly questions that cannot be answered in principle, such as what happens after death, there are others that cannot be answered with words, but only by what speaks to us at a heart level, by what inspires us, soothes our pain, or brings us joy.

There is also a saying that being in conflict is like taking poison and waiting for the other person to die. When we center ourselves in what is heartfelt, poignant, and profound, we connect with others at the same level. As a result, we can perceive, through the noisome cacophony of conflict communications, what our opponents' hearts are actually saying and refuse to become their enemy. To do so, and to resolve conflicts at a heart level, we need to learn how to initiate and sustain heartfelt, poignant, profound conversations. In general, mediators can do so by

- searching for alternatives to the platitudes that normally fill conflict conversations;

- asking questions that reveal what is deeply desired, even if it is initially opposed;

- listening closely to mood, cadence, rhythm, and silences, and metaphors in conflict stories;

- ignoring the scripts others have written to keep conversations safe, and moving them off-track into unfamiliar territory;

- taking risks, surfacing what is hidden, and speaking the unspeakable by saying what others are afraid or unwilling to say;

- asking questions that require insight or reflection, such as "What did you learn from that experience?" or "Why is that important to you?";

- interrupting circular conversations with questions that spiral dialogue inward toward the center of the problem;

- asking people to identify the issues they really need to talk about, and what we could do to make their conversation more useful and satisfying;

- asking questions like "What are we *not* talking about that we still need to discuss?" or "Why are we avoiding that conversation?"; and

- speaking directly to people's hearts.

Heartfelt conversations cut through ordinary speech to reveal a commonality of caring that lies directly beneath the surface of hostile communications. We can access that caring by asking poignant, touching, profound questions, focusing attention on satisfying our opponent's deepest concerns, and asking risky, dangerous questions. The choice to open our hearts in conflict should not be decided by who our opponents are or what they did, but by who we are and how we want to live. When we act congruently with our values and become unconditionally openhearted, we no longer experience the same order of conflicts and are able to transcend them.

Ten Paths to Transcendence

Transcendence cannot be encompassed in ten, twenty, or one hundred paths. Nevertheless, I have tried to make the following methods as brief, easy, practical, and effective as possible, though many prove complex and difficult in practice. They are presented sequentially to encourage a sense of discernment and inquiry about how they occur, while in practice they often resist ordering. Here, then, are ten paths to transcendence for mediators, each of which will afterward be explained in detail.

1. Engage in committed, openhearted listening, as though your life depends on what you are about to hear.

2. Use a spotlight of narrow, focused attention and a floodlight of broad, sweeping awareness to clarify what is taking place beneath the surface.

3. Use dangerous empathy to search for the center of the conflict within yourself, then ask questions to discover whether the same might be true for others.

4. Use dangerous honesty to communicate your deepest understanding to others.

5. Use your heart to locate a heart space in the conversation, then open and expand it.

6. Craft a question that asks people to speak and listen directly from their hearts.

7. Work collaboratively to redesign and reform the cultures and systems that produced or reinforced the conflict.

8. Clarify and reinforce what was learned from the conflict, and use it to improve and evolve to higher levels of conflict and resolution.

9. Move the conversation toward forgiveness and reconciliation.

10. Design and execute a ritual of release, completion, and closure.

It is important to recognize three critical limitations before reviewing these paths. First, as in quantum mechanics, it is impossible to pin heart-based communications down precisely, and at a certain level of exactness, additional efforts to do so will only make them more jittery and uncertain. Second, it is possible to follow each path faithfully, yet fail because we did not go deep enough into our own hearts, or harbored personal judgments, or sent mixed messages. Third, other people's decisions to participate in heartfelt conversation do not belong to us, and they may not be ready to follow any of the paths we open. Our role is to create an alternative path, then let them choose whether to follow it.

1. Engage in Committed, Openhearted Listening

Committed listening originates in the heart, and is oriented toward meaning. This is fundamentally different from routine listening or hearing, which originates in the mind and is oriented toward facts. Most listening in conflict is adversarial, as when we listen for holes or openings in people's arguments, or for what is wrong with them and what they are saying, rather than collaborative, as when we listen for what is right with them and what they mean to say. Listening is a matter of intention, and can be done in a variety of ways.

- *Contextual listening,* as when we listen for background information, unspoken assumptions, and unmet expectations.

- *Active listening,* as when we actively participate in discovering what others are trying to tell us and communicate our interest in their remarks.

- *Responsive listening,* as when we engage in conversations or dialogues that flow back and forth between us.

- *Creative listening,* as when we search for innovative solutions or try to come up with novel approaches to solving a problem.

- *Empathic listening,* as when we listen as though we are the one who is speaking.

- *Undivided listening,* as when we are no longer aware of our presence as a listener, but completely merge with the speaker and their story.

- *Committed listening,* as when we listen as though our lives depend on understanding what others are saying.

- *Listening with the heart,* as when we listen with an open heart to the heart of the one who is speaking.

As people tell stories about their conflicts and describe what happened to them, listening in these ways can help us locate the heart of their story and transform. Mediator Ken Dvoren wrote the following description of what listening with the heart means to him:

> When I'm conversing with someone, I find myself wanting to be listened *to* more than I want to listen. The person I'm talking with appears to want the same thing, and so a subtle competition ensues. When I decide to listen to the other with interest and empathy, I move beyond myself and notice that rather than feeling neglected or diminished, I'm actually expanded. My identity, who I sense myself to be, now includes them, so that as I give to them, I am also receiving.

> When I'm in conflict with someone, the stakes are even higher. I not only want to be heard but also to be agreed with and to be *right*. And it's even harder to listen to the other, because if I do I might understand them, and if I understand them I might agree with them, and if I agree with them I might think I have to give them what they want, and if I do then I won't get what I want. But if I take what feels to be the very real risk of truly listening, the same remarkable event occurs. As my identity expands to include them, I start to appreciate their values and interests, and when I consider meeting their needs, I realize I will also be meeting my own. And I have finally met my brother.

2. Use Narrow, Focused Attention and Broad, Sweeping Awareness

A second path consists of using a narrow spotlight of pinpointed, focused attention, and a broad floodlight of sweeping, unfocused awareness to clarify what is taking place beneath the surface of conflict. Awareness can be divided into two parts: pointed, laser-like concentration on a narrow, critical area; and expansive, generalized awareness of a wide-ranging undivided whole. Both are useful, especially in combination. For example, imagine crossing a busy two-way pothole-filled street with a full glass of water without spilling a drop. The only way to succeed is by merging these two forms of awareness, focusing simultaneously on each car and pothole, and on the task as a whole. This may sound simple, but even a small loss of attention can make it impossible. The most important source of lost attention in conflict is ego, along with its ablest enforcers: anger, fear, shame, guilt, and pride.

When we feel ashamed or proud of what we did in the past, or angry or frightened about what will happen in the future, we withdraw energy and attention from what is happening in the present and lose concentration. To communicate with the heart, we need to cultivate curiosity, attentiveness, agility, and acceptance in the present. The poet e. e. cummings stated this idea more eloquently as a wish: "May your mind walk around hungry and fearless and thirsty and supple."

3. Use Dangerous Empathy

Using dangerous empathy means searching for the heart of the conflict within ourselves by vividly imagining what it might have been like for others. This means understanding what could cause us to feel or act the way they did. The information gained through empathy will not provide an answer, but will sometimes provide a question that can take them into the heart of their conflict.

Recent research has revealed that mirror neurons are partly responsible for triggering empathy in primates and people. Thus, when we observe someone eat, throw a baseball, smile, or experience pain, the neurons responsible for coordinating these actions inside us fire involuntarily, stimulating an empathetic response. Functional MRI studies have shown that, while most subjects easily extend empathy to people who are in pain, some (mostly men) take pleasure in watching a mild electric shock be administered as punishment to those they observed cheating.

While ordinary empathy is easily extended to people we regard as similar to ourselves, dangerous empathy stretches our identity to include people whose behaviors we find incomprehensible, burdensome, or abhorrent. For mediators, this means dropping our pretense of objectivity, neutrality, expertise, and professional truth, admitting our humanity (including distasteful qualities within ourselves), and endeavoring to become omni-partial and on both people's sides at the same time, no matter how difficult this may seem.

At a heart level, there is no such thing as objectivity, neutrality, expertise, and abstract truth. Rather, these are professional disguises, used to create emotional distance from clients, camouflage fears, conceal biases, discount criticisms, and dress up subjective ideas in order to impose them on others. By presenting ourselves as objective neutral experts who know what is true, we limit our capacity for empathy, discount subjectivity, and minimize the value of dissenting perspectives. And, as Shakespeare has Macbeth proclaim, "Who can be wise, amazed, temperate and furious, loyal and neutral in a moment? No man."

Historically, objectivity and neutrality emanate from the law, where any combination of power and subjectivity can lead to tyranny, injustice, and oppression. The law makes a conspicuous display of objectivity, neutrality, expertise, and abstract truths, partly because these qualities advertise formal independence from powerful vested interests, and partly because people might otherwise refuse to obey. Yet while judges routinely exercise power in the name of objectivity, neutrality, and abstract truth, they also inevitably rely on their own conscious and subconscious subjective experiences, values, and ideas, transforming them into universal standards that allow them to lecture litigants on how they ought to behave.

Mediators, on the other hand, operate by consensus, placing the power to resolve conflict in the hands of the parties. As a result, we are permitted to be subjective, vulnerable, human, and wrong, which is essential in order for opposing parties to experience us as unbiased and empathetic and to trust that their heart-based communications will be heard, honored, and appreciated.

When I find myself thinking judgmentally and unable to place myself on both people's sides at the same time, it is usually because they have pushed my emotional buttons, making it more difficult to find their hearts inside my own, reach out to them, understand their deeper issues, or work through mine. When I notice and own my judgments and biases, I become more effective in understanding theirs, can perceive what lies at the heart of their conflict, and know what I need to do to mediate more effectively.

Many people resist or are frightened of empathy because they do not want to become vulnerable in the presence of their opponents, or be forced to surrender their anger, or dissuaded from behaving badly. Many mediators believe that exercising empathy or opening their hearts will make them appear unprofessional and deny them the safety of neutrality, expertise, and distance. The opposite is true. Neutrality, expertise, and professional distance close our hearts, blind us to the subtler sources of conflict, and make us less skillful in reaching people and assisting them in reaching resolution, transformation, and transcendence.

There are many varieties of empathy. There is, for example, *physical* empathy, which allows us to experience sympathetic bodily pains and pleasures; *intellectual* empathy, which allows us to identify with other people's thoughts and ideas; *emotional* empathy, which allows us to resonate with their feelings; *spiritual* empathy, which allows us to understand their intentions, sincerity, and life energy; and *heart* empathy, which allows us to access heart truths. My daughter Elka wrote a poem that conveys the feeling of empathy:

> diamonds in our eyes remember
> critical pressure -
> what it was like to be coal.
> suspended above our humanity
> on a cross or a pedestal
> we are clinging to the rails,
> we are lowering our gaze
> like a rope
> down into the crowd.

4. Use Dangerous Honesty

After using dangerous empathy to learn what is in people's hearts, we can use dangerous honesty to communicate what we learned. Ask yourself honestly: have you ever gained a useful insight while listening to someone describe a conflict and said nothing? Most of us are reluctant to tell painful truths to others, partly because we believe they will interpret our comments as judgments or hostility. Yet our inability to communicate what we observe can prevent them from learning what their conflict took place to teach them and us from becoming more skillful in communicating potentially painful information.

Telling the truth in conflict requires a Golden Rule, inviting us to communicate as we would have others communicate with us. Often, this means framing insights as questions, asking them in gentle and supportive ways, making sure we establish strong empathetic connections before we speak, listening with our hearts for what the other person most wants to say, lowering our voices, slowing our pacing, and being prepared to accept a greater, perhaps less skillful honesty in return.

The more dangerous it feels to communicate something, the more likely it may be to trigger transcendence, since what we fear most in conflict is change and loss. For this reason, the most dangerous truths are those we already subconsciously know to be true, but deny, disguise, resist, and defend against, precisely because of their far-reaching implications. None of this would make any sense if the truth were not dangerous. And in conflict, as in society, as Oscar Wilde observed, "An idea that is not dangerous is unworthy of being considered an idea at all."

5. Locate and Open a Heart Space

A fifth path is to use your heart as a sense organ to locate a heart space in the conversation, then open and expand it, as described in the previous chapter. The only practical instruction I can offer is to focus attention on opening your heart, listen as it responds to whatever is being said, and ask yourself what you think that person most wants or needs to hear. When your heart vibrates with some poignant truth, or another person's pain or pleasure, or wants to shout or laugh or cry, it is likely that their heart just opened and revealed its innermost secrets.

6. Craft a Question That Asks People to Speak and Listen From Their Hearts

A sixth path to transcendence is to ask a question that emanates from your heart and invites the parties to speak and listen from theirs. The deeper purpose of listening and empathy in conflict resolution is to lead us to questions that can touch people's hearts and encourage open, honest communication. There is no single question that will work in every situation, and it is necessary to design each one using empathy, honesty, and intuition to probe what lies beneath a seemingly superficial statement. A list of these questions, *How to Initiate Heartfelt Conversations,* appears on pages 270.

7. Work Collaboratively to Redesign and Reform Cultures and Systems

A seventh path to transcendence is to work collaboratively to redesign and reform the dysfunctional cultures, contexts, environments, and systems that caused or reinforced the conflict. Many conflicts reoccur after having ostensibly been resolved because the hostile cultures, contexts, environments, and systems that triggered or supported them were not also transformed. Preventing future conflicts requires us to collaboratively examine the behaviors and conditions we have accepted as necessary or taken for granted, accurately identify the systemic elements that contributed to our conflict, apply design principles to increase the possibility of early resolution, and act to improve these elements, even in small ways.

As an illustration, chronic conflicts regularly occur in health care facilities between doctors, nurses, staff, administrators, patients, and families. Most of these flow not from substantive disagreements over how to achieve medical goals, but from administrative hierarchies, bureaucratic procedures, insulated departments, physician/nurse miscommunications, racial and cultural differences, high-risk outcomes, overwork, low wages, lack of training in handling intense emotions, abrasive or manipulative personalities, unmet expectations, labor/management disagreements, and lack of conflict resolution alternatives.

These conflicts directly impact the quality of health care and productivity. They undermine teamwork and morale, increase resistance to improvements, raise costs, waste time, alienate patients, interfere with healing, and occupy the conscious and unconscious attention of everyone at work, creating additional burdens on a system already groaning under the weight of reduced resources and increasingly stressful work.

Instead of trying to resolve each isolated, seemingly interpersonal, conflict that emanates from these complex, compound sources, it makes sense to treat them as chronic and use a systems design process to staunch their flow, for example, by developing

- conflict audits to identify and analyze the primary sources of conflict within the facility;

- comprehensive lists of methods for resolving chronic disputes;

- preventive models for comprehensive dispute resolution that describe in detail the stages and steps in preventing, managing, settling, and resolving each kind of dispute;

- plans for hospital-wide conflict resolution programs that support conflicting parties in using a range of formal and informal, internal and external problem solving, mediation, and arbitration processes;

- management structures, systems, and processes that support inclusion, empowerment, equity, collaboration, and consensus, and other organizational techniques for reducing conflict;

- training programs for managers, employees, and union leaders in conflict resolution and ways of implementing and sustaining preventative systems;

- changes in policies and procedures to encourage widespread use of these approaches;

- regular feedback, evaluation, learning, and improvement; and

- resources for ongoing learning and support.

As William Ury, Stephen Goldberg, and Jean Brett write in *Getting Disputes Resolved*, the elements of a system that reinforce and reproduce conflict can be identified, researched, analyzed, categorized, and prioritized, allowing hospitals to identify:

- predictors of conflict;

- preventative measures;

- safety nets and support systems;

- outlets for constructive expression of differences;

- loopbacks to informal problem solving and negotiation;

- internal mechanisms for preventing, managing, and resolving conflict;

- procedures for resolution;

- methods for making them effective; and

- forums for final resolution outside the courts.

Systems design techniques can activate both individual and collective transcendence through organizational learning and evolution based on the lessons distilled from conflicts.

8. Clarify and Reinforce What was Learned, and Use it to Improve and Evolve

An eighth path to transcendence consists of clarifying and reinforcing what was learned from the conflict and using it to improve and evolve to higher levels of conflict and orders of resolution. In my experience, every conflict contains a hidden, metaphorically coded lesson that the parties either already subconsciously know or quickly recognize once it is clarified and their defenses are dropped.

It is possible for mediators to ask people directly or indirectly what they think their conflict is trying to teach them or what they have already realized or learned as a result of their dispute. I sometimes ask people, after resolving their issues, if they would be willing to meet with others who did not participate in the mediation to describe what they learned from their conflict, how they came to resolve it, and what they think might be done to prevent future conflicts.

Learning from conflict sometimes means working collaboratively with their opponent to make improvements or take simple corrective actions that could make a difference. Occasionally it means apologizing for their thoughtlessness or acknowledging the other person's good intentions. Sometimes it means inviting their opponent to ask questions about things they don't understand or can't surrender. Sometimes it means helping them microscopically alter their behaviors so they no longer act in ways that can be interpreted as hostile, unpredictable, or inauthentic.

I call this *microsurgery*, in which people minutely and precisely analyze the sources of their conflict, approach each sub-issue separately and meticu-lously, microscopically, and painstakingly identify tiny collaborative steps they can take, individually or collaboratively, to prevent them from occur-ring again. I write these up as agreements and ask the parties to sign and post them, and meet periodically to assess their progress.

9. Move Toward Forgiveness and Reconciliation

A ninth path to transcendence is to move the conversation in the direction of forgiveness and reconciliation. [This step is addressed in greater detail in *Mediating Dangerously: The Frontiers of Conflict Resolution*, Jossey Bass/Wiley Publishers Inc., 2001.] In this context, it is important to recognize that every heart-based conversation points finally and fundamentally in the direction of forgiveness and reconciliation, which are essential for people to complete their conflicts, reclaim their energy, and move forward in their lives.

Forgiveness and reconciliation are large-scale outcomes as well as small-scale openings and transformations that often go unnoticed. In many inti-mate relationships, small forgivenesses and reconciliations can occur sever-al times a day, usually without much skill or forethought. What is most important is for people to complete their conflicts, leaving nothing left over to make their next dispute more difficult to resolve. To do so, they need to do and say whatever will allow them to feel complete and to become peo-ple who are able to learn from their conflicts and successfully transcend them. Ultimately, this requires self-forgiveness, self-reconciliation, and a positive reintegration of their opponent within themselves, in the form of wisdom, learning, empathy, and evolution or transcendence.

10. Design and Execute a Ritual of Release, Completion, and Closure

A tenth path to transcendence consists of collaboratively designing a ritual of release, completion, or closure, as described in Chapter 6. Without rituals, it is easy for people to fool themselves into thinking they have transcended their conflicts, allowing old patterns to draw them into renewed hostilities.

In the end, transcendence cannot be predicted or compelled. While these ten techniques have worked for me, they may not work for you. It is important to find your own way of being in conflict and, if possible, to open your heart and help others do the same. In doing so, I hope you will discover, as I have, that the heart is a reliable source of insight, uniquely capable of revealing who we are and showing us what we most need to know.

With these tools, we may ultimately recognize that what divides us is less important than what holds us in a common embrace, whether what divides us is grand or petty, international or familial, profound or silly. We may then discover that at the heart of every conflict lies the possibility of its conversion into forgiveness, reconciliation, and love, as described in the following case study.

Washing Our Sins—A Case Study

Roberta was driving home from work on the freeway when her windshield suddenly shattered. She slammed on the brakes and narrowly averted a collision with the cars around her. A police investigation revealed that two young kids aged 12 and 14 had been throwing rocks at passing cars from a freeway overpass. They were arrested, but because it was their first offense, the prosecuting attorney's office referred the case to a juvenile victim-offender mediation program as part of a pilot project to determine whether mediation could produce better results than the criminal courts.

It took some effort to convince Roberta to mediate, as she was afraid at first to meet her attackers. Ultimately, she agreed to mediate with the two juveniles, Phil and Tim, together with their aunt who was raising them because their mother was working out of town and their father had disappeared. Phil and Tim were also reluctant to meet with Roberta, but their only alternative was to face prosecution in Juvenile Court and a possible jail sentence.

I opened the session by thanking everyone for being willing to meet and talk honestly about what happened. I expressed a hope that we would be able to achieve something more through direct conversation than by formal court proceedings. We agreed on a set of ground rules, which included everyone's right to stop the conversation if it was not working, and either correct it or end the process and return to court, where we would lose the ability to speak confidentially and directly to each other.

I asked Roberta to begin, to be completely honest, and to tell Phil and Tim what they had done to her and how it made her feel. She pointed a finger directly at them and said in a tense, angry, accusatory voice, "You little sons of bitches, you almost killed me! I am going to be a grandmother next month and you almost killed me, you little sons of bitches," and she began to sob. Phil and Tim, who were frightened just to attend the mediation, were now completely terrified and also began to cry. The victim they had never stopped to imagine, except as a faceless nonentity, had suddenly turned into a real, angry, frightened grandmother whom they had nearly killed.

On seeing Phil and Tim burst into tears, Roberta realized that the "hardened criminals" she had imagined were just children. She softened her tone and told them more openly and vulnerably about her fear and sadness, and asked them, "How could you have done this to me?" Their aunt tried to enter the conversation to defend them, but I did not want to let them off the hook, and asked her to hold her comments and let Phil and Tim answer the question themselves. I said that Roberta was entitled to hear directly from them why they had done it.

It took several moments of silence for them to recover enough to speak. At last, Phil, the fourteen-year-old, spoke. Sobbing, he told Roberta he was sorry, that he hadn't meant to hurt anyone, that they had just been playing and he hadn't thought about the harm they might cause. Tim said, "It's all my fault. I was the one who threw the rock. I'm sorry," and they both began to cry again.

On hearing their willingness to accept responsibility for what they had done, Roberta softened even more, and began to speak to them directly in a sympathetic tone about what they had done, insisting that they take responsibility for the damage they had caused. I asked the aunt if she wanted to speak, and she said that Phil and Tim were good boys, but were having a hard time as their father had disappeared and their mother had to work full-time to support them, which was why she was not present. Roberta was sympathetic, but did not feel this excused their actions.

I asked Roberta what she thought Phil and Tim might do to prove to her that they were willing to accept responsibility for what they had done. She said what she really wanted before the mediation began was for them to pay for a new windshield, but she now understood their circumstances and saw that they were not old enough to find paying jobs.

She thought for awhile and offered instead that they might come to her house once a week for three months and wash her car. I asked Phil and Tim what they thought about this idea, and they eagerly agreed. We set a date, wrote up their agreements, and ended the mediation with the idea that it was now up to them to reverse the harm they had caused by being responsible for repairing the damage as best they could, and that the criminal case would not be dismissed until Roberta certified that they had fulfilled their agreements.

At first, Roberta was anxious about inviting Phil and Tim to her house, but when they came, behaved respectfully, and worked hard to clean her car, she began to relax. It became clear to her while they were washing her car that they were also washing away their sins and cleansing their guilt, and she began to experience forgiveness.

The second time they came, she offered them some milk and cookies. The third time, she invited them into her house and they talked about school and their lives. At the end of the three months, they had begun to be friends, and Roberta decided to pay them an allowance to take out her garbage and perform small tasks around the house.

Several years later, when Phil was about to graduate from high school, Roberta asked him what he was going to do, and he said he didn't know. She encouraged him to go to college, but he said he couldn't afford it. Guess who agreed to pay his tuition.

Now imagine the same story without mediation. Imagine what might have happened to Phil and Tim in the criminal justice system. Imagine them in prison, and what their lives would have been like afterward. Imagine how Roberta would have felt about the trial and sentence, and what the lack of real closure would have meant to her life, as opposed to what actually happened.

It would have been impossible for any of the participants to imagine at the beginning how this conflict would end, not just with restitution, but with redemption, transcendence, and real forgiveness. By communicating deeply and honestly and with open hearts, they were able to resolve their personal conflict and to transcend the conditions that had created it, revealing the possibility of a far greater social evolution.

Their resolution revealed in miniature how mediation can produce far more effective results in criminal cases than those obtained by prosecution. The parties were each able to find at the center of their conflict a path leading directly to their own transformation and transcendence, allowing them to evolve to more advanced levels of conflict and resolution and escape the prejudicial self-fulfilling prophecies common to their social environments. It provides the best example of what it really means to transform a conflict and achieve personal and social transcendence.

SECTION IV:
REFLECTIONS ON THE THEORY
AND FUTURE OF CONFLICT RESOLUTION

The great modern theoretical innovations reach across disciplines and, just as important, are vitally anchored in the present, the present as a historical and social actuality with a whole genealogy preceding it. Four characteristics define this series—some particular humanistic or social problematic, a historical perspective requiring the creation of an inventory, the convergence of several approaches, and an acute awareness of and sophistication in theory, together with an avoidance of theoretical elaboration for its own sake. Convergences occur as practices, not as mere theoretical gestures.

–Edward W. Said

Chapter 11   Toward a Unified Theory of Conflict Resolution

We—sentient creatures—are in part living in a world the constituents of which we can discover, classify and act upon by rational, scientific, deliberately planned methods; but in part...we are immersed and submerged in a medium that, precisely to the degree to which we inevitably take it for granted as part of ourselves, we do not and cannot observe as if from the outside; cannot identify, measure and seek to manipulate; cannot even be wholly aware of, inasmuch as it enters too intimately into all our experience, is itself too closely interwoven with all that we are and do to be lifted out of the flow (it is the flow) and observed with scientific detachment, as an object. It ... determines our most permanent categories, our standards of truth and falsehood, of reality and appearance, of the good and the bad, of the central and the peripheral, of the subjective and the objective, of the beautiful and the ugly, of movement and rest, of past, present and future, of one and many; hence neither these, nor any other explicitly conceived categories or concepts can be applied to it— for it is in itself but a vague name for the totality that includes these categories, these concepts, the ultimate framework, the basic presumptions wherewith we function.

– Isaiah Berlin

Like the proverbial blind men describing an elephant, mediators have for years explored different aspects of dispute resolution while remaining largely unaware of their concealed interconnections, hidden unities, and the shape of the whole. As a result of these early explorations and an accumulation of practical experience, we are now in a position to speculate on the veiled symmetries and underlying connections that link the various elements described in earlier chapters and to speculate on how they express, contribute to, and form part of the whole.

In contemplating the elements that might unite conflict resolution as a whole, we are immediately confronted with four difficulties. The first flows from Isaiah Berlin's insight that what we are attempting to elucidate is so closely interwoven with who we are that we cannot separate it from the whole of our being and experience. There is little we can do to address this difficulty, other than to recognize the truth of our limitations and do our best to clarify what we have learned.

The second difficulty is that every theory, style, specialization, and branch of conflict resolution perceives the world from its own particular subjective standpoint. Mediators with a legal perspective tend to focus on issues that mean little to mediators with psychological, organizational, labor/management, divorce, family, environmental, spiritual, political, commercial, and community perspectives, and vice versa, making it difficult for them to learn from each other.

The third difficulty is that we have adopted and become accustomed to a fairly timid, immature, reactive approach to resolution. We wait for conflicts to happen, for parties to invite us in, for issues to emerge, for opportunities to arise. This patience and willingness to accept whatever happens is useful in mediation, as it makes us flexible and intuitive, but it does not add significantly to our ability to think proactively, design preventatively, or integrate what we have learned.

The fourth difficulty is that conflict resolution, while ancient in lineage, is still quite young as a profession, and is still deeply engaged in the process of defining itself. There has not been time for diverse forms of practice to settle and steep, for innovation and exploration to become sufficiently self-reflective, or for evolutionary adaptation and professional expansion to deepen our capacity for critical self-examination and preventative or strategic intervention.

Thus far, we have failed to resolve these difficulties. Perhaps this is because our understanding of conflict resolution is still relatively superficial and we are not yet ready to craft a comprehensive unified theory. Perhaps it is because we realize that overcoming these difficulties will be arduous and require us to break new ground. Perhaps it is because the practice of conflict resolution is highly subjective, making it easy to become lost in our own private worlds. Perhaps it is because our economic self-interest as conflict resolution professionals encourages us to distinguish ourselves professionally from others by establishing fixed boundaries, competitive attitudes, and divisions of labor.

Regardless of the reasons, it will ultimately be useful for us to develop a theory of the whole that includes all the diverse forms of practice that characterize our field. This will require us to understand the subtle connections—not only between physical, intellectual, and emotional components of conflict—but, more problematically, those related to spirit and heart, including forgiveness and reconciliation, and those related to systems, contexts, cultures, and environments, including organizational, social, and political conflicts.

Some mediators will consider these topics secondary, superfluous, fallacious, risky, touchy-feely, unnecessary, or unimportant. Yet it will be impossible for us to formulate a comprehensive, unified, integrated understanding of conflict resolution as a whole or to fully grasp any of its parts unless we include an analysis of these difficult areas.

Do We Need a Theory of Conflict Resolution?

It may be argued that it is unnecessary, even misguided, to try to develop a theory of conflict resolution. Why invent a theory when our technique is doing fine as it is; in other words, "if it ain't broke, why fix it?" Why not just use intuition, which is often a reliable guide to what is happening in conflict, and not clutter our minds with intellectual abstractions that draw attention from the process? Why promote theoretical approaches that encourage arguments over meaningless abstractions rather than focus on flexibility, innovation, and technique? Here are a few quick responses to these three objections.

1. If it ain't broke, why fix it?

First, it may actually *be* broke and we haven't noticed. Second, as a living, organic process, conflict resolution needs to evolve as a field, which is the same as fixing it. Third, when we stop trying to fix it we stop caring about it. Fourth, it's not about whether conflict resolution is "broke," it's about improving it. Fifth, if we don't try to fix it we are likely to grow accustomed to its dysfunctions and ways of fixing it may escape our attention. Sixth, it really doesn't matter whether it's broke because it is challenging, satisfying, and enjoyable to fix it anyway.

2. Why not just use intuition?

Intuition is highly useful in conflict resolution, but it is best to combine it with reason and analysis and learn to use our heads and hearts at the same time. Intuition is not an argument against reason, but against the exclusivity of reason as a way of knowing the world. The brain's hemispheres operate differently, one reasoning and the other intuiting, and by working together they provide more useful and accurate information than either could by working alone. Whole brain approaches allow mediators to act more rapidly and flexibly.

3. Why encourage abstract theoretical approaches over flexibility and technique?

Theories are paradigms that easily become ossified with age and end in dogmatism and blind acquiescence if they are not continually updated and overthrown by newer, more accurate theories. The aim of every theory is to expand perception and awareness, clarify underlying problems, and introduce fresh possibilities. Theories can make what was impossible or unthinkable seem natural, logical, and inevitable. Ideally, they explain what we are doing, why we are doing it, and how we might do it better. They give us fresh ways of experiencing commonplace realities. They point to testable hypotheses and predictable practices, and unify the disparate elements of isolated, individual experiences. They connect ostensibly unrelated events, relationships, and processes, and allow us to form an integrated understanding of the operations of the whole.

Developing a unified theory would thus mark a stage or milestone in our understanding and define a paradigm for future generations to revise and contradict. It would express our commitment to thinking scientifically as well as artistically about the intricacies and complexities of our work. It would encourage us to integrate our understanding of its two deeply interwoven yet contradictory aspects: those that are *internal*, where we explore emotion, awareness, intention, attitude, spirit, heart, and self; and those that are *external*, where we explore systems, structures, strategies, processes, contexts, cultures, relationships, and environments. The issue is therefore not theory instead of practice or practice instead of theory, but their creative, synergistic combination.

Parallel Modes of Understanding

The first step in developing a unified theory of conflict resolution is to critically examine the methods by which we intend to examine and craft it.

There are dozens of ways of trying to understand conflict resolution, or any subject, many of which appear contradictory, but actually complement each other. We can, for example, try to understand a problem using reductionism or holism, analysis or imagination, history or fantasy, abstraction or experience, intellect or emotion, logic or intuition. We can apply science or art, objectivity or subjectivity, divergence or convergence, contrast or commonality. We can look digitally or analogically, sequentially or summatively, in isolation or relationship to context and environment. Each approach will provide different answers and, when combined, reveal hidden symmetries that deepen our understanding.

In essence, the left hemisphere of the brain is a scientist while the right is an artist. Each of these modes of understanding augments and enlarges the ways we experience conflict and resolution. Each generates radically different results, takes us to different locations, and influences what we are capable of imagining. Each allows us to develop a different set of practical techniques and a deeper, more integrated understanding of the whole.

When we attempt to understand conflict resolution using only logic, reductionism, history, and science, we make its emotional, holistic, experiential, and artistic aspects less accessible. As a result, we may decide to settle disputes without resolving the underlying reasons that gave rise to them, or fail to recognize the presence of a subtle, yet attainable potential for heartfelt conversation that could lead to transformation or transcendence. When we abandon logic, reductionism, history, and science, we may become mired in mysticism, sink into sentimentality and naiveté, and lose whatever parts of resolution rely on reason, science, strategy, technique, and planning. Yet there is a science to every art and an art to every science, and what works best is not one or the other but both in combination. And beyond their simple combination lies the possibility of their seamless, synergistic, holistic integration, marking the beginning of wisdom.

Thinking About the Way We Think

Using slightly different terms, in addition to these two fundamental approaches to comprehending anything—which are to reduce, dissect, and analyze its separate parts, distinguishing similar from dissimilar phenomena, and to combine, unify, and integrate disparate phenomena, analyzing them as a single, unified whole—there is a third approach, which is to integrate them by performing both operations simultaneously.

While dissection, distinction, and reductionism tend to destroy holistic thinking by reducing it to a series of smaller sequential parts, unification, integration, and holism tend to cancel reductionist approaches by consolidating discrete parts into a single whole and focusing only on the sum of their parts. Doing both simultaneously integrates these seemingly opposed complementary approaches to understanding, allowing us to understand phenomena as both discrete and continuous, stable and moving, analog and digital, different and similar, objective and subjective, quantitative and qualitative, particle-like and wave-like.

The principal advantage of reductionism is that it allows us to form a detailed understanding of each separate component making up the whole. Its principal disadvantage is that particle-like approaches encourage us to see things discretely, in isolation, disregarding their interconnections. The principal advantage of holism is that it allows us to explain the interconnections between seemingly distinct phenomena and identify potentially synergistic combinations. Its principal disadvantage is that wave-like approaches encourage us to minimize or disregard what is distinct in each element and disregard their differences.

If we subdivide reductionism and holism once more, we can derive four simple, distinct ways of understanding that allow us to describe conflict resolution and a number of other phenomena at a more detailed level. The following diagram highlights these four methods of analysis, offering examples from physics and mathematics in regular type and locations, elements, and styles of conflict resolution in italics.

Four Approaches to Description

Content	Relationship	Process	Context
Reductionism	Dynamics/Change	Analysis	Holism
Individual	Interaction	Form	Integration
Facts/Logic	Meaning/Metaphor	Timing/Fairness	Impact/Ecology
Point or Line	Function or Limit	Equation or Symbol	Space or Field
Particle	Energy	Wave	Environment
Discrete	Continuous	Comparative	Unbounded
Arithmetic	Calculus/Analysis	Algebra	Geometry
Intellect	*Interests*	*Emotions*	*Spirit, Heart, and*
Positions	*Recognition and*	*Feelings*	*Systems Design*
	Empowerment	*Facilitative Style*	*Learning, Prevention*
	Transformational		*Transcendent Style*

Thus, an orientation toward content or reductionism in conflict resolution will encourage a focus on intellect and positions, suggesting the adoption of an evaluative or directive style of mediation; an orientation toward process or analysis will encourage a focus on form and the adoption of a facilitative style, and so on. Combining these orientations will encourage an eclectic style that shifts from one approach to another as circumstances and intuition suggest.

Each of these ways of describing conflict invites a different set of observations, experiences, truths, and understandings to emerge. Each requires a different set of skills to make it effective. None is mutually exclusive or more accurate than others, and each may at best address a particular kind of conflict. Would it not then make sense for us to become fluent in *all* of these styles and approaches and select those that work best for each conflict? In combination, might they not reveal underlying symmetries that integrate these seemingly diverse approaches into a single, interrelated whole?

Before considering how to combine these elements and move toward a unified theory of conflict resolution, it will be helpful to clarify our understanding of the dynamics of conflict, not merely in its human manifestations, but as it occurs in nature, and briefly consider what science has discovered regarding chaos, criticality, entropy, symmetry, spectra, and fields. Thinking about these abstract, complex, difficult scientific ideas and regarding them as metaphors will allow us to find novel ways of understanding conflict behaviors and innovative conflict resolution techniques.

Chaos, Criticality, and Conflict Resolution

We all allow that conflict can become chaotic. Yet the science of chaos, considered as a metaphor, can deepen our understanding of the method by which conflict turns chaotic. In physics, chaos is defined as sensitive dependence on initial conditions, meaning that it is inherently unpredictable. At the same time, chaos is deterministic, in the sense that it is not simply random, or poorly defined, or merely disordered. Chaos regularly occurs, for example, in periods leading up to a phase transition, as when water begins to change into steam or ice.

By analogy, we can consider the transition from impasse to resolution as a phase transition. A first-order phase transition is one in which, for example, the molecular composition of water remains the same while its form changes suddenly from liquid to steam or ice, giving it completely new properties. Settlement can also be regarded as a first-order phase transition in which the content of the conflict remains the same and only its form changes. Resolution can be regarded as a second-order transition in which the content of the dispute is continuously or completely redefined. This analogy can help us understand how transformational and transcendent moments in mediation might unpredictably alter the form and substance of a conflict.

During a phase transition, bifurcations in potential outcomes increasingly draw predictable motions toward a strange attractor, spontaneously breaking their symmetry. Systems then automatically arise out of a need for balance along the critical boundaries that separate one phase from another, increasing its complexity. A system forms when individual elements interact and self-organize to maintain themselves in dynamic equilibrium during a period of criticality. This self-organized criticality characterizes systems that are approaching chaotic, far out of balance, poised, or critical states. Quantum criticality occurs when the temperature of an ordinary phase transition in certain materials is tuned to occur near absolute zero, for example, by applying a magnetic field. Quantum indeterminacy then radically alters the material's properties so that electricity continues to flow, even though its individual electrons do not.

Continuing with this metaphor, when the energy or information that is constantly flowing into and out of a system begins to drive it toward a phase transition, chaos causes the underlying symmetry, form, and structure of the system to dominate its less important characteristics. During moments of criticality, even seemingly minor changes can produce dramatically different outcomes.

At the precise moment of phase transition, as when water turns into ice, a critical juncture occurs in which miniscule changes in temperature cause the entire system to suddenly shift into a qualitatively different state, reflecting a new form of symmetry. In a sand pile, the addition of a single grain of sand can drive the pile toward a critical state, resulting in an avalanche, catastrophe, and phase transition from ordered and pyramidal to disordered and flat. It is impossible to predict in advance which grain of sand will initiate this shift, as the outcome sensitively depends on the precise location of every other grain of sand in the pile.

In these critical moments, the content, properties, and details of the system become increasingly irrelevant, and only three things matter: the number of dimensions of the system (which are not just two or three, but the fractions lying between them), the overall orderliness of the system, and the relative size of the largest orderly structure within it.

In this way, science reveals that chaos, criticality, and phase transition are influenced by fractal structures that may appear two-dimensional, yet actually occupy a dimension lying somewhere between two and three. Fractal structures are self-similar on all scales, allowing a coastline to look essentially the same when seen from a thousandth of an inch, a yard, and a mile. Fractals reflect the fact that self-organized systems near criticality and phase transition occupy a space that is between dimensions.

By analogy, it is impossible to predict with any precision what statements or actions during a conflict will drive a family system that has self-organized to maintain equilibrium into a critical state that is far out of balance, leading toward the avalanche, catastrophe, and phase transition of divorce, eventually resulting in the creation of a new family system, possibly revealing a higher level of order.

Conflicts can similarly be said to possess fractal-like structures that occupy a space between dimensions and to be self-similar on all scales, revealing commonalities between petty interpersonal squabbles and momentous political controversies. Criticality and chaos in conflict resolution can be seen to increase as mediators move deeper into the heart of a conflict, causing it to become less stable and predictable, introducing new attractors and allowing small, sensitive changes in the parties' attitudes or behaviors, and in the dimensions, orderliness, and emotional clarity of their communications to result in significantly different outcomes.

Conflicts can arguably cause psychological, familial, organizational, social, and political systems to self-organize as criticality approaches and they near the juncture to a first-order phase transition in form or a second-order phase transition in which higher forms of symmetry and order allow the content or meaning of the conflict to be redefined and transcended.

Conflict Resolution as a Hedge Against Entropy

A second useful scientific metaphor can be found in the idea of entropy, based on the Second Law of Thermodynamics, which is a measure of disorder and loss of energy due to random motion, and of the loss of information. Anthropologist Gregory Bateson has defined information as "any difference that makes a difference," which holds special meaning in conflict resolution where only a very few differences between people make a difference in their relationship.

At a quantum level, the famous Uncertainty Principle discovered by Werner Heisenberg confirms that information about certain opposing pairs of conjugate qualities cannot be precisely determined simultaneously. Thus, the more information we gather about a particle's position, the less we can possibly know about its momentum. Similarly, though somewhat more difficult to understand, the more we know about the time an event occurred, the less we are able to know about the amount of energy involved.

By analogy, conflict routinely results in entropic disorder and a loss of important information—about the human nature of one's opponent, collaborative possibilities in problem solving, and what adversaries may have in common. Also, the more opposing parties know about what their opponent did wrong, the less they seem to know about their interests or what they might do to resolve the conflict. Many people even forget who they *are* in conflict and do things they do not understand, recognize, or like.

While systems do not spontaneously become more ordered, they easily become more disordered, making it easier to break an egg than to create one. Because resolution is a more highly ordered state than conflict, greater energy is required to bring it into existence. Thus, without any additional expenditure of energy, it will always be easier for resolution to break down and result in conflict than for conflict to break down and result in resolution.

It is similarly easier for people to lose track of what they really want and need than to recognize what they might achieve by communicating more constructively regarding their differences, collaborating, and finding solutions to their problems. As mediators, it is far less time consuming to ignore the systemic organizational and familial defects and political, economic, and social anomalies that fuel interpersonal conflicts than to use system design techniques to prevent future disputes before they occur.

Entropy measures how much of a system's energy is lost through work, including, by analogy, the work of communicating critical information, resolving conflicts, learning, and evolving. While overall entropy and disorder always increase, systems can evolve to higher states of order, or negative entropy, by dissipating disorder into their environment. This allows them to create greater complexity and order in one area in exchange for greater simplicity and disorder in another. In a similar way, by expending energy on conflict resolution, we can improve difficult communications, minimize the loss of socially useful information, and create higher levels of organization in relationships, though doing so will always require greater effort.

Conflict resolution can therefore be regarded as a hedge against psychological, organizational, social, and political entropy; as a means of clarifying, concentrating, and organizing important information; and as a method for dissipating the chaos and cacophony of conflict communications and transforming them into learning, evolution, and transcendence.

Entropy can also be understood as a kind of background noise or static that diminishes the clarity and integrity of conflict communications, turning intelligible messages into unintelligible ones and distorting their meaning. Entropy increases with the length and seriousness of conflict, adversarial attitudes and behaviors, use of power- or rights-based processes, and the level of physical, mental, emotional, and heart-based dissonance in conflict communications.

Entropy can be reduced by increasing the amount of order in a conflict system, and by improving the clarity and integrity of communications, allowing the parties to receive even incomplete or blurred communications intact. This can happen, for example, when mediators use empathy to reveal and clarify each party's true intent, ask questions to fill in missing details, illuminate or transform the meaning of conflict stories and communications, reframe negative comments, use heart-based interventions to reveal what both sides truly want, or engage in collaborative efforts to improve on-going relationships.

Chronic systemic conditions aggravate conflict and trigger an enormous loss of useful, important information. Significant losses of information can occur, for example, in systems that encourage gross disparities in wealth and power, autocratic or dictatorial decision making, bureaucratic relationships, debilitating discriminations, or hierarchical communications, each of which increases the level of entropy within the system and stimulates personal, social, and political conflict.

Considering entropy as a metaphor allows us to apply many of the techniques developed for reducing entropy and static in electronic information transfers to conflict communications. For example, we can use redundancy, selective emphasis, and repetition to reinforce elements that define a communication's meaning. Or we can use facilitation, mediation, and public dialogue to provide a structure for highly chaotic emotional communications. Or we can use open, accurate, recurrent feedback to measure what works in communications and relationships. Or we can stimulate personal and organizational learning as a way of decreasing entropy in subsequent communications.

Recapturing lost information through structured, facilitated, or mediated communications can dissipate the otherwise chaotic energy of conflict and transform it into greater resolution complexity, systems design, and learning processes that encourage evolution to higher levels of conflict and resolution. Heart-based communications can powerfully decrease entropy and relational disorder by clarifying, at a deep level, how people feel, what they mean, and who they are.

The Symmetry of Conflict

In physics, symmetry is defined as invariance, meaning that things do not alter or change when moved or rotated in relation to some element in their environment. A symmetry operation is one that can be performed without altering the appearance of an object. For example, mirror symmetry occurs when an object like a square looks the same after being rotated 90, 180, 270, or 360 degrees. A circle possesses a higher order of symmetry because it can be rotated through an infinite number of angles without altering its appearance. Symmetries can be broken and reduced or increased, as the symmetry of a circle is broken and reduced by cutting it in half, and the symmetry of water is altered by turning it into ice or steam. Spontaneous symmetry breaking often accompanies chaos and criticality and defines the onset of a phase transition.

Conflict can be said to possess a kind of symmetry of its own. Indeed, we can think of the symmetry of harmonious relationships as being broken by conflict, resulting in a lower degree of symmetry between the parties. We may also observe a *mirror* symmetry of opposition between polarized issues and parties; a *circular* symmetry created by repeatedly going round and round the same arguments; and *translational* emotional symmetries of mutual escalation and de-escalation, reciprocal cycles of blaming, and failure to acknowledge the interests of opponents that characterize many disputes.

In physics, all symmetries are said to suggest the presence of a law of conservation, since some element of a square, for example, must be conserved if it appears the same after being rotated 90 degrees. Thus, energy is conserved when an action does not change with respect to time and looks the same whether it is moving into the past or the future. It is not conserved and is lost to entropy when that symmetry is broken and the arrow of time moves in only one direction. Similarly, linear momentum is conserved when actions do not vary in space, angular momentum when they do not vary with the direction of rotation, information when they do not vary in scale, and so on.

Applying these ideas as metaphors allows us to understand, for example, why most conflicts would not change their appearance if the parties were to switch sides. Their symmetry of opposition conserves the content of their conflict and the substantive issues over which they are fighting. Similar symmetries can be said to conserve *form*, or the ways people fight; and *scale*, or whether the conflict is between individuals, organizations, communities, or nations.

We can identify symmetries in the behaviors parties engage in that do not vary with culture or personality; symmetries in the interests of the parties that do not vary with the nature of the issues; and symmetries in the emotions experienced by the parties, such as anger or fear, which can be thought of as conserving deeper, heartfelt desires that, if resolved, might result in higher orders of relational symmetry.

These symmetries might be used to predict, for example, that methods that have proven effective in resolving marital disputes might also be useful in resolving business partnership disputes, as the intimacy of these relationships suggests a conservation of emotions, behaviors, and underlying interests.

They might also help us understand why opposing parties sometimes act so similarly, and why our interventions need to be symmetrical, or balanced.

With regard to scale, we can describe a conflict as symmetrical if the issues or the parties' behaviors do not vary significantly with the size of the dispute, but reveal similar features at all gradations. Many complex physical systems are now seen to possess underlying architectures, or scale-free networks, governed by shared organizing principles that respond similarly regardless of size. Such networks have been found to exist within ecosystems, languages, and social relationships, and can be identified in conflicts as well. Connections inside these networks are formed through scale-free nodes or hubs that operate democratically through participation and choice, rather than hierarchically through command and control. [For more information on how scale-free networks can be used to resolve organizational conflicts, see Kenneth Cloke and Joan Goldsmith, *The End of Management and the Rise of Organizational Democracy*, Jossey Bass / Wiley Publishers Inc., 2002.]

Symmetries allow us to predict, for example, that conflict systems in families, organizations, and societies will naturally gravitate toward equilibrium and impasse in order to conserve their operations; that this equilibrium will be reinforced by repetition, causing the system to become increasingly resistant to change; and that targeting the nodes and hubs of networks and repeatedly reinforcing alternative messages and stories that emphasize resolution might change the system as a whole, allowing it to respond less reactively to small-scale interpersonal conflicts and to work proactively to prevent large-scale disputes.

Symmetries have been used by physicists to unify three of the four fundamental forces of nature, first allowing electricity and magnetism to be described in a single set of equations, then providing a mathematical formalism for integrating weak and strong nuclear forces. At present, many physicists are attempting to extend these symmetries to include gravity as well, through the mechanism of supersymmetry and string or M theory. In a similar way, conflict symmetries can lead us to develop a deeper theoretical understanding of the unities underlying seemingly disconnected aspects of conflict resolution.

The Spectrum of Conflict

Just as we can identify a spectrum of electromagnetic waves that proceed from ultraviolet to infrared, we can imagine a spectrum of conflict that extends from petty, minor disagreements to wars of annihilation, and a spectrum of resolution that extends from impasse and de-escalation to forgiveness and reconciliation. We can also imagine each conflict as revealing a spectrum of *ideas* regarding the parties, their opponents, and their issues, ranging from respectful to revengeful; a spectrum of *emotions* ranging from mild irritation to homicidal rage; a spectrum of *interests* ranging from survival to desire for intimate relationship, and so on.

In recent years, it has been demonstrated that certain fundamental human emotions, (anger, sadness, shame, fear, joy, surprise, and love) are universally recognized through distinct facial expressions, and interpreted in exactly the same ways by people in widely dispersed cultures and locations. Each emotion can be seen to exist along a spectrum that extends, in the case of sadness, from minor unhappiness to catastrophic grief and life-threatening depression. The same can be said of ideas, interests, and other elements in conflict.

Thus, each conflict might be seen as the unique interweaving of a spectral range of ideas, emotions, and interests that connect or separate, attract or repel, cancel or amplify those of the opposing party. Each interweaving spectrum creates a pattern that links warp and woof in a distinct, united way, and partially obscures its origins. In a similar way, each mediated conversation can be seen as an interweaving of these spectra in a joint search for causation and meaning. Mediators might clarify the deeper meaning of conflict conversations by isolating and revealing these spectra, and analyzing how they became interwoven.

In physics, white light can be broken into a spectrum and analyzed using refraction, diffraction, and interference, revealing a range of colors. Similarly, mediators can use refraction, diffraction, and interference to separate and analyze the elements of conflict and identify their distinct frequencies. In physics, some parts of the spectrum of light are absorbed by different chemical elements, revealing themselves through omissions that can be identified using spectrographic analysis. Similarly, we can notice how parties in conflict reflect and absorb selectively from a spectrum of ideas, emotions, and interests; how they omit telltale facts from their stories; and how they react when their omissions are noticed or corrected.

Perhaps the most stunning spectrum in nature is the rainbow, which results from a combination of raindrops, sunlight, an observer, and a precise angle of observation. In a similar way, we can think of mediation as an effort to locate a precise angle of observation that is able to refract people's statements about their ideas, emotions, and interests, in order to reveal their hidden colors.

The Field of Conflict

A field in mathematics and physics is not a *thing*, but an activity, a pattern, a process, a relationship in motion. A magnetic field, for example, is defined by the lines of force that emanate from the opposition of positive and negative magnetic charges. These fields are not confined to a physical magnet, but extend outward into the entire universe. In a similar way, gravitational fields are created by the curvature of space-time, binding planets and the sun in a single, invisible process. Gravity, then, is simply the shape, form, or geometry of the field of space-time.

In a similar way, every conflict is a combination of polarization and unification, antagonism and collaboration, separation and integration, and all the relationships that are possible between them. These symmetrical, scale-free, oppositional forces spread outward over space and time, combining tension and unpredictability, criticality and self-organization, entropy and order. Together, they create a field defined by the interaction between them, allowing us to see conflict as a product of the shape, form, and geometry of the field of interpersonal relationships.

Everything exists in some relationship to the field, context, space, or environment in which it arises, to such an extent that it is impossible to imagine one without the other. Energy produces a field because it requires something to push against, a negative to accentuate each positive. The idea of a field allows us to consider what is intrinsic, or inside, in combination with what is extrinsic, or outside, within a single set of interactions that take place both locally and globally.

If we recognize that conflicts are not discrete events, but radiate a kind of energy defined by the tension between opposition, polarity, contradiction, and negation on the one hand, and duality, unity, synergy, and oneness on the other, we can imagine these elements extending along magnetlike polarized lines that define the field of conflict in much the same way that invisible field lines can be observed by placing iron filings on a sheet of paper covering a magnet. It is these lines that a field-theoretic approach to conflict resolution should seek to identify.

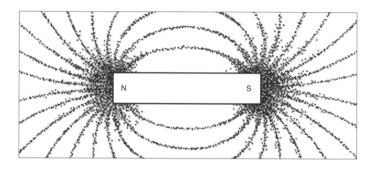

Thinking of conflict as a field offers us fresh insight into its universal nature, reveals hidden connections between its seemingly isolated parts, elements, steps, and stages, and allows us to stitch together a composite, holographic picture of the whole. These may lead to more sophisticated resolution techniques, explain the diversity of approaches that characterize conflict resolution, and clarify the principles that might succeed in uniting them.

A conflict field can be said to consist of the opposite poles defined by the content of a dispute as well as the process of communication, the style of negotiation, the emotions of opposing parties, and the relationship between them. It will be influenced by cultural differences, systemic dysfunctions, and environmental conditions that form the context of the dispute and by the totality of these forces and possible interaction between them, from impasse through transcendence. It will include the forces of opposition and unity, and everything that *might* result from their combination, including outcomes that depend sensitively on each party's character, intention, and attitude, which cannot be predicted in advance of their interaction.

Extending this analogy, we can hypothesize that field lines of caring or concern will unify the parties' differences at the *equator* of their dispute and divide them at its *poles*. This will allow mediators to pinpoint the principal vectors that define a conflict's direction and magnitude at each location in what we can refer to as conflict space, enabling us to shift the parties' conversations toward the broad regions of unity that lie between their oppositely charged, antagonistic poles, or vice versa, depending on what works best.

It is difficult to regard field theory as more than a metaphor in conflict resolution because of its mathematical complexity, generality, and concern with average behaviors. To be more accurate in applying this idea to conflict resolution, we would need to include the possibility that, as conflict approaches a state of chaos or criticality, complex interactions and relationships can quickly shift from linear to chaotic, allowing, for example, the flapping of a butterfly's wings in one location to influence the weather in another.

These are only a few of hundreds of mathematical and scientific metaphors that may prove useful in revealing unnoticed remarkable connections between conflicts in nature and those between human beings. While these connections cannot directly instruct us regarding the deeper principles that may underlie and unite the various forms of conflict resolution, they powerfully suggest the presence of deeper simplicities and underlying principles that might be mined and clarified over time.

Toward a Unified Theory of Conflict Resolution

In each of the scientific metaphors explored above, seemingly disconnected, disordered, inexplicable phenomena were recognized to be intricately interconnected, ordered, and explicable as a result of the development of a unifying theory. In a similar way, much of the incongruity in conflict behaviors and more perplexing aspects of the resolution process suggest the presence of an underlying set of unifying principles.

Before identifying some of the unifying principles that connect different forms of conflict and resolution practice and that might lead us in the direction of a unified theoretical approach to conflict resolution, it is important to begin with a caveat. Too little is known at present about conflict resolution to do more than suggest that there is a need to develop a unified theory based on the principles, techniques, and practical experiences outlined in this and previous chapters.

Nonetheless, in the interest of stimulating thinking and work on this important topic, I believe it will be useful to begin drawing connections between seemingly unrelated phenomena, identifying links that can deepen our understanding and suggest techniques capable of crossing the artificial boundaries separating different kinds of conflict and diverse styles, processes, and approaches to resolution. What follows, therefore, is a first effort at clarification, offered in the hope that it will be critiqued and improved in subsequent iterations.

In the chart that follows, I have endeavored to summarize and connect many of the patterns, processes, relationships, and symmetries that link the diverse elements, stages, steps, styles, dimensions, forms, locations, and components of conflict and resolution described in preceding chapters.

Elements in a Unified Theory of Conflict Resolution

Indispensable Component of Conflict	Likely Results of Component	What is Needed, Wanted, or Missing	Possible Strategies for Intervention	Conflict Location
1. Two or More People (or internal parts of the same person)	Diverse Interests, Isolation, Distrust, Competitive Relationships	Communication, Openness, Positive Intent, Common Goals	Ground Rules, Listening, Storytelling, Empathy, Common Interests	Body
2. Disagreement over Form, Process, Relationship, or Outcomes	Unresolved Issues, Differences over Facts, Competing Issues, Personal Solutions	Engagement, Logical Analysis, Neutral Identification and Discussion of Common Interests	Brainstorming, Collaborative Negotiation, Creative Problem-Solving, Dialogue	Mind
3. "Negative" Emotion, e.g., Anger, Fear, Jealousy, Shame, Guilt, or Grief	Unexpressed or Hostile Emotions, Incomplete or Inadequate Compassion and Letting Go	Emotional Closure, Introspection, Venting, Empathy, Acknowledgment, Self-Esteem, Rituals, Completion	Venting, Acknowledgement, Caucusing, Emotional Processing, Rituals of Closure	Emotion
4. Lack of Awareness of Self and Other, Antagonistic Spirit, Intention, or Energy; Intolerant or Unforgiving Aim, Attachment, Embittered Life Force, Soul, or Chi	Chronic Conflict, Illness, Injury, Blindness, Misery, Confusion, Spiritual Imbalance, Feeling Stuck, Incessant Suffering	Forgiveness, Mindfulness, Insight, Expanded Awareness, Compassion, Authenticity, Acceptance, Release Apology, Letting Go	Honesty, Empathy Introspection, Centering, Meditation, Rituals, Shift from Negative to Positive Energy	Spirit
5. Closed-Hearted Attitude, Hostile, Self-Centered, or Withholding Outlook or Relationship	Dysfunctional Relationships, Depression, Self-Centeredness, Broken Heart	Reconciliation, Compassion, Positive Attitude, Heart-to-Heart Dialogue	Openhearted Communication, Confession, Learning, Acceptance of Self and Other	Heart
6. Adversarial, Bureaucratic, or Highly Competitive Context, System, Culture, or Environment	Inimical Social Conditions, Systems &/or Structures; e.g., Inequity, Hierarchical, Bureaucratic and Autocratic Relations	Systemic Change, Collaborative Relationship, Cultural Sensitivity, Equity, Equality, Community, and Democracy	Transform System, Alter or Adapt to Environment, Balance Power, Build Participation and Consensus	System, Context, Society

What follows is therefore a summary and a simplification, reflecting my view of how conflict and resolution are interconnected through a six-fold, hexagonal symmetry that characterizes the whole.

Likely Level, Percent, Style of Resolution	Principal Methods and Forms of Resolution	Forms of Interaction, Process	Dimensions and Degrees of Change	Degree of Release or Closure
Stop the Fighting (20%) *Conciliation*	Physical Separation, Listening, Calming Tone of Voice	Monologue, Conciliation, Coaching	1: Line (0)	Stasis, De-escalation
Settle the Issues (60%) *Settlement*	Adversarial Negotiation, Caucusing, Compromise	Debate, Brainstorming, Problem Solving	2: Plane (45)	Ending
Resolve the Underlying Reasons for the Dispute (90%) *Resolution*	Emotional Venting, Acknowledgement, Dialogue, Apology, Surface Interests, Collaborative Negotiation	Introspection, Dialogue, Empowerment, Recognition, Requests and Promises	3: Cube (90)	Completion
Reach Forgiveness (98%) *Transformation*	Memory, Empathy, Ownership, Release False Expectations, Choose to Reclaim Energy	Expanded Awareness, Authenticity, Acceptance, Release	4: Hyper-cube (180)	Closure
Reconcile (100%) *Transcendence*	Deep Empathy, Dangerous Honesty, Speak Directly from the Heart	Open, Poignant, Affectionate, Profound	5: Spiral Inward (360)	Disappearance
Synergy, Community (100%+) *Systems Design*	Prejudice Reduction, Systemic Change, Organizational Democracy	Learning-Based Collaboration, Consensus, Public Dialogue	6: Hologram or Field (all dimensions at once)	Prevention - Continuous Iterative, Open-Ended

[Source: Kenneth Cloke, *The Crossroads of Conflict: A Journey into the Heart of Dispute Resolution*, Janis Publications, 2006]

From this diagram, we can see that each of the elements of conflict discussed in earlier chapters is linked with the others, revealing why the range of resolutions open to mediators extends naturally from impasse to reconciliation in a unified, holistic way. As a consequence, we can more clearly understand why resolution techniques that prove useful in reaching settlements are unlikely to contribute to forgiveness, how each variety of intervention culminates in a different level of closure or completion, and why spirit, heart, and systems design should be regarded as essential elements in the pantheon of respected, objective, professional approaches to conflict resolution. While infrequent and difficult to achieve, the whole of conflict resolution cannot be fully understood without reference to the subtle, pervasive influence of these higher dimensional qualities.

Similarly, this chart allows us to assess the impact of systems, contexts, cultures, and environments on conflict, and to preventatively redesign them. It therefore includes, as a natural and inevitable component of conflict resolution, the examination of dysfunctional systems and invites us to consider the broad array of cultural, organizational, social, economic, political, and environmental influences that are critical in coming to a complete operational understanding of our field as a whole.

The Consequences of a Unified Theory

A number of consequences are likely to flow from the development of a unified approach to conflict resolution. First, while mediators often focus on particular kinds of conflict or follow particular styles or approaches to resolution, a unified theory will encourage us to recognize that we are seamlessly connected and united, not only by intention, but by the nature of conflict resolution itself.

Second, rather than feeling bound to follow any single approach or style of resolution, or believe that we can only assist in resolving particular kinds of conflicts, we may be able to recognize that our skills can be made much stronger through cross-training and being exercised in multiple ways in diverse arenas and manifestations of conflict.

Third, instead of training prospective mediators to focus on one or another style, technique, or approach to conflict resolution, we will be encouraged to recognize that we can become far more effective by conducting trainings in all styles, techniques, and approaches, support beginning mediators in understanding the advantages and disadvantages of each, and learn how to choose those that will work best for them.

Fourth, a unified understanding of conflict resolution can encourage mediators to improve the ways we interact, communicate, debate, and relate to one another professionally. If we understand that what each of us does in conflict resolution is a unique combination of personal and abstract elements that require diverse levels of understanding, skill, and presence, we may listen to each other's experiences and perspectives more openly and constructively.

The development of a more accurate, inclusive, and comprehensive theory will, as mentioned, be a collective enterprise requiring considerable research, thinking, and practical work by future generations. It will not be easy to unravel the complex roles of systems, context, culture, and environment in shaping interpersonal and social or political conflicts, yet it is my belief that doing so will allow us to become more skillful in resolving even mundane commercial and family disputes.

It is not my intention, therefore, in proposing the development of a unified theory to in any way constrict creativity or suggest a uniform set of techniques or procedures, or limit spontaneity in responding to the chaos of conflict. Rather, it is to enlarge options, increase the range of choices, suggest novel ways of incorporating what doesn't fit into a consistent, unified framework, and use them to develop more powerful, iterative, overarching descriptions of the whole. Ultimately, it is to discover the hidden, almost mathematical equations that govern the art and science of what we do that cannot be made simpler, more beautiful, or more profound.

In closing, it is important to realize that it is not theory or technique that are fundamental, but the human lives of people in conflict. When facts contradict theory, it is the facts that should be retained rather than the theory. The central facts in every conflict are the people who experience it. Therefore, the best advice was given by Carl Jung, who wrote, "Study your theory; practice your techniques inside out, and when in the presence of a living soul, respond to the soul." To do so, it is necessary to journey deep into the heart of conflict, clarify its hidden meanings, and use it as a guide to resolution, transformation, and transcendence. In this, I believe, lies our future as a profession.

Chapter 12 Conclusion: The Future of Conflict Resolution

Real generosity toward the future lies in giving all to the present.
– Albert Camus

For the most part, as conflict resolvers, we respond reactively to disputes that already exist, or have existed for some time, and only when asked to do so by both sides. Yet by the time we intervene, many of these disputes will have already reached impasse, and the parties' communications and relationships will have deteriorated to a point of no return, resulting in significant losses, reluctance to mediate, recidivism, and an inability to reach closure.

Would it not make more sense for conflict resolution initiatives to be implemented *preventatively* in advance of impasse? To redesign systems so as not to generate chronic conflicts? To obtain permission to mediate in *advance* of the outbreak of hostilities? To train mediators and conflict resolutionists in every school, neighborhood, workplace, and government agency, and to encourage them to intervene *before* people suffer, or cause others to suffer, irreversible damage?

To understand how it might be possible for us to respond more preventatively and proactively as individuals and as a profession to predictable, imminent, incipient, and chronic conflicts, it is important to understand what unites us professionally and to articulate the core values that, together with a unified theoretical framework, can help us focus our efforts and act more strategically, with real generosity toward the future. In doing so, it will be useful to look backward for a moment at our history as a profession.

A Brief History of Conflict Resolution

Conflict resolution is nearly as ancient as conflict. Even among primates, certain individuals routinely attempt to calm others down, settle disagreements, and restore unity to the group as a whole. We can therefore think of conflict resolution as at least as ancient, universal, and enduring as conflict, with roots that extend into every culture, time, and place.

In more recent years, conflict resolution has emerged as a distinct profession around the globe, with its own language and rules. Yet at the same time it has become what I like to think of as a mongrel discipline comprised of elements drawn from a variety of diverse, sometimes incompatible domains of experience, understanding, and practice, each of which has made it more vigorous, comprehensive, street smart, and versatile.

Historically, in the United States, professional conflict resolution began with efforts during the First and Second World Wars as an effort to mitigate the destructive effects of adversarial labor-management practices in order to keep wartime production running smoothly. To achieve these results and reduce the human suffering that was brought on by the Depression, the government began to restrict anti-labor practices and encourage arbitration, mediation, and collective bargaining in order to prevent and settle strikes.

Decades later, in the aftermath of urban riots following the assassinations of Malcolm X and Martin Luther King, Jr., Congress approved funding for neighborhood justice centers in several major cities, inspiring similar projects, such as San Francisco's Community Boards Program, which linked conflict resolution with community organizing, prejudice reduction, and improving cross-cultural relationships. Later, filing fees for civil cases allowed monies to be set aside for community mediation programs, permitting them to stabilize and expand their reach.

The growth of a large peace movement in opposition to the war in Vietnam also had an impact on the awareness of people generally regarding the waste and futility of adversarial approaches to solving global problems. It became increasingly clear that there were insufficient skills, methods, and resolve to mitigate an increasingly repressive backlash against the political and cultural changes brought about during the 1960s. As a result, many peace activists became interested in conflict resolution, bringing with them a strong sense of values and an orientation toward democracy and community.

Roger Fisher and William Ury at Harvard Law School's Program on Negotiations added an international perspective to the profession, helping design the Camp David negotiations, systematizing work in interest-based negotiations, and assisting in reducing international tensions. Bill Ury, along with Steve Goldberg, Jeanne Brett, and others, helped expand grievance mediation, organizational alternative dispute resolution (ADR) programs using the powerful idea of conflict resolution systems design. The Federal Mediation and Conciliation Service and others used conflict resolution to strengthen labor-management collaboration and win/win bargaining.

Simultaneously, mediation began to be introduced in divorce and family disputes, with conciliation courts being formed to resolve bitter custody battles. These efforts linked conflict resolution with psychology, particularly its humanist, client-centered, Jungian, and Gestalt varieties. As a result, many psychotherapists became mediators, bringing with them a rich understanding of the underlying emotional issues in conflict and powerful techniques drawn from their disciplines for responding to intense emotions that might otherwise result in escalation and impasse, including brief and narrative forms of therapy. Gestalt therapy's focus on the whole, the present, the relationship between self and environment, the quality of contact between disputants, the creation of systems, the impact of biases, and clarity of intent contributed significantly to the development of dispute resolution. Jungian therapy's emphasis on symbolism, ritual, synchronicity, metaphor, and connection through meaning helped deepen the ability to understand what was occurring beneath the surface of conscious attention.

The Hewlitt Foundation provided funding for many large-scale mediation programs. Universities and law schools began developing undergraduate, graduate, and certificate courses in dispute resolution. Academic researchers began investigating the new phenomenon. Peer-based school mediation programs, led by New York's School Mediation Alternative Resolution Team (SMART) program, together with countless others, introduced mediation in the public schools, supported by the National Association for Mediation in Education (NAME).

Victim-offender mediation programs began working with juvenile offenders and their victims and to develop techniques oriented to restitution and redemption. These programs expanded their emphasis on restorative justice through community sentencing, family circles, and similar work, initially with indigenous aboriginal communities in New Zealand, Australia, and Canada.

Attorneys and judges also took up conflict resolution, initially as a means of settling simple personal injury lawsuits and complex commercial cases, reducing judicial backlogs, and mitigating the destructive effects of adversarial litigation. Through the insight of Harvard Law Professor Frank E. A. Sander, this led to an innovative idea about how lawsuits might be processed better and the development of the "multi-door courthouse."

As a result of these developments, many lawyers became mediators, bringing with them skills in legal analysis, ethics, judicial principles, and contract drafting and interpretation techniques that have proved useful adjuncts to dispute resolution. This has led to the development of collaborative law practices and a fundamental shift of the legal system away from costly, pointless, adversarial combat. It has also led to an increasing legalization of mediation programs and an emphasis on certification that has divided the profession.

Responding to an increasing emphasis on settlement and the growth of evaluative practices, Joseph Folger and Robert Baaruch-Bush wrote the immensely influential *The Promise of Mediation*, describing a transformational approach to mediation, Harvard University's Program on Negotiations created an Insight Initiative, and the Association for Conflict Resolution (ACR) formed a spirituality section.

In the last few decades, conflict resolution has expanded exponentially, increasing its effectiveness and extending its influence worldwide. From modest beginnings in the US, mediation has become a worldwide phenomenon, producing outstanding mediation programs in Canada, Ireland, Argentina, the Netherlands, and many other countries. This expansion has enabled us to develop powerful, subtle, intricate techniques, to learn how to work more effectively in diverse cultures and communities, and to successfully resolve more and more difficult and intractable conflicts.

The Mongrel Profession

As a result of this expansion, conflict resolution has separated into a number of divergent styles, subject matter areas, techniques, and philosophical camps, which have gradually grown more competitive and at odds with each other. This differentiation was initially reflected in the rise of competing professional organizations focused on different areas of practice. Yet these differences have also contributed to the growth, diversity, and strength of the whole, producing extraordinary synergies.

We can see, for example, that conflict resolution has been informed in critical and important ways by at least the following professions and disciplines, which continue to be mined for insights and practical contributions:

- Law
- Labor-Management Relations
- Dialogue
- Group Facilitation
- Systems Theory
- Learning Theory
- Myth and Ritual
- Mindfulness Meditation
- Communication Theory
- Neurophysiology
- Economics
- Game Theory
- Coaching and Mentoring

- Psychology
- Negotiation
- Arbitration
- Non-violence
- Prejudice Reduction
- Race and Gender Studies
- Buddhist Philosophy
- Spiritual Practices
- Art and Aesthetics
- Anthropology
- Community Organizing
- Physics and Mathematics
- Creative Problem Solving

- Neuro-Linguistic Programming
- Evaluation and Assessment
- Management Theory
- Team Building
- Sociology
- Theories of Justice

- Feedback Techniques
- Quality Improvement
- Organizational Culture
- Collaborative Processes
- Political Theory
- International Relations

Each of these disciplines and professions offers rich resources for the exploration and resolution of conflict, yet none is capable by itself of being the sole source of conflict resolution theory and practice. For example, every conflict has an emotional component. Consequently, it is nearly impossible not to use *some* emotional skills in resolving conflict. The same can be said in varying degrees of the other disciplines listed above. Our choice, therefore, is not whether we will incorporate elements from other disciplines in conflict resolution, but whether we will do so consciously, collaboratively, proactively, strategically, and in ways that accentuate their underlying unity.

Each new discipline has added to our understanding of the whole. Each has brought a fertile set of theories and techniques with it. Each has been modified and customized to increase our ability to resolve conflicts in general, and has become so incorporated into the practice of mediation as to become increasingly indistinguishable from it. This integration is reflected in the formation of a single, unified professional organization, the Association for Conflict Resolution (ACR), which draws together researchers and practitioners from all of these disciplines and fields. Yet without a unified, integrated understanding of how these parts are connected, it will be prove difficult for these combinations to result in fresh synergies.

Mediating Among the Mediators

As individual practitioners, we have lacked the influence, skills, techniques, and understanding needed to fully integrate this multitude of diverse styles, approaches, and professional experiences into a single, unified practical and theoretical whole. While many mediators entertain visions of a unified future, these are largely grounded in the hope or faith that we will recognize the merits of each other's contributions and find ways of communicating across the experiential and conceptual distances that separate us.

The mediation profession now includes, at a minimum, retired judge mediators, attorney mediators, collaborative law office mediators, commercial mediators, insurance mediators, health care mediators, ombudsmen, organizational mediators, labor-management mediators, therapist mediators, divorce and family mediators, marital mediators, school mediators, peer mediators, community mediators, victim-offender mediators, restorative justice mediators, evaluative mediators, facilitative mediators, transformational mediators, narrative mediators, spiritually oriented mediators, international mediators, and a group of eclectic mediators who float uneasily between them.

As a result of drawing successful practitioners from such diverse backgrounds, mediation as a profession is entering a state of crisis, torn between inconsistent approaches and visions for the future and divided into a number of discrete camps. Retired judges and attorney mediators, for example, tend to view their conflict resolution experiences completely differently from therapist and community mediators, who see themselves as distinct from narrative and transformational mediators. Divorce mediators approach their work with a different orientation than labor-management mediators, victim-offender mediators, and international mediators. Mediation, it seems, lies in the eye of the beholder.

Certainly there are many points of agreement that link these different orientations and approaches. Most will agree, for example, on the usefulness of classic techniques like setting ground rules, surfacing interests, and maintaining confidentiality, while implementing them in completely different ways. Most will agree that each conflict is different, each mediator is different, each institution, organization, and subject matter is different, each mediation is different, and all of these are constantly changing.

This inevitable fluidity justifies us in adopting a wide variety of styles and approaches to resolution. Moreover, each style and approach has proven remarkably successful in resolving certain kinds of disputes for those who use it, and no one has yet been able to demonstrate that any one approach is naturally superior to any other. As a result, each has tended to advance its own specialized perspectives and experiences and sometimes ignored or dismissed those of others. While it is easy to recognize multiple truths in mediation, it has sometimes proven more difficult to do so in professional interactions with other mediators.

One of the underlying sources for continued divisiveness is that we have not formulated an agreed-upon theoretical understanding of conflict resolution that subsumes and integrates all of these practices and grounds them in a unified set of methods and techniques. It is natural and important for any emergent discipline to experience competition over styles, techniques, strategies, and interpretations. These early struggles encourage a search for what works best and help clarify the essence and limitations of the field. Indeed, out of this competition has emerged examples of what each approach does distinctly and successfully and what is common between them, just as parties in conflict discover interests that unite them.

Yet periodic efforts to draw precise boundaries that distinguish conflict resolution from its contributing disciplines or prohibit entry to those without a professional license are ultimately doomed to failure. Not only do these efforts divide us and make us more competitive and territorial, they mistakenly focus attention on boundaries that were originally designed to reduce the supply of available professionals and discourage poaching by outsiders, including mediators not trained in their specific techniques and cultures. While doing so clearly increases effective demand, resulting in higher fees for services, it also freezes core ideas and techniques and obstructs cross-fertilization. Worse, it deters us from attempting to understand and unify conflict resolution as a whole.

As a result, mediators have occasionally fretted and bickered over the invisible boundaries that separate and insulate these disciplines from one another, vainly endeavoring to pinpoint precisely where one ends and the other begins. It is better, in my opinion, to *embrace* our mongrel origins, opportunistically extract whatever we can that might prove useful from every other profession, and seek their integration in a provisionally bastardized and synthetic but ultimately holistic form.

Indeed, part of the excitement and energy of conflict resolution derives from its capacity to learn from other professions and transform specialized theories and techniques into multidisciplinary, goal-oriented practices. We have done so largely by listening and recruiting mediators from other areas of expertise and by experimenting and adapting their techniques.

For mediation to remain open and alive and continue embracing innovation, diversity, and cross-fertilization, it is necessary for us to acknowledge and affirm our mongrel heritage, clarifying what unites us both in theory and in practice, and to recognize that these are core values that inform every aspect of what we do and critically define who we are.

Core Values in Mediation

The first challenge in any profession is to develop a diverse, complex, inconsistent array of methods, practices, models, and theories in order to investigate and crystallize every aspect of what is learned. The second challenge is to synthesize, integrate, and unify these disparate lessons in a single, holistic, internally consistent set of theories and practices. The third challenge is to engage each other in dialogue over how these theories and practices might be linked through a set of core values that provide ethical grounding and strategic orientation for charting the future.

Values are essentially priorities. They are choices that are present in everything we do and do not do, everything we resist and are willing to tolerate. When taken seriously, they are based on real alternatives with a genuine consideration of consequences. They are openly and publicly expressed, acted on repeatedly, and upheld, even when they run counter to personal self-interest.

Every organization, profession, behavior, and attitude possesses an underlying set of values that is initially unconscious, unacknowledged, and unexplored. At the heart of every person and relationship is a set of values that defines their identity, culture, and potential, and affects every aspect of what they do, whether they are aware of and agree with them or not. These values surface whenever there is conflict, yet are always in the background waiting to emerge.

Values are attributions of meaning or significance to things that might otherwise appear ordinary. If we value education, it may be because we were, are, or could be denied it, and therefore attach importance to it. Thus, values represent a developmental relationship between ourselves and our futures, measured by what is important to us at a given moment relative to our other needs, and by its potential to contribute to our future learning and evolution. We grow as our values are conceived, committed to, struggled and sacrificed for, secured, generalized, taken for granted, and forgotten because they have become integral parts of who we are, allowing us to graduate to higher values.

What is important or valuable in one set of circumstances may change as we transition to another, and for this reason, there can be no final, complete, absolute, and permanent set of values for everyone and all times. While values may not be absolute and may vary with time, place and circumstances, in any given circumstance it is possible for a relative value to turn absolute, as, for example, when a white lie regarding fair weather is told to a fisherman heading out to sea.

At a deep level, we all communicate values by what we say and do and, more importantly, by who we are. When we try to define values, we create definitions rather than values, and it becomes easy to slip into preaching, moralizing, and imposing our values on others. While rules and morality can be preached and imposed on others, values and integrity are personal, subjective, chosen, open to change, and diluted by exhortation and coercion.

When values are preached and imposed as though they were morals, they easily become contradictory and hypocritical. Yet it is possible to minimize hypocrisy and duplicity by shifting from externally imposed moral structures to internally accepted values, and from preaching and enforcing compliance to dialogue and reaching consensus. Ultimately, values require each individual to identify for themselves the areas where their walk does not match their talk.

When values are collapsed into morals, they begin to serve opportunistic ends and give rise to two opposing dangers. When no actions are considered better or worse than others, there is a danger of moral relativism, based on complicity and condonation, which gives people permission to engage in ethically reprehensible actions. A mediator may slip into moral relativism, for example, by failing to intervene when one party engages in grossly abusive behavior.

On the other hand, when one action is considered better or worse than others, there is a danger of moral imperialism, based on intolerance and arrogance, which gives permission to dominate others through self-appointed moral superiority and to make oneself the arbiter of other people's choices. A mediator may slip into moral imperialism, for example, by imposing their values on the parties, even if it is the value of their own transformation.

Building on the work of cyberneticist Heinz von Forester, I believe there are three orders of values. First, there is a specific value itself, such as honesty or respect; second, there is the value of having values; and third, there is the transformation of values into integral, inseparable aspects of who we are. The first consists largely of declarations whose aim is to advertise a value orientation and protect against unethical behaviors. The second consists largely of understandings whose aim is to encourage learning, improvement, and evolution to higher levels of integrity. The third consists largely of behaviors whose aim is to make values such an integral part of character that they flow naturally from who we are rather than what we declare or understand.

In reaching these second and third orders of values, it is not merely our identification of core values that matters, but the process by which we identify and discuss them, the ways we express them in behaviors, how we revise and encourage them, and what we do when we or others do not observe them. [For a more detailed discussion of values, see Kenneth Cloke and Joan Goldsmith, *The End of Management and the Rise of Organizational Democracy*, Jossey Bass / Wiley Publishers Inc., 2002.]

Beneath many commonly articulated mediation values it is possible to locate a set of meta-values that I see as representing our best possible future as a profession. The most elementary of these, in my view, ask us to

- accept conflicts as opportunities for learning and improvement, requests for dialogue, and invitations to improve content, process, and relationships;

- support unity *and* diversity, and reject false dichotomies of inclusion or exclusion, superiority or inferiority, correctness or heresy, victory or defeat;

- bring deep levels of honesty, empathy, and unconditional integrity to conflict conversations;

- accept and acknowledge intense emotions, and seek to satisfy everyone's interests;

- consider ourselves to be on both parties' sides at the same time;

- encourage dialogue, consensus, collaborative negotiation, and heartfelt conversations leading to resolution, forgiveness, and reconciliation; and

- search for preventative and systemic solutions.

While not everyone will accept these values, merely articulating them, debating, and engaging in dialogue over them, collaboratively defining how to implement them, and deciding to commit to live by them affirms the second order value of having values—not only by what we say, but how we say it and who we become while we are saying it. We keep values alive by revising them, bringing them into people's conscious attention, living them as fully as possible, and developing theories and practices, processes and relationships that encourage others to live by theirs.

Our Challenge

In the end, we cannot resolve, transform, or transcend conflicts by acting inconsistently with our values or by manipulating others, making choices that do not belong to us, or sacrificing someone else's future to improve our own. When we act unilaterally and exclusively to resolve shared conflicts, we discourage our opponents from accepting responsibility for implementing solutions, cheat them out of partnership and collaboration, and make them feel they have failed.

We therefore need to redefine success in conflict resolution to include being able to work inclusively, collaboratively, and preventatively with one's opponents on an interpersonal level as well as organizationally, socially, and politically in ways that increase our capacity to satisfy diverse, conflicting interests. At its deepest level, being able to work together means journeying into the heart of dispute resolution, strengthening heart connections, and promoting forgiveness and reconciliation both locally and globally.

I believe there are five fundamental future-oriented goals we can attempt to achieve during our lifetimes. We can strive to love others and ourselves as deeply and unconditionally as possible. We can work to become better human beings. We can endeavor to learn more about life, the universe, and everything in it. We can seek to gain insight into the subtle nature of human interactions and relationships. And we can seek to leave the world a better place than we found it. Mediation, miraculously, allows us to practice all five.

Our challenge as mediators is therefore to evolve in significantly new directions both internally and externally. Internally, this means becoming as adept and skillful as we can in resolving, transforming, and transcending conflicts in all their locations and dimensions, including those that arise within ourselves and our profession. Externally, it means assisting people everywhere to develop the skills they need to resolve disputes, design conflict resolution systems to prevent and resolve personal, organizational, social, and political disputes based on interests, and work collaboratively as a profession to bring these changes into existence.

The ultimate aim of conflict resolution is not to end conflicts, but to help people become better, more openhearted human beings, to resolve conflicts in ways that end in forgiveness and reconciliation, and to integrate peace with justice on a global scale. While the possibility of doing so may seem remote at present, we no longer have a choice. Our capacity to destroy life has increased steadily alongside our swelling technological prowess. Every day we become more dependent on each other for survival and we desperately need to learn how to prevent and resolve conflicts so as to avoid human and environmental catastrophe.

To create a better future, it is ultimately necessary to stand in opposition to whatever causes injury and harm in the present; even to place oneself in conflict with those who find such damage acceptable. In conflict resolution, this means pushing the boundaries of what we have accepted as given or inevitable and critiquing the ease and tolerance with which war and injustice are accepted.

In the end, our challenge is to recognize that mediation cannot be separated from the mediator, that we *are* the technique, the future we create, and the lessons and values we model in mediation. We therefore need to improve not only our skills and techniques by learning to move patiently and inexorably into the heart of conflict, but also our theoretical understanding of the whole of conflict resolution, including the role of attitude and intention, spirit and heart, system and environment. In this, I believe, lies the future of mediation.

A Closing Thought

Many years ago, I read an interview with a man who was a champion pole vaulter. While competing in the Olympics, he missed two vaults in a row. Despondent, and with only one opportunity left to succeed, he sought out his coach, who gave him an extraordinary piece of advice. The coach asked him to imagine the sound of his pole hitting the ground as the first note in a love song. He followed this advice and made a spectacular vault, but what struck me was how the stimulus of imagining the first note in a love song allowed him to open his heart and let his body be guided by it, rather than by his fear or desire to succeed.